The
Bible
and
Moral Injury

The Bible *and* Moral Injury

Reading Scripture Alongside War's Unseen Wounds

Brad E. Kelle

Abingdon Press™
Nashville

The Bible and Moral Injury:
Reading Scripture Alongside War's Unseen Wounds

Copyright © 2020 by Abingdon Press

LCCN: 2019952930
ISBN: 978-1-5018-7628-8

20 21 22 23 24 25 26 27 28 29—10 9 8 7 6 5 4 3 2 1
MANUFACTURED IN THE UNITED STATES OF AMERICA

To those who came home, those who didn't, and those who are still trying

Contents

Contents

Contents

Foreword

Since its inception, moral injury has been an intersectional, cross-disciplinary term with significant work appearing in the social sciences, classics, philosophy, religion, literature, and medicine. With Brad Kelle's excellent work, deeply grounded in this earlier wealth of materials, we have a major engagement with the Bible, a document that also crosses disciplines and cultures. The Bible holds sway in two major religions, in literary and historical studies, and in secular culture. This nuanced, illuminating book on moral injury will be valuable to anyone with an interest in the Bible and its cultural influences. It will also be helpful to clergy, chaplains, and mental health professionals who will find resources for addressing those who suffer moral injury, including those who are not religious.

Among the strengths of this work are that it offers comprehensive research into definitions of moral injury and engagement with their strengths and weaknesses. It also pays careful attention to other works on moral injury and what they contribute not only to his interpretations of biblical texts, such as a re-reading of the story of Saul, but also to contexts beyond military moral injury. Finally, it delivers a subtle, compelling examination of how moral injury opens new ways of interpreting biblical texts and how biblical texts can inform understandings of moral injury, lamentation, somatic trauma work, and the ways ancient biblical cultures used collective rituals for returning war fighters.

One of the most profound, unsettling, and important aspects of this book is its honest and unflinching examination of how the Bible can inflict moral injury on its readers. Kelle offers copious examples of a jealous, murderous, warring God who violates foundational moral values. The faithful who must contend with such abhorrent texts may, he reveals, experience moral injury and turn against faith. Rather than dismissing the texts or eliding how truly awful they are, he suggests the texts, in our current context of war, may "keep the actual experiences of war ever before those who read them, urging a sense of shared moral responsibility and an appreciation of war's inescapable costliness."

For a society gripped by endless war, yet largely oblivious to the suffering of those sent to fight and of those they fight, this book is an invitation to think more collectively and honestly about our relationship to war, done in our name, by reading the Bible for what it is: a complex, contradictory, vexing, inspiring, and valuable source for understanding moral injury. Accepting that invitation might lead us to addressing our own collective moral injuries in hopes of peace.

Rita Nakashima Brock, PhD
Senior Vice President and Director of the Shay Moral Injury Center
Volunteers of America

Preface and Acknowledgments

Writing about war and the moral toll it can take on human lives is a weighty task. To involve the Bible in that effort only adds to the weightiness. My journey into this subject matter began more than a decade ago, when I was the founding chairperson of the Warfare in Ancient Israel Section at the Annual Meeting of the Society of Biblical Literature (SBL). Many years of research and publication on various elements of warfare in the Old Testament and ancient Israel and Judah eventually led to a focus on trauma theory and its significance for interpreting biblical texts, especially those associated with violence, destruction, and exile. I first encountered the emerging notion of moral injury within psychology and military studies during the time that I was working on trauma hermeneutics. I sensed there was potential there for creative and beneficial intersections with biblical studies, but I also gained a renewed sense of the personal and moral ambiguity, disillusionment, and even anguish that can come from looking closely into the realities of war. As I've read accounts of the experience of moral injury and watched the research on it develop within psychology, moral philosophy, ethics, theology, religious studies, and pastoral care, I've become more convinced that the study of the Bible (both academically and devotionally/pastorally) can benefit from and contribute to this important ongoing work. But I've also become more convinced that there is a cost to the study of this subject matter.

There is no way to work on moral injury and the Bible's war and violence texts and remain unaffected by the moral uncertainty and emotional discomfort that such things create.

In light of the weightiness and newness of the topic of the Bible and moral injury, I've been very fortunate to receive support from a variety of personal and institutional sources. I appreciate my faculty colleagues and students in the School of Theology and Christian Ministry at Point Loma Nazarene University (PLNU), who encouraged me in the work and readily engaged in beneficial conversation about my ideas, always making them better. I received a sabbatical from PLNU in the spring 2019 semester during which the bulk of the book was written, and I'm particularly thankful for the support of my dean, Mark Maddix, in both undertaking and completing this project. A dean who understands the value of research and publication and tangibly encourages their pursuit is a gift indeed! I am especially grateful to my colleague Samuel M. Powell for taking time from his own impressive publication and research (and teaching!) tasks to read and help shape my work. Although I alone bear responsibility for the shortcomings that surely remain here, every word of this book is better because Sam gave it his time and attention. Thanks also to the editorial team at Abingdon Press, especially David Teel, who first accepted the proposal for this book, and now Michael Stephens, who has seen it through to completion. Finally, and above all, I'm grateful to my wife, Dee, and our now nineteen-year-old son, Grayson, for their encouragement and patience with yet another book project.

In addition to these personal and institutional means of support, I've particularly benefited from working on moral injury while living in San Diego. Yes, there are palm trees and beaches! But this is also a military town. And it's the location of the nation's first residential program for active duty military personnel devoted to repairing the psychological wounds of war, including moral injury. I am grateful to the civilian and military personnel at the OASIS (Overcoming Adversity and Stress Injury Support) program associated with Naval Base Point Loma and the Naval Medical Center San Diego, especially the supervising clinical psychologist Mardi Smith and chaplains LCDR Glen Orris and LCDR Stephen Brown, for their willingness to share their time and work and to help me think through this project. I am also grateful for the biblical scholars who've participated with me in sessions on moral injury at the SBL Annual Meeting over the last three years. Conversations with conscientious scholars such as Joseph McDonald, Amy Cottrill, Jenny Matheny, Nancy Bowen, and Kelly Denton-Borhaug have shaped my own thinking in substantial ways. Publications of mine that emerged from some of these sessions underlie parts of this book. Portions of chapters 3, 4, and 5 have appeared in print previously and are used here by permission (see notes provided in those chapters). Regrettably, I didn't have access to Zachary Moon's important new book, *Warriors Between Worlds: Moral Injury and Identities in Crisis* (Lexington, 2019) in enough time to engage it fully in my work here, and it appears primarily in citations.

Finally, I must confess that this book has been both a joy and a challenge to write. As I noted above, the subject matter of moral injury and the Bible's war and violence texts takes a psychological and emotional toll. Looking long into the grim realities represented by these things comes at some cost, yet surely not the same cost as actually experiencing them. As much as I might want to take a pacifist stance or a conscientious objector position, hoping that all may be free from the experiences of war, I realize that the present reality is otherwise for many who live in my own community and throughout the world. Yet the sincere work being done on moral injury and repair from so many quarters is cause for hope that there are critiques of war that can be made and there is healing that can be found by those whose sense of self and the world has been wrecked by the realities of violence. I believe the study of the Bible can contribute to these goals, and toward that end I offer this work. Later parts of this book will explain that the experiences of moral injury aren't limited to soldiers and military settings. But service members and veterans throughout history have known directly and personally what many of the rest of us are just learning to take seriously—namely, the moral wounds inflicted by war and the moral struggles involved in trying to come home from it. So, I dedicate this work to soldiers past, present, and future—those who came home, those who didn't, and those who are still trying.

Is there a way to liberate [hu]mankind from the doom of war?

—*Albert Einstein*[1]

Chapter 1
Introduction

The soldier's heart, the soldier's spirit, the soldier's soul are everything.

—General George C. Marshall[1]

Unseen Wounds, Moral Injury, and Scripture

Not all wounds of war are physical or visible. In recent years, psychologists, caregivers, counselors, chaplains, and pastors have increasingly recognized that the injurious effects of war on combatants and noncombatants include psychological, emotional, relational, and even ethical consequences. And these consequences often manifest themselves in inward experiences such as fear, grief, stress, shame, guilt, and anger, and outward experiences such as the loss of relationships, resources, and social functioning. Contemporary study has used the label *unseen wounds* to designate these real, but often hidden, dire effects of war. In the current context, researchers and caregivers identify war's most common unseen or hidden wounds as Military Sexual Trauma (MST), Traumatic Brain Injury (TBI), and, especially, Post-traumatic Stress Disorder (PTSD). In different ways, each of these wounds embodies the harmful consequences that participation in war (both directly and indirectly) can have on persons—consequences that can last for a lifetime and affect families and communities.

Psychologists, researchers, and other caregivers have recently identified another of war's unseen wounds, which has come to be referred to as *moral injury*. The following chapter will outline the current understandings and definitions of moral injury; but in short, we may say that moral injury is a nonphysical wound that results from the violation of a person's core moral beliefs (by oneself or others). Put more technically, moral injury refers to the deleterious effects of war participation on moral conscience and ethical conceptions—the wrecking of a person's fundamental assumptions about "what's right" and how things should work in the world—that may result from a sense of having violated one's core moral identity and lost any reliable, meaningful world in which to live.

As chapter 2 will show, moral injury remains an emerging concept. But the starting point for this work has been the insistence that although this label is recent, the experience that it represents is ancient.[2] The recognition that the dangers and damages of war aren't limited to observable physical injuries appears in diverse literary, artistic, religious, and philosophical contexts throughout various historical periods. The challenge to such recognition is that modern (especially Western) societies often resist the acknowledgment of these injuries, avoid the facts, memories, and testimonies about them, and fail to recognize war's harmful effects on morals, ethics, self-image, and family and communal systems.[3]

In spite of modern society's resistance, work on moral injury has emerged at a staggeringly fast rate since 2009, with academic analyses, clinical studies, firsthand accounts, and other discussions appearing in works from clinical psychology, military studies, moral philosophy, chaplaincy resources, general-audience books, and popular press publications such as the *New York Times* and the *Huffington Post*. For some, moral injury has taken its place as the "inevitable wound of all war" and the "signature wound of today's wars."[4] Two characteristics of the burgeoning work on moral injury provide segues to my efforts in this book. First, those working on moral injury have identified relevant themes and experiences in some of the sacred texts of the world's religions. Second, work on understanding and addressing moral injury thus far has had a decidedly multidisciplinary character, with insights coming not only from psychology and military studies but also from religion, theology, and moral philosophy.

The purpose of this book is to ask whether the study of the Bible—in academic, ministerial, or other contexts—can benefit from and contribute to the study of and work with moral injury. More specifically, I seek to explore two questions: (1) What can moral injury research contribute to the interpretation of biblical texts? and (2) What can the study of the Bible (both academically and devotionally/pastorally) contribute to the ongoing efforts to understand and address moral injury? My approach is to explore with case studies the interpretation of biblical texts (especially war-related narratives and ritual depictions from the Old Testament) in conversation with research on moral injury being done in other fields.

In some ways, this book forms a biblical studies companion to the recent publication (also by Abingdon Press) of Larry Kent Graham's *Moral Injury: Restoring Wounded Souls*, which examined moral injury from the perspective of pastoral theology and counseling.[5] As mentioned above, I seek to go beyond simply interpreting biblical texts through the lens of moral injury to see what the critical study of biblical texts can contribute to the moral injury conversation. I don't argue that the biblical texts provide moral and ethical answers to the experiences of moral injury. But I suggest that engaging the stories, rituals, laments, and other texts in the Bible can be an instrument that allows soldiers, veterans, chaplains, and others to explore the moral and religious dimensions of war participation in new and profound ways, perhaps moving toward new kinds of self-understanding and conclusions. My thesis is that the engagement between the Bible and moral injury generates a two-way conversation: on the one hand, moral injury can be an interpretive lens that brings new meanings out of biblical texts, especially those associated with war and violence; on the other hand, the critical study of biblical texts can make substantive contributions to the ongoing attempt to understand, identify, and heal moral injury.

Starting Points

There are several starting points for the discussions in the chapters that follow. First, this book's engagement with the Bible and moral injury is a Christian engagement. I write as a Christian, but with the hope of a broader audience as well. More specifically, I write as an Old Testament scholar, professor, and Christian minister within the Wesleyan theological tradition. As our postmodern situation has reminded us, our interpretations of texts are influenced by the communities in which we encounter those texts. Far from being something to lament, this context-bound reality gives us creative and meaningful lenses for viewing the biblical texts, celebrating the ways that such ancient and foreign texts take on local and particular significance. I came to the study of moral injury after previous research on warfare in ancient Israel and the Old Testament, and especially through the use of trauma and trauma literature as a way to engage the Old Testament's war and violence texts, particularly in the prophetic books.[6] Because of my own background and training, the discussion of the Bible and moral injury in the following chapters will concentrate on the Old Testament, although the concluding chapter will suggest how the New Testament texts might be included in this engagement.

Along these lines, I approach the Old Testament with a theological perspective that reads it as part of Christian scripture. This way of reading sees the Old Testament as part of a larger, inspired canon that can shape the imagination and practice of its readers toward the character and ways of God's intentions for human life and all creation. Far from being a set of moralistic answers or a collection of outmoded ancient cultural expressions, the biblical texts—viewed as Christian scripture—fund new and authoritative ways of imagining who God is, who we are as human beings created in God's image, and how, then, we should live together in God's world. Seen this way, the ancient Israelite texts found in the Old Testament can become fresh resources for understanding and working with moral injury, even as dimensions of moral injury can reshape some of the ways we read and use these texts in contemporary settings, especially those related to warfare and violence. Approaches to the Bible in both Christian confessional communities and academic biblical scholarship, however, indicate that the best way for the biblical texts to function in this manner is through an interdisciplinary approach that brings perspectives from other fields of study to bear on the understanding of the texts, even as insights generated by biblical interpretation are offered to other fields in the mutual work of understanding and application.

A second starting point concerns my intended audiences. This book is predominantly oriented toward Christian ministers, chaplains, counselors, and interested laypersons who are concerned with moral injury and seek to serve those affected by it. Members of these groups often look to the Bible as Christian scripture to find teachings, stories, poems, and perspectives to put into dialogue with other resources that inform their work as Christian moral healers and guides. While several recent publications have addressed moral injury care for chaplains and Christian ministers in general, I hope this book's engagement with various Old Testament passages and themes will provide specific textual resources and encounters to fund that work.[7]

The book also has another intended audience—namely, those working on moral injury outside of Christian ministry, biblical studies, or any necessarily religious context, especially within clinical psychology, veterans' care, and other counseling settings. My hope is that the treatment of the Old Testament texts offered here will provide an additional resource for understanding, articulating, and addressing moral injury both for their treatment work with people from Christian backgrounds and for the more general inquiry into the nature and dynamics of moral injury and the responses to it. As chapter 2 will discuss, works on moral injury have previously emphasized the usefulness of ancient texts such as the *Iliad* and

Odyssey for this engagement, but little sustained attention has yet been paid to the biblical texts. Additionally, recent moral injury study has included pleas for other academic disciplines to contribute to the work and perhaps yield a broader understanding than any one approach could do on its own. As Meagher and Pryer assert, contributions from psychologists, ethicists, veterans, theologians, pastors, Native American healers, yoga instructors, or others may all play a role: "Whatever sheds light, whatever helps, is worth knowing and sharing—this at the very least is a sound point of departure."[8] Given its cultural and religious significance as one of the world's sacred texts, and the number of US service members and veterans who identify as Christian or Jewish, surely the Bible—through the work of critical biblical scholarship—can contribute to the study of moral injury, even as perspectives from moral injury provide new insights into biblical texts.

These intended audiences suggest a third starting point. There are several motivations for the work I try to do here with the Bible and moral injury, which begin with the aforementioned effort to provide a new and previously underappreciated set of possible resources for those trying to understand and work with moral injury in various contexts. I'm motivated to try to build on the limited engagement with biblical studies that has happened in moral injury work thus far.[9] Perhaps above all, however, I'm motivated by the human realities and costs associated with the experiences of moral injury among service members and their families. It is common these days to hear of US veterans committing suicide at the average rate of more than twenty per day.[10] While the overall numbers aren't certain and not all veteran suicides are related to the psychological and moral effects of war, researchers working on moral injury have increasingly gathered data indicating that moral injury may play a significant role in the US military's high suicide rate, especially as a consequence of the American wars in Iraq and Afghanistan, lasting now more than fifteen years. A recent clinical and empirical study, for example, gives data to support a link between heightened suicidality and experiences of perceived moral injury in service members who didn't receive care aimed at moral and ethical struggles.[11] Pryer records that from 2003 to 2012, the suicide rate in the Navy and Air Force doubled, while it more than doubled in the Marine Corps and tripled in the Army.[12] He acknowledges that not all of these suicides are linked to combat experiences. Even so, although moral injury has been an unnamed consequence of war for thousands of years, the intensification of suicides and other war-related struggles likely results from the uninterrupted state of war over the last decade and a half, as well as the absence in modern contexts of the very ways of dealing with the moral and emotional effects of war that are visible in certain ancient cultures and writings. The problem has been intensified because the US military "rarely even acknowledges that moral distress can lead to suicide," and this has allowed the moral consequences of war to be ignored both in prewar decision-making and postwar care.[13]

Beyond suicide, however, a 2017 sample of active duty marines who saw ground combat in Afghanistan found that 25 percent said they had violated their own moral code and 33.3 percent said they felt betrayed by someone they trusted—two key components of moral injury (see ch. 2).[14] Likewise, the 2013 National Health and Resilience in Veterans Study showed that 10.8 percent of combat veterans acknowledged moral transgressions by themselves, 25.5 percent acknowledged transgressions by others, and 25.5 percent felt betrayed by those they trusted.[15] This study also revealed pressing emotional health and social justice concerns, as it indicated that veterans who acknowledged moral transgressions by self and experiences of betrayal had higher suicidal ideations and attempts, and veterans from underrepresented racial and ethnic groups and lower socioeconomic status had an increased likelihood of suffering potentially morally injurious experiences.

All of this gives the engagement with moral injury, including through the medium of the biblical texts, an urgency for helping people and perhaps even saving lives. There is a need to find ways to "neutralize a recognized moral danger or at least to warn others about it, to comfort others who are morally injured while encouraging their rebuilding work... [and] to expand our store of information" about moral injury.[16] The urgency and need for resources are especially pressing, I believe, for those who work with morally injured persons and families within the context of Christian ministry and chaplaincy. Many US service members come from Christian backgrounds and have Christian moral frameworks, and they often seek moral repair within that same context. Likewise, they and their Christian ministers and chaplains often look to the Bible for potential help in this work. Surveys of Veterans Administration (VA) and Department of Defense (DOD) chaplains indicate that many service members and veterans feel more comfortable talking with chaplains and ministers than with psychologists about combat-related moral and ethical issues (perhaps due to stigmas attached to psychological and emotional struggles within military culture), and that nearly half of all VA chaplains in 2013–2014, for instance, reported "frequently" working with personnel suffering from moral injury.[17]

The Bible and Moral Injury: A Two-Way Conversation

My work in the pages that follow begins by asking what moral injury research can contribute to the interpretation of biblical texts, and what the study of the Bible (in academic, ministerial, and other contexts) can contribute to the ongoing efforts to understand and address moral injury. Let me conclude this introduction by briefly expounding both sides of this potential two-way conversation and providing an overview of the subsequent chapters.

Moral Injury as a Frame of Reference

The first part of my thesis suggests that moral injury can be a heuristic or interpretive frame of reference through which we can read biblical texts in new ways.[18] In physics, for example, a frame of reference is a framework that is used to observe and describe a physical phenomenon. (For example, imagine two people standing, facing each other on either side of a sidewalk. If a skateboarder rides down the sidewalk between them, for the person on one side of the sidewalk, the skateboarder is moving to the right; for the person on the other side, the skateboarder is moving to the left. The two people constitute two different frames of reference from which to describe the skateboarder's movement.) By placing data into a certain frame of reference, interpreters are able to describe it in a particular way. In fact, reframing a collection of data into different frames of reference yields new meanings that aren't necessarily visible from other frameworks. The point is that frames of reference are ways of gathering and viewing certain materials that bring out new dimensions of meaning. Whether physicists or Bible readers, observers can switch frames of reference and see different emphases and insights. My invitation in this book is for us to consider what meanings emerge from the Old Testament when we read it within the frame of reference provided by the emerging understandings and work on moral injury.

Seen in this way, moral injury invites us to read biblical texts with an eye for what these ancient writings offer to our thinking about moral conscience and consciousness. We can become attuned to characters and stories that resonate with issues raised by moral injury—characters who display the characteristics of violating their moral conscience or experiencing betrayal, and stories that illustrate the consequences of and attempts to deal with these experiences. We can look for war-related rituals, poems, or prayers that connect to experiences of moral injury and attempts to come to grips with them.[19] In all these ways and more, the moral injury frame of reference can help us see things we might have missed in our readings of biblical characters, stories, rituals, and prayers—especially the human dimensions of Christian scripture. Moral injury provides a window into the human experiences, realities, and dynamics that stand behind these ancient sacred texts and the communities that created and preserved them, particularly the reality of human pain caused by loss, death, moral violation, and betrayal.

One particular impact of this moral injury heuristic involves the ways that the Bible is used within the larger Christian discussions of participation in war. Although I won't focus on that issue in this book, Meagher's recent work, *Killing from the Inside Out,* brings moral injury concerns to bear on the development of ethics concerning war in the Christian tradition.[20] He argues that the development of the Christian doctrine of "just war" departed from the ways that ancient civilizations such as Greece and Rome thought about the ethics of killing in war and has actually prohibited the Christian church from recognizing and dealing with moral injury. Meagher concludes that the acceptance of the just war doctrine has covered, excused, and denied the morally problematic effects of war and has made Christians incapable of seriously considering war's morally injurious elements. Whatever the merits of Meagher's larger thesis and argumentation, he shows that by reading the Bible through the frame of reference provided by moral injury, readers can see elements of moral injury preserved in the sacred texts and thus raise questions about the Christian just war doctrine.[21]

Another particular way that the moral injury frame of reference can provide new insight concerns the perennial challenge raised by the Bible's depictions of war and violence. One of the most commonly discussed issues in reading the Old Testament in particular, especially within Christian communities of faith, is how to deal with the passages that depict violence, war, and killing done by God's people at God's command, and sometimes directly by God.[22] The frame of moral injury can give contemporary readers a new perspective from which to engage these ethically difficult texts, perhaps by asking, Do the biblical warfare and violence texts morally injure their readers? Chapter 6 will take up this issue in detail. At this point, I simply note that the lens of moral injury indicates that the "theological problem" for many readers is how these texts violate their sense of a right and stable moral world—a world where God is good and works to bring life and where the chief moral values are "do not kill" and "love your neighbor." Insights from moral injury may allow contemporary readers to articulate why the biblical warfare texts are morally injurious, how they've been used throughout history to justify violent and hateful actions, and whether any of the proposed ways to heal moral injury in soldiers might also help with reading the texts.

Biblical Interpretation's Contributions to Moral Injury Work

The other part of my thesis suggests that the study of the Bible can contribute to the ongoing efforts to understand and work with moral injury that are being done by psychologists, veterans, philosophers, chaplains, and others. Engagement with Old Testament texts in the following chapters aims to demonstrate this idea, and the concluding chapter (ch. 7) will discuss the possible contributions from biblical studies in sum (especially as pathways for possible future study). Let me highlight at the outset, however, that the possibility of biblical studies making contributions begins from the commonly expressed need within moral injury work for broader methodological input and greater methodological precision. Frame describes moral injury as "a notion seeking a parent discipline...a foster child still hoping that someone will call it their own."[23] I'm not convinced that moral injury needs a single "parent discipline," and biblical studies need not try to claim moral injury all for itself. Yet, biblical studies can surely be one of the academic disciplines that contribute to what is rightly a multidisciplinary search for understanding and resources.

Let me preview possible contributions that will appear in the following chapters (and especially ch. 7). Perhaps the most readily apparent contributions involve perspectives related to faith and spirituality. First, however, I would note that the chapters that follow hope to show that the critical study of the Bible can also contribute a distinctively humanities dimension to moral injury work. So far, moral injury study has been dominated by mental health, psychology, and related therapeutic contexts, resulting in it often being "medicalized" and creating a kind of clinical and scientific reductionism (see ch. 2).[24] By contrast, the perspectives of historians, philosophers, theologians, sociologists, and textual scholars can provide different dimensions by allowing access to human experiences and reflections that can help modern persons see and articulate their own experiences. The biblical texts in particular—as ancient writings from historical communities and cultures—purport to describe human lives and experiences that point to the historical and cultural breadth of the moral struggles involved in war. The biblical writings can place moral injury into contexts of human experience that clinical psychology and even moral philosophy cannot—contexts of rituals, penance, confession, and narratives about complex moral agency and characters.

To return to the more apparent contributions of faith and spirituality, recall that many US service members self-identify as Christians, come from Christian backgrounds, or at least express interest in spirituality.[25] Based on this identity, many of these soldiers and veterans would naturally expect the Bible and its interpretation to speak to proper morality and values, including how those convictions operate in experiences of war and how people find comfort and healing when they feel they've violated those convictions. Several recent studies within moral injury work have paid particular attention to spiritual and faith-based dimensions and have indicated that veterans generally welcome the incorporation of religion and spirituality into psychological counseling concerning moral injury.[26] These perspectives indicate that religious communities that utilize the Bible as a sacred text can contribute perspectives of moral theology and Christian communal practices to the psychological approaches to moral injury.[27] As we'll see, biblical texts can help those interested in moral injury consider how a person of faith experiences moral violation; what the personal, communal, and religious effects of such an experience are; what the morality of war in and of itself is, and how one responds to having participated in it; what the Bible teaches about forgiveness and healing; and the place of prayer, honesty, grief, and confession for those affected by war.

Beyond the preceding preview, one additional potential contribution that biblical studies can make deserves special attention at the outset. The definition of moral injury as a violation of a person's core moral beliefs and the deleterious effects of war participation on moral conscience assumes that a person has a set of fundamental convictions about "what's right" and how things should work in the world. In other words, moral injury presumes that a person has a core moral identity and ethical framework that can be violated in such a way that the person no longer sees it as reliable or functional. And this is the identity and framework that the healing work on moral injury seeks to recover and restore.[28] Far from being a sign of weakness or pathology, then, suffering moral injury indicates that a person has some sense of conscience, established moral sensibilities, and ethical expectations that have been upset by the experiences of war.

Most moral injury studies have assumed that people have some set of ethical principles or conception of moral goodness (including, for example, the inherent value of life and the need to resist evil); however, they've largely avoided discussion of the source of these frameworks. Where does this sense of a moral self come from and who has responsibility to safeguard and, if necessary, repair it? There are differing views within recent moral injury studies on whether such moral and ethical convictions derive from innate (natural) attributes, religious beliefs, cultural norms, or the ideals of particular organizations.[29] For instance, some have suggested that military culture itself (learned primarily through the indoctrination of basic training) provides the starting ethical framework that gives soldiers a certain understanding of morality, a particular sense of self, and guidelines for proper actions.[30] In this view, military culture supplies its own ideals, beliefs, and values (e.g., selflessness, dedication to duty, willingness to sacrifice, defense of the social order) that shape the identity of the person and form a set of moral codes against which acts are judged as right or wrong and toward which restoration after violation moves. Moon has recently provided helpful nuance here by arguing that people possess "moral orienting systems" that are dynamic matrices of values, beliefs, and behaviors shaped over time by various formative experiences and relationships.[31] In his view, military recruit training reengineers this existing moral system and indoctrinates soldiers with a military moral orienting system with new values, beliefs, and behaviors meant to enable functioning within the military.

It is precisely concerning this question of the source and content of the initial moral framework that biblical studies might make a new contribution to moral injury work. Views that see military culture as providing the moral framework often treat morality as a set of rules rather than a holistic identity grounded in an understanding of who one is (and how one is called to live) and shaped in terms of virtue, goodness, and responsibility within relationships.[32] Moreover, those working with service members in clinical counseling, especially treatment done inside of military units and contexts, often treat religion (and its sacred texts) as merely a utilitarian means to comfort struggling soldiers and return them to combat readiness. By contrast, the Bible might constitute the source and provide the content of a starting moral sense of self and the world, at least for those who identify as part of communities of faith that view the Bible as a sacred, authoritative, and life-defining text. The biblical writings offer a particular way in which readers define themselves as persons, structure their world, and live in relationship to the world and others. The damaging of this initial moral sense may be the cause for some of the experience of moral injury and the object that needs to be recovered and restored in the work of healing.

As a caveat, I don't mean to suggest that the Bible provides modern communities with a simplistic set of moral principles or values that can be cherry-picked in isolation or made to align with values endorsed by military culture. Rather, the Bible as a whole, with its diverse stories, teachings, and poems about complex moral situations and complex moral characters, provides what we might call a theological anthropology—that is, a set of particular theological ways of viewing the nature of the world, what it means to be human, and the character of relationships among God, humans, and the world. These understandings yield a moral framework that is more complex than any list of rules or values. Seen in this way, the Bible—in all of its irreducible diversity of genres, styles, and viewpoints—can offer those working on moral injury a common language or shared grammar for talking about moral dimensions of the inner life that some writers have suggested is missing from current moral injury conversations.[33] The biblical writings don't have to be the only language or grammar for discussing human moral dimensions involved in moral injury, but they can be one, especially for those whose notions of morality and ethics are already formed by a background in Christian communities of faith and the importance of the Bible within those communities.

What, then, is the moral sense of self and the world that the biblical writings offer as a starting moral or ethical framework within which moral injury might be experienced and healed? In general terms, the biblical writings put forward a particular understanding of who we are as persons and toward what end or goal (Greek, *telos*) we are called to live as individuals and in community. In biblical terminology, these realities constitute the "image of God" in which all human beings were created (Gen 1:26). Specifically, in the biblical writings, the vision of the moral self is that humans are created by God to live in life-giving relationships with God and others. These relationships should imitate God's own ways and exhibit values, abilities, and practices such as empathy, compassion, and the ability to recognize what is good and life-giving and what isn't.[34] In addition, the Bible's moral framework puts forward the conviction that humans are created by God to live toward the particular end or goal of knowing and loving God and others in the fullest way possible. In biblical terminology, we are created as moral persons to "love the Lord your God with all your heart, and with all your soul, and with all your mind" and to "love your neighbor as yourself" (Matt 22:37, 39; see also Deut 6:5; Lev 19:18). All actions, practices, and beliefs are to move us toward this goal, and we experience a fulfilled life the more we live into these divinely ordained ends. By contrast, when we are drawn away from pursuing these ends by our own actions or those of others, we sense (or sometimes fail to sense) that our moral selves are fragmented, our relationships distorted, our purpose amiss, and our fulfillment frustrated.

Overall, then, biblical studies may contribute something especially distinctive to work on moral injury in the specific case of questions concerning the moral and ethical framework from which moral considerations begin. This contribution adds to psychological perspectives by offering a holistic theological conception of the nature of human persons as moral beings in relationship, with a fundamental orientation toward a particular, guiding telos. As Kinghorn explains, the common psychological approaches to moral injury, while perceptive and helpful, typically don't treat moral injury as "anything other than an immanent, psychological phenomenon involving not a fragmentation of a teleological whole but transgression of a soldier's own internalized rules and assumptions."[35] The biblical contribution to the question of initial moral frameworks, however, names the moral struggles of war "not simply as psychological dissonance but as a tragic and perhaps even sinful reminder that the peace of God is still not yet a fully present reality" in our lives and our world.[36]

Those who engage biblical texts in these ways don't have to reach precise or identical conclusions concerning moral and ethical frameworks. They can, however, consider the Bible's conceptions of the moral self in relationship and the particular ends toward which persons are to live as one way to describe the foundational moral or ethical framework that is upset in moral injury and repaired in moral healing.

Overview

From these starting points the following chapters will explore the twofold thesis that moral injury can be an interpretive frame of reference that brings new meanings out of biblical texts and that the critical study of biblical texts can make substantive contributions to the ongoing attempt to understand, identify, and heal moral injury. Chapter 2 will provide a basis by discussing current understandings of moral injury drawn from various fields (psychology, military studies, moral philosophy, and more), including current conceptions of the nature, causes, symptoms, and means of healing moral injury. The discussion will highlight two main trajectories of how biblical and other ancient texts have already been engaged in the context of moral injury work and what possibilities arise from those engagements.

Each subsequent chapter will treat a specific element within these trajectories of engagement, discussing what has already been done with that element in moral injury work, offering a case study from the Old Testament, and reflecting on the possible new perspectives raised by the intersection of the biblical text and moral injury. Chapter 3 will look at one trajectory of engagement that consists of creative rereadings of literary characters and narratives within ancient texts as exemplars of warriors and experiences related to moral injury. The chapter will explore how the story of King Saul (1 Sam 9–31), with its often-cited tragic dimensions, might be read as the tale of a morally wounded warrior and how biblical interpretation might, in turn, contribute to moral injury work that seeks new and illuminating readings of literary, especially tragic, characters. Chapter 4 will discuss a second trajectory of engagement that consists of exploring war-related rituals and symbolic practices in ancient texts for their connections to moral injury and the attempts to deal with its experiences and effects. This chapter will focus on postwar rituals and practices that appear in the Old Testament, especially the ritual purification of warriors, captives, and objects after battle (e.g., Num 31) and the various kinds of redistribution of spoils from battle (e.g., Gen 14:17-24; Num 31:25-47; Josh 22:7-9). The discussion will look for textual elements in the rituals and practices that suggest the recognition of and need to deal with the experience now associated with moral injury.

In an extension of the rituals and practices trajectory, chapter 5 will single out the practice of lament, especially as expressed in the Old Testament's lament and penitential psalms (both individual and communal).

The discussion will explore the possible connections between ancient Israel's expressions of lament and the emerging emphasis on imaginative confession or disclosure, compassionate dialogue, and forgiving moral authorities within current moral injury work. Chapter 6 will then move to a broader question on which perspectives from moral injury may provide new insights for biblical studies: "Do the biblical warfare and violence texts morally injure their readers?" This discussion reconsiders the difficult issue of the interpretation of the Old Testament's texts depicting divine and divinely sanctioned violence by exploring whether elements within moral injury yield a new way to understand what is theologically troubling about these biblical texts (especially for Christian readers) and whether any of the proposed ways to heal moral injury in soldiers can help with interpretation. Chapter 7 will conclude by summarizing the ways that moral injury provides a reading lens for biblical texts and the possible contributions that the study of the Bible can make to the ongoing work on moral injury. This discussion will briefly highlight the consideration of moral injury within contexts other than warfare and the possibilities that New Testament texts may offer to the engagement between moral injury and the Bible.

Chapter 2
Moral Injury and Biblical Interpretation

*I fear I am no longer
alien to this horror.
I am, I am, I am the horror.
I have lost my humanity. . . .
The monster and I are one.*

—*Camillo (Mac) Bica* [1]

This chapter is a basic overview of the current understandings of moral injury, especially as they have developed within psychology, military studies, and veterans' work. Since my focus in this book is not on moral injury per se but on the engagement between the Bible and moral injury, the overview here isn't intended to be comprehensive, technical, or definitive. The aim is to provide an adequate sketch of current views in order to establish the basis for the creative engagements explored in the following chapters. Readers who want more thorough discussions of the definition, causes, symptoms, and possible treatments of moral injury should explore the references provided in the notes that accompany this chapter. Beyond the basic overview, however, this chapter introduces how moral injury studies have thus far used biblical texts and how biblical interpretation has thus far engaged elements of moral injury work.

Understanding Moral Injury (Definitions, Symptoms, and Healing)

The label *moral injury* describes, in a basic sense, the result of the violation of a person's core moral beliefs (by oneself or others). Put more technically, moral injury refers to the deleterious effects of war participation on moral conscience and ethical conceptions—the wrecking of a person's fundamental assumptions about "what's right" and how things should work in the world—that may result from a sense of having violated one's core moral identity and lost any reliable, meaningful world in which to live. In other words, moral injury is particularly concerned with perceived violations (by oneself or others) of one's own sense of morality, and the impact that such violations have on a person's view of themselves or the nature of the world. As Brock and Lettini explain, "Moral injury results when soldiers violate their core moral beliefs [or have those beliefs betrayed by others], and in evaluating their behavior negatively, they feel they no longer live in a reliable, meaningful world and can no longer be regarded as decent human beings."[2] Seen in this way, moral injury involves acts of moral compromise or the violations of values and beliefs that potentially threaten soldiers' abilities to admire or even recognize themselves or trust in the morality of others and the world.

This basic description, although accurate, masks the complexity and diversity present within current moral injury studies. There has been a flood of publications exploring moral injury over the last decade, with numerous studies appearing even during the writing of this book.[3] Although earlier works acknowledged and engaged the possibly injurious moral and ethical effects of war on those who participated in it, sustained, clinical, and research-based studies of moral injury began to appear in earnest in publications in 2009.[4] In recent years, studies have appeared within clinical psychology, VA-sponsored treatment programs, and other academic fields, both religious (e.g., pastoral care, chaplaincy, and Christian counseling) and nonreligious (e.g., moral philosophy). Today, attention to and discussion of moral injury appear not only in academic settings and scholarly writing, but also in current press and media (e.g., the *Huffington Post*, the *New York Times*), as well as popular culture avenues (movies and television).

Syracuse University initiated the Moral Injury Project in 2014, and Brite Divinity School at Texas Christian University opened the Soul Repair Center in 2012. Volunteers of America now sponsors the Shay Moral Injury Center. Veterans themselves have produced films and documentaries. Note, for instance, the documentary *Almost Sunrise*, which features Tom Voss and Anthony Anderson, and chronicles the 2013 journey of the two veterans as they walked from Wisconsin to California to raise awareness for PTSD and moral injury. The Department of Defense and other military and government agencies have paid increasing attention to the possibilities of moral injury in recent years.[5] Perhaps most notably, the Naval Medical Center in San Diego, California, sponsors the first-of-its-kind residential program called Overcoming Adversity and Stress Injury Support (OASIS), with a particular focus on work with moral injury. Even some popular science fiction, such as Orson Scott Card's 1986 book, *Ender's Game* (later made into a movie), explores issues of guilt and the search for atonement related to actions in war.[6] At the general level, each of these ways of engaging moral injury is considering the morality of war and the ethical problems raised by participation in it.

The emerging and wide-ranging nature of the work being done on moral injury in recent years has produced a situation in which there is currently no single definition or unanimously shared understanding of it. At present, we can identify events and experiences that are potentially morally injurious, describe some of the characteristics of being morally injured, and employ various strategies for healing. We cannot yet, however, accurately predict all the kinds of events and experiences that might cause moral injury, identify which characteristics of being morally injured are "necessary and sufficient" for that determination, or know with certainty what methods of repair work, with which people, and in what ways.[7] Nash

[handwritten margin note: Movements toward awareness + healing]

and Acampora provide a helpful analogy for the present state of our attempts to understand, identify, and work with moral injury: "We are still proverbial blind men and women unwittingly describing the parts of an elephant that are close enough to touch, yet we have no idea how the trunk, ears, tusks, and tail might possibly fit together on one beast, or even whether what we perceive are truly aspects of just one entity."[8]

This analogy might exaggerate, but it accurately expresses that the effort to understand and work with moral injury at present is marked by ongoing debate and unsettled questions, especially concerning how to define moral injury, how to identify its causes and symptoms, and how best to help those affected by it.

Definitions

Moral injury doesn't have a single, agreed-upon definition (see the appendix at the end of the book), and this book will not try here to resolve all of the unsettled questions in the way that a work solely dedicated to understanding moral injury per se might try to do. Part of the struggle with finding a precise definition stems from the fact that in its origins and usage, the designation *moral injury* has functioned primarily as a working label to highlight certain unspecified and ill-defined effects of war participation not covered by well-established clinical diagnoses such as PTSD. Orris describes moral injury in its origins as a "provisional construct," designed to point to the "impact of certain stressor events commonly encountered in war, yet excluded from the current definition of posttraumatic stress disorder (PTSD), especially the psychological consequences of moral violations."[9]

The effort to identify moral injury as distinct from PTSD was, in fact, the starting point for early attempts at definition and understanding.[10] At the most fundamental level, PTSD is a psychological disorder—a fear-victim response—that results from an injury to the areas of the brain that regulate emotions. It is a psychological adjustment disorder that focuses on the impact of "life-threat trauma" and the ways that experiencing threat from and harm by others prevent the victim from adjusting back to a sense of safety and trust.[11] The use of insights from trauma theory in general and PTSD in particular has been a significant part of biblical interpretation since the 1990s, especially among scholars working on Old Testament prophetic texts that are associated with the experiences of destruction and exile.[12]

Over the last two decades, studies of the effects of war have begun to question whether the categories of trauma and PTSD account sufficiently for aspects of war's aftermath that go beyond emotional wounds and adjustment difficulties, particularly aspects related to moral and ethical sensibilities and feelings of shame and guilt. Beginning especially with Shay's works centered on Vietnam veterans, studies have pointed toward the need to identify some of war's effects that do not fit comfortably in typical medical and mental health approaches.[13] Moral injury has thus developed as a distinct category that attempts to shift the focus from the results of experiencing or witnessing actual or threatened death and injury to the consequences of perpetrating or inflicting violence or killing on others within war contexts. Seen in this way, moral injury moves from analysis of "the long-term phenomenology of individuals *harmed by others* (and other unpredictable, uncontrollable, and threatening circumstances)" to the "potential harm [to the agent] produced by perpetration (and moral transgressions) in traumatic contexts."[14]

Debate continues today over the precise relationship between moral injury and PTSD.[15] Recent studies build on the distinction in various ways and articulate the relationship between moral injury and PTSD differently. Some identify moral injury as complementary to but distinct from PTSD, while others imply that moral injury can cause PTSD, or that moral injury works alongside PTSD so that an event can be both traumatic and morally injurious.[16] It seems clear that moral injury and PTSD overlap in key ways (especially in shared symptoms such as anger, depression, and anxiety) but also have unique components. An increasing number of researchers argue that moral injury can exist apart from and as distinct from PTSD, especially since moral injury considers the experiences of shame and guilt that need to be addressed in specific ways and can be easily obscured by a focus on fear-related brain disorders.[17]

As we turn from this background to current definitions of moral injury, one way of seeking understanding is to attend to the descriptions of veterans. Unlike technical and clinical definitions, veterans' accounts often explain moral injury and the experiences that cause it in ways that are anecdotal, imprecise, emotive—yet powerful. For example, a thirty-year-old Navy corpsman told his psychologist that all he could think was "Die woman, die," as he watched an Iraqi woman, who had earlier killed one of his marines in a firefight, lay dying after he returned fire on her. As a corpsman, his role was now to save her, but all he felt was anger and a desire for her to die. "It bothers me that it doesn't bother me, Doc. Is that wrong? Am I evil?" he asks his counselor.[18]

A marine named Nick reported another experience. After he spotted someone moving behind a wall and firing at him and his marines, Nick saw the shooter was a young teenage boy. "With only a split second to decide, he squeezes the trigger and ends the boy's life."[19] Also reflecting the impact of dealing with children, Stephen Canty reported his experiences at a vehicle checkpoint in Afghanistan. He recalled the approach of a middle-aged man riding a moped with two bruised and crying young boys on the back. The marines there knew that the boys had been raped. But because they had no weapons, Canty said, "By our mission here they're good to go—they're OK! And we're supposed to keep going on missions with these guys. Your morals start to degrade."[20] Even a chaplain recounted the experience of moral betrayal during his time in Iraq: "Seeing the devastation of Iraqi cities and towns, some of it caused by us, some by the insurgents and the civil war that we brought about, hit me to the core.... I felt lied to by our senior leadership. And I felt those lies cost too many thousands of American lives and far too much destruction."[21]

Many more veterans' accounts are available.[22] Even these examples, however, show that issues related to morality, ethics, meaning, and value are key elements of the soldiers' experiences. Readers can see the struggle with a self-understanding that begins with confident feelings that one is good, acts honorably, and that justice is attainable—and yet ends with worries that perhaps one hasn't done what is right, has contributed to the problem, and encountered a world that is incoherent and lacks any reliable moral order. Perhaps most notably, as Bica insists, soldiers' accounts show that the moral and ethical conflict being described should be seen not as an illness, condition, or disorder, but as an "injury"—a "wound" of war.[23]

Alongside these anecdotal ways to define moral injury, more technical, precise, and clinical definitions have now been proposed by psychiatrists, psychologists, and other researchers. The initial, formal articulations appeared in several clinical psychology publications between 2009 and 2013.[24] Even earlier, though, the more narrative works of psychologist Jonathan Shay on the intersections between the experiences of American veterans of the Vietnam War and the literary depictions of warriors in the *Iliad* and the *Odyssey* introduced the concept of moral injury as an overlooked element in the study of war-related experiences.[25]

The progression from Shay's initial work to that of the later clinical studies resulted in a significant shift in the definition of moral injury that shapes current efforts at understanding and identification. Shay's original formulation focused on the soldier's experience of betrayal of trust by authorities as the primary element of moral injury. He defined moral injury as a betrayal of "what's right" by someone who holds legitimate authority in a "high-stakes situation."[26] In Shay's definition, there is a social and interpersonal element to moral injury because the soldier has been morally injured by the betraying actions of another, especially those in military or governmental authority. The individual may have engaged in morally questionable actions, but they did so because they were betrayed by someone who held legitimate authority and yet acted immorally and unethically. The "what's right" that gets violated here is not just the soldier's inner convictions, but the right ways that one should treat and be treated socially, relationally, and interpersonally within military structure and in high-stakes situations.[27] Defined in this way, moral injury began as a critique of military structure and leadership (especially in the context of the Vietnam War), with an important social and political dimension meant to challenge policies and conditions seen as harmful to soldiers. Moral injury provides a mechanism to critique the cultural conditions and policies that lead to war and harm its participants.[28]

From this starting point, definitional work on moral injury next developed primarily within clinical settings, especially within military psychology. Here, the primary defining focus of moral injury shifted to acts done by the soldier that violated her or his fundamental moral convictions.[29] The most widely accepted clinical definition appeared in the work of Litz et al.: "Perpetrating, failing to prevent, or bearing witness to acts that transgress deeply held moral beliefs and expectations may be deleterious in the long-term, emotionally, psychologically, behaviorally, spiritually, and socially."[30] For Litz et al., "morals" are the fundamental assumptions about how things should work and how one should behave in the world. This definition allows for the one who violates these moral convictions to be someone other than the soldier (since moral injury can be caused by simply "bearing witness" to acts); but in practice, this definition has typically resulted in an emphasis placed almost entirely on the soldier and her or his own actions as the cause of moral injury.[31] The political and social criticism of military, governmental, and cultural practices present in Shay's initial definition was somewhat lost in these more clinical understandings.[32]

More recent and emerging definitions of moral injury try to take account of both the aspects of betrayal and perpetration. Litz himself has recently revised his original definition so that it now distinguishes between two types of moral injury: "perpetration-based moral injury" and "betrayal-based moral injury."[33] Overall, at present, definitions typically identify three broad types of moral injury: (1) perpetration (of acts done legitimately or otherwise that are morally injurious), (2) failure (by self or others), and (3) disillusionment (ranging from specific to broad).[34] Acts of perpetration may include offensive and defensive aggression, lack of restraint, acts of revenge, inflicting of collateral damage, and actions undertaken in ambiguous situations. Failure-based moral injury may involve self-blame for inaction that could've saved a fellow soldier or feelings of a lack of control and predictability in the world. Disillusionment-based moral injury may involve the perception that an authority is incompetent, unethical, or indifferent (e.g., making risky decisions or acting out of self-interest), or an individual's increasing recognition that she or he has a capacity for violence and evil.[35]

Based on the above observations, many formal definitions have appeared in recent publications. Here are only a few examples that stand alongside the two initial formulations of Shay and Litz et al., especially those that best capture the generally shared sense at present (see the appendix at the end of the book for a fuller listing). For example, another definition by Litz (this time with Maguen) brings together most of the variables and nuances of moral injury noted above:

> In the context of war, moral injuries may stem from direct participation in acts of combat, such as killing or harming others, or indirect acts, such as witnessing death or dying, failing to prevent immoral acts of others, or giving or receiving orders that are perceived as gross moral violation. The act may have been carried out by an individual or a group.[36]

The understanding provided by a veteran highlights the ways that moral injury can be experienced even when accepted cultural or governmental standards are followed: "Killing hurts the killer, too, even in self-defense or in the line of duty and . . . no *justification*, legal, political, religious, or otherwise, can heal those wounds."[37]

Some recent definitions especially emphasize the corrosive impact of moral injury on one's sense of self, character, and identity. Levine defines moral injury as

> a persistent existential crisis that erodes the very fabric of their sense of self . . . a spiritual and existential ambivalence that leads to a deep identity crisis due to the fact that they have perpetrated, witnessed, or failed to prevent battlefield events that run against the grain of identified or unidentified, but viscerally felt and "known," personal moral or ethical views and commitments.[38]

Likewise, Larson and Zust label moral injury as a "complex 'soul' wound...[that] produces a chain of emotions and maladaptive behaviors that corrode character and damage an individual's capacity for living."[39] Graham describes moral injury as "the erosive diminishment of our souls because our moral actions and the actions of others against us sometimes have harmful outcomes."[40] In the most recent comprehensive treatment grounded in the field of moral philosophy, Sherman defines moral injury as "experiences of serious inner conflict...that can overwhelm one's sense of goodness and humanity" and stresses that these experiences aren't limited to "moral transgressions" but may also involve "a generalized sense of falling short of moral and normative standards befitting good persons and good soldiers."[41]

The most comprehensive recent definition that describes moral injury as a phenomenon links it with trauma, and points the way to exploring its specific symptoms. It reads as follows:

> Phenomenologically, *moral injury* represents a particular trauma syndrome including psychological, existential, behavioral, and interpersonal issues that emerge following perceived violations of deeply held moral beliefs by oneself or trusted individuals (i.e., morally injurious experiences). These experiences cause significant moral dissonance, which if unresolved, leads to the development of its core symptoms.[42]

Among the current definitions and conceptions of moral injury, there remain some unsettled questions and ongoing issues. One of the most significant issues is that the US military resists acknowledging officially the reality of moral injury or using that specific label. Instead, military publications such as the Navy's and Marine Corps's *Combat Operational Stress Control* identify the experience as "inner conflict" and "moral damage" and discuss it as one of their "combat operational stress" injuries.[43] Another ongoing discussion in current studies concerns whether moral injury necessarily implies wrongdoing by the person and the need for forgiveness. Some works maintain that it is possible to draw a distinction between feelings of having been morally compromised by actions or circumstances and the fact of having committed acts that are judged as wrongs in need of pardon.[44] This issue is relevant to the ongoing consideration of the role of forgiveness in the healing of moral injury (see discussion below) and will be discussed further in chapter 5 in connection with the practice of lament.

A final open question concerns the extent to which moral injury can be a communal experience. Most studies have focused on moral injury as an individual reality without much attention to how it might be experienced by social, cultural, or ethnic groups, who might then seek healing together as a group.[45] The postwar rituals often cited in reference to healing moral injury, including those from ancient texts such as the Old Testament, tend to reflect a communal dimension that isn't often discussed in definitions of moral injury (see ch. 4).

Causes and Effects

At the most basic level, moral injury is caused by doubt. As Bica explains, moral injury can result when doubts arise "regarding the necessity and justness of the enterprise and the nobility and righteousness of the warriors' involvement."[46] Circumstances, events, and experiences can poke holes in what Larson and Zust call the common cultural "myth" that if soldiers fight within the rules of engagement in a "just war," their consciences should be untroubled.[47] Just war theory as it has developed within Christian tradition is a moral code. Even so, the experience of soldiers suggests that sometimes an action that is justifiable according to a formal theory (e.g., just war or international law) conflicts with moral intuitions (e.g., all life is sacred) and feels like a violation of something at the core of who we are as humans. Modern Western societies may declare that if something is "legal" than it must be "moral," but soldiers may not experience war's realities in that way.[48]

All of these observations show that the assumptions people hold about themselves and their world can contribute to the experiences of moral injury. In a classic work on trauma, for example, Janoff-Bulman made the big claim that well-adjusted persons operate with the assumptions that the world is benevolent and meaningful, and they themselves are worthy individuals.[49] Whether or not this claim can be sustained for all well-adjusted persons, the realities of war can raise doubts about these kinds of operative assumptions and thus constitute a general cause of the experience of moral injury.

More specifically, building on the two initial definitions by Shay and Litz et al., one clinical study has now formulated the "Moral Injury Events Scale," a nine-item self-report questionnaire designed to identify potentially morally injurious events, and has emphasized two primary causes of moral injury: (1) the transgression of moral codes by self or others, and (2) betrayals of trust.[50] At the most basic level, these kinds of events reduce confidence in previously held moral beliefs and one's own and others' motivation and ability to live in just and ethical ways. The initial study by Litz et al. proposed that the core cause of moral injury is a person's inability to contextualize, justify, or accommodate morally challenging actions into her or his understanding of self and the world.[51] The potential for moral injury, then, unfolds through a progression that begins when one commits an act (or witnesses or fails to prevent an act) that transgresses one's moral convictions and thus creates moral dissonance and conflict. But a broader perspective suggests that the potential injury isn't simply about transgressions. Rather, it's the phenomenon of being caught between two moral imperatives, each of which is good but can't be simultaneously followed (e.g., to defend one's family or country, and to honor and protect all life as sacred).[52]

The conditions that follow dictate whether the person experiences moral injury. If the person comes to see the transgressive act as "global" (i.e., not context dependent), "internal" (i.e., the result of something within her or his own character rather than a particular circumstance), and "stable" (i.e., enduring beyond a specific time and place), the likelihood that she or he will experience the kinds of shame, guilt, and loss of trust associated with moral injury significantly increases.[53] As we'll see, many of the portrayals of moral injury in ancient, even biblical texts, as well as the proposed rituals and practices for healing, revolve around how to help soldiers see their experiences in ways other than global, internal, and stable.

Two additional considerations are relevant for moral injury's causes. First, some recent explorations have suggested that discussions of the causes should include the possibility that moral injury doesn't even require actions; rather, just being in the environment of war or the military can cause moral injury. Bica asserts that simply living amid the prolonged violence, death, trauma, and anxiety of war "erodes our moral being, undoes character, and reduces decent men and women to savages capable of incredible cruelty."[54] The environment itself is toxic, as it transmits ideologies and demands actions that conflict with moral approaches to living. Seen in this way, military culture itself, apart from combat, is a potentially morally damaging environment. Bica claims that basic training strikes the first blow of moral injury, using "sophisticated indoctrination techniques of value manipulation, moral desensitization, and psychological conditioning aimed at destroying/overriding their humanity and their moral aversion to killing."[55] Basic training tries to dismantle the recruit's previous beliefs, values, and ethics and replace them with those that serve the needs of the military, forcibly putting into place a new "moral system" that may contradict and override the ways soldiers have understood themselves and accounted for their world.[56] In Christian terms, this process may constitute the transformation or, perhaps, distortion of the "image of God" as the created moral and relational identity of human persons (see discussion in ch. 1).

Second, Kilner has recently added a consideration for discussing the causes of moral injury that is especially relevant to biblical and theological perspectives.[57] Alongside the commonly recognized causes of betrayal by authorities and perpetration by the soldier, moral injury can be caused by a sense of divine betrayal. Firsthand experiences of large-scale and seemingly meaningless violence lead some soldiers to the sense that God has been overcome by evil, is unjust by allowing such evil, or must not exist. This sense of betrayal by God can lead to loss of faith in God, doubts about the reality of goodness and justice, and anger at God.[58]

The effects of moral injury may be viewed as consequences or symptoms.[59] They can be internal (distorted values and condemnations of self) and external (lost sense of an ordered and just world or loss of social relationships). They can be emotional, psychological, spiritual, and social. Researchers have now developed two primary matrices for the purposes of identifying specific effects of the experience: the "Moral Injury Symptom Scale—Military Version"[60] and the "Expressions of Moral Injury Scale—Military Version."[61] The effects include changes in ethical behavior and attitudes, changes in spirituality, reduced trust in others and social contracts, and feelings of guilt and shame.[62] Specific consequences here may include despair, self-harm, self-condemnation, and suicide; social and emotional detachment, numbing, or alienation; loss of faith or religious beliefs; inability to forgive self or others; or disillusionment with institutions and authority. A specifically theological consequence of moral injury, especially for those who come from deeply religious backgrounds, involves doubt about God. These doubts may take the form not only of questions about the very existence of a "higher power," but also doubts about God's character, worthiness, and purpose that can lead to questions about personal worth and vocation.[63] At a more general level, returning soldiers may struggle to have a nuanced understanding of what happened, what their responsibility actually is, and to what extent the experience was their fault.

A Theological Conception of Moral Injury

In addition to work in chaplaincy and pastoral care contexts, the field of academic theological studies has recently begun to engage moral injury. Brian Powers's work provides the most extensive and detailed example, using one particular Christian theological tradition.[64] He uses the theology of Augustine of Hippo (354–430 CE)—which conceives of sin as human will exercised in the pursuit of created things (good but finite things) that are wrongly loved in place of God—to argue that moral injury is not just acting in a way that violates one's moral convictions or rules; it is the loss of any meaningful moral world at all. In Powers's view, this loss occurs because military involvement—with its culture, values, and morality—distorts the person's understanding of what constitutes a moral world and moral character in specific ways.

Powers' thesis

First, participation in military culture and wartime actions results in "a 'flattening' of any sense of moral order—the creation of a moral world in which all that mattered was the pursuit of the enemy."[65] Put in the terms of Augustinian theology's conceptions of original sin and human will, military participation systemically and comprehensively transforms a person's original, internal convictions of what is right into the "pursuit of distorted and poisoned moral goods."[66] In other words, military culture and combat experience realign a person's moral orientation so that she or he "wills" the pursuit of a new "good"—namely, the defeat of an enemy through violence. This realignment begins, Powers explains, in the reconditioning accomplished in basic training, as military culture instills the "good" of killing through techniques such as dehumanizing the enemy and teaching reflexive (unthoughtful) obedience to commands.

Moral injury then occurs at a later point, sometimes during and sometimes after a person's participation in war. Due to the kinds of experiences noted above as causing moral injury (betrayal, disillusionment, ethically questionable circumstances and acts, and so on), a soldier may conclude that the new moral orientation they have adopted—and the new "good" toward which they have dedicated their willing—are false goods that don't stand up to moral scrutiny or produce good and life-giving results.[67] The person feels like they've lost any sense of a moral world or the proper good toward which they should commit their will. Moral injury is the realization that one has committed her or his "active willing in a powerful and compelling moral orientation that is understood at some point to be false."[68]

new, false goods

Healing and Repair

Contemporary work in psychology, counseling, and chaplaincy has proposed and practiced a number of ways to respond to moral injury and its effects, with some attention also given to possible prevention.[69] The goal is to address moral concerns and formulations, not simply to achieve functionality, so they're more rightly characterized as "moral healing" or "moral repair," rather than "treatment." This kind of recovery has proven to be more of an ongoing process than a cure or easily definable endpoint. At their core, the various approaches to moral repair attempt to respond to the primary cause noted above—namely, that moral injury occurs especially when a person comes to view a potentially morally injurious act as "global" (i.e., not context dependent), "internal" (i.e., the result of something within her or his own character rather than a particular circumstance), and "stable," (i.e., enduring beyond a specific time and place).[70] Proper healing and recovery practices try to frame potentially morally injurious acts and events as context specific, time bound, and at least partially the result of external demands that do not define the soldier's character forever, even as they acknowledge that bad actions may have been done and that appropriate grief, forgiveness, and atonement may be beneficial.

Approaches to moral repair attempt to accomplish this goal by using particular practices and promoting specific perspectives.[71] Two major clinical programs for working with moral injury have been developed and are being researched in practice: "Impact of Killing" (a six-session module) and "Adaptive Disclosure" (an eight-session intervention).[72] Four items appear frequently in these approaches: (1) learning forgiveness (especially for guilt and shame) for self and others through accepting appropriate responsibility and receiving compassion from a moral authority; (2) contextualizing events as having been products of and confined to specific circumstances; (3) distributing proportions of blame fairly and correctly among oneself, others, circumstances, and other factors; and (4) engaging in acts of repair and hope that give a sense of renewed humanity and a better world. In contrast to psychological approaches in other kinds of therapy that were designed to correct distorted thoughts or beliefs in the patient, these practices acknowledge that the soldiers' beliefs about their wartime actions are accurate, and they need ways to deal with the reality of those beliefs.[73] Hence, the goals are to help the soldier accept that wrong was done but that it need not define her or his life, to find ways of experiencing a sense of cleansing and forgiveness, to receive compassionate support for sharing their story, to reintegrate as a positive member of their community, and to engage in actions that reestablish the individual as a morally good person and the world as a place where good exists.[74] Litz et al. summarize the healing approaches as follows: "Moral repair...must involve acceptance of inconvenient truths, after drawing them into as objective a focus as is possible, and tolerance of painful moral emotions, so that a new context can be created for the traumatic events going forward (e.g., by making amends, asking forgiveness, or repairing moral damage symbolically)."[75]

Among these approaches to moral repair, the two means of prevention and healing discussed as most significant are symbolic purification and communalization. Symbolic purification involves specific postwar practices, perhaps even ceremonial rituals, to give returning soldiers a sense of cleansing and transition. The aim is not to excuse morally troubling acts but to allow them to be judged as such, and yet also allow soldiers to work through feelings of guilt or shame and transition from the social and moral adaptations that characterize warfare contexts.[76] Additionally, several book-length treatments and clinical studies have pushed the notion of communalization and the role of the community to the center of work on moral injury healing. The earlier works of Shay argued that prevention and repair are best accomplished as communal efforts involving things such as long-term cohesion of soldier units and the use of religious and social communities of support.[77] More recently, Sherman's comprehensive work grounded in moral philosophy identifies ways of recovery that revolve around building community and shared participation.

To communalize war-related acts is to engage in concrete practices that reframe the acts as communally, rather than individually or personally, owned and executed.[78] To communalize is to place moral repair not in the hands of mental health professionals but "in the society, in the community, and in the family—precisely where moral questions should be posed and wrangled with."[79] Here, morally wounded service members can tell their stories to those who can be trusted to receive them and thus reconnect with the communities from which they have been estranged by their participation in war.

The goal of communalization is to find practices that give soldiers a sense that the moral burden and responsibility are equally distributed among soldiers, leaders, and their community, even those who remained outside of the direct conflict, and that the combat has some larger significance. Current moral injury literature describes some of these practices in modern contexts as soldiers gathering in small groups (often in faith communities), making lists of all persons and institutions involved in responsibility for war events, and performing acts of repair, re-creation, and service in the community; these practices represent the opposite of war's acts of destruction.[80]

Moral Injury and Biblical Texts: Past Work and Present Trajectories

There are two elements that provide the remaining background for the specific engagements between moral injury and the Old Testament in the following chapters. Moral injury studies from various fields have already used biblical texts in some limited ways, and works within the discipline of biblical studies have very recently engaged elements of moral injury work. More detailed examples of each of these elements will appear in the chapters that follow, but the discussion here provides the general contours of what has happened thus far.

Past and Present Engagements

First, some moral injury works from disciplines such as psychology, military studies, historical studies, moral philosophy, and even journalism have referred to biblical texts, especially in their discussions of the effects and healing of moral injury. Sometimes these uses have been minor, simply drawing principles from teachings of scripture and applying them to moral repair and recovery. For example, Grimsley and Grimsley identified forgiveness as a biblical principle and used it as a key for healing moral injury.[81] More frequently, however, references to the Bible have appeared when moral injury works have discussed the potential role of rituals and symbolic practices in moral repair. Several psychologists and other researchers have identified rituals from biblical texts as possible models. For example, Shay explicitly mentioned the Israelite purification rite described in Numbers 31 (see ch. 4), and others have referenced this and similar postbattle biblical practices in this regard.[82] Other psychologists, approaching the Old Testament writings as artifacts of an ancient culture, have identified certain biblical characters, especially Saul, David, and Job, as allegories for soldiers' experiences (see ch. 3), not unlike Shay's initial work noted above with the ancient Greek mythological characters of Achilles and Odysseus.[83]

Moral injury works from fields closer to but still distinct from biblical scholarship, especially religious studies, pastoral theology, and Christian ethics, have also used biblical texts in their discussions. Like their nonreligious counterparts, these uses have also often been undeveloped, simply drawing principles from teachings of scripture and applying them to moral repair and recovery, although others have pointed to biblical rituals and characters as potential models and lessons. For example, Lee suggested that scripture can provide "meaning-making" instructions for finding hope, forgiveness, and purpose.[84] Many of these works have particularly referenced the Psalms, especially the so-called lament and penitential psalms, as potential resources for the elements of grief, confession, and forgiveness in moral repair. Childs, for example, noted that biblical lament psalms may provide the much-needed language that allows those suffering moral injury to speak honestly about their experiences as a means to healing.[85] Others have mentioned reading certain psalms as ways to express feelings of shame, guilt, betrayal, and anger, or the incorporation of lament into corporate rituals and public memorials related to moral injury.[86] A recent study of moral injury in relationship to biblical texts and classical Jewish writings represents one of pastoral care's most extensive engagements with the Bible, especially from within Jewish tradition.[87] This study surveys biblical narratives and characters, as well as Jewish rabbinical and liturgical texts, for references to spiritual brokenness and wounds, although most of the examples involve nonmilitary contexts (e.g., Cain and Abel in Gen 4).

Although moral injury works have sometimes referenced biblical texts, neither works from Christian and pastoral contexts nor those from psychology, military studies, and moral philosophy have typically done so in substantial, systematic, or sophisticated ways. And they haven't typically used biblical texts in keeping with the approaches of professional biblical scholarship. Very recently, however, a small number of works within the discipline of biblical studies per se have engaged elements of moral injury in dialogue with the interpretation of biblical texts. These new—and admittedly few—works provide the most immediate background for what I attempt to do in the Old Testament case studies that follow.

Some biblical studies works have attempted to further the conversation about possible Old Testament rituals and symbolic practices that might be reexamined with moral injury in mind, analyzing the relevant passages in their textual, historical, and cultural contexts in ancient Israel and the ancient Near East, as well as through the use of ritual theory, as academic biblical studies typically would do.[88] Some of these works have also considered how the rituals described in biblical texts might, in turn, be resources for understanding the dynamics of moral injury or for developing practices of moral repair.

Thus far, however, biblical scholars have mostly used moral injury as an interpretive lens to bring out new meanings from biblical narratives. In other words, the focus so far within biblical studies has remained on the biblical texts themselves, rather than on what or how the biblical texts might contribute to the formulations of moral injury and its healing. And most of these works have focused on characters within biblical stories, offering creative rereadings through the lens of moral injury's experiences, akin to what Shay did with Achilles and Odysseus. These studies form a counterpart from the field of biblical studies to the moral injury works mentioned above that operate in other fields but refer to certain biblical characters (e.g., Job, Saul, David) as possible allegories and analogues.

The most recent, book-length collection of these works is the volume edited by McDonald entitled *Exploring Moral Injury in Sacred Texts*. This volume's topics go beyond the biblical texts, including considerations of the intersections between moral injury and Judaism, Christianity, Islam, and Buddhism. But the volume contains several studies devoted to particular biblical narratives and characters. For example, Bowen reconsiders the disturbing acts in the Sodom story in Genesis 19 as the possible consequences of previous moral injury suffered in the war described in Genesis 14. She also rereads the subsequent reconnection between some Israelites and Lot's descendants (in Moab) described in the book of Ruth as a narrative example of moral repair.[89] Similarly, Blumenthal reinterprets David in the books of Samuel and Kings as a basic model of the experiences of return and repair after morally injurious actions.[90] As a New Testament example, Yandell reads the Gerasene demoniac in Mark 5 as a veteran of the Roman military. He explains the man's isolation, self-harming, and aggression in terms of the consequences of moral injury through war participation.[91]

Trajectories for Moving Forward

Among the works from psychology and military studies that attempt to understand moral injury and its causes, effects, and healing, as well as among the engagements with moral injury that have thus far taken place within professional biblical studies, two primary trajectories have emerged concerning how ancient texts such as the biblical writings have been and might be fruitfully used. These trajectories offer the most immediate potential to chaplains, ministers, counselors, and other readers of Christian scripture for creatively considering what moral injury research can contribute to the interpretation of biblical texts (especially warfare and violence texts) and what the study of the Bible (both academically and devotionally/pastorally) can contribute to the ongoing efforts to understand and address moral injury.

The first trajectory found in both general moral injury writings and biblical engagements with moral injury undertakes creative rereadings of literary narratives and characters as portrayals of morally injured warriors. As discussed above, the use of Greek mythological figures stands alongside the interpretations of biblical characters in this regard. The next chapter will offer an Old Testament case study in this trajectory that focuses on rereading the character of King Saul (1 Sam 9–31) as the tale of a morally wounded warrior and the effects of moral trauma on character, social trust, and personal survival.

The second trajectory found in both moral injury writings and biblical engagements with moral injury explores the identification, importance, and implementation of postwar rituals and symbolic practices that attempt to deal with aspects of moral injury. As noted above, various moral injury studies have looked to rituals and practices from ancient and traditional societies and their writings, hoping to connect these with the felt needs of morally injured persons for forgiveness, purification, communalization, and hope. And these studies have appealed to researchers to look for more potentially useful models among rituals and practices in ancient texts. Chapter 4 will offer some case studies in this trajectory by surveying the Old Testament's postwar rituals and symbolic practices, as well as their parallels in ancient Near Eastern texts and cultures, to consider how moral injury shapes our understanding of those textual depictions and what that analysis might offer to reflection on the moral and ethical dynamics of soldiers' responses to battle. Chapter 5 will extend this trajectory with an Old Testament case study devoted to the practice of lament. The focus will be on the Old Testament's so-called lament and penitential psalms, especially in connection with moral injury approaches such as "Adaptive Disclosure," which emphasizes the use of confession and dialogue with a compassionate moral authority who can grant forgiveness.

Chapter 3
Moral Injury and the Case of King Saul (1 Samuel 9–31)

[Whoever] fights with monsters should be careful lest he [or she] thereby become a monster. And if thou gaze long into an abyss, the abyss will also gaze into thee.

—*Friedrich Nietzsche* [1]

The Old Testament case study in this chapter is the first attempt to explore the thesis that the engagement between the Bible and moral injury generates a two-way conversation. The interpretations of some of the Bible's war-related stories and ritual descriptions undertaken here and in the following chapters illustrate how moral injury can be an interpretive lens that brings new meanings out of biblical texts, and how the critical study of the Bible can make substantive contributions to the ongoing attempt to understand, identify, and heal moral injury.

Toward that end, I offer here a rereading of the story of King Saul (1 Sam 9–31) in dialogue with the perspectives of moral injury.[2] Within biblical studies, interpreters have viewed Saul, Israel's first king, not only as a negative, less-than-admirable character, but more specifically as a tragic figure, reading the story of his kingdom's rise and fall in the literary category of tragedy known from ancient Greek literature. Through the engagement with moral injury, however, Saul's story, with its often-noted tragic dimensions, might be read as the tale of a morally wounded warrior and might, in turn, contribute to our understanding of moral injury.

The discussion below represents an example of the first of the two primary trajectories noted in chapter 2 that have emerged concerning how ancient texts have been and might be fruitfully used in work on moral injury. As mentioned in the preceding chapter, these trajectories offer the most immediate entry points for chaplains, ministers, psychologists, biblical scholars, and other interested persons to consider creatively what moral injury research can contribute to the interpretation of biblical texts (especially warfare and violence texts) and what the study of the Bible can contribute to the ongoing efforts to understand and address moral injury. The interpretation of the story of King Saul here represents the trajectory that undertakes creative rereadings of literary figures as portrayals of morally injured warriors and thus as instructive and illuminating metaphors for the postwar experiences of real soldiers—a trajectory that has appeared in Shay's and other researchers' use of Greek mythological figures, as well as in some biblical scholars' recent interpretations of certain biblical characters and stories.[3] Although Shay asserts that Homer's *Odyssey* is the earliest known account of a soldier's moral and psychological struggles after war, Saul's story might provide another example of a morally injured warrior whose symptoms and struggles are cast in the theological matrices of the biblical narratives concerned primarily with David and Israelite kingship.[4]

What follows isn't a comprehensive analysis but an initial, exploratory, and suggestive venture that illustrates how readers of the Bible might look for characters in warfare contexts who transgress their moral conscience or otherwise suffer moral injury, as well as for stories that illustrate the consequences of such transgressive experiences. The first part of the chapter reviews the background of these kinds of literary reinterpretations in moral injury work in general. The heart of the chapter works through the various parts of Saul's story in dialogue with moral injury's dynamics, experiences, and consequences. The chapter concludes by considering the potential insights that emerge from this encounter between the biblical story and moral injury.

Background: Ancient Texts, Literary Characters, and Moral Injury

There are several avenues of study that lead to this reading of the Saul story in dialogue with moral injury. The first is the way that moral injury research, from its beginnings in psychology and veterans' care to its present formulations in chaplaincy and Christian ministry, has undertaken creative rereadings of literary figures, especially those found in ancient Greek myths and tragedies, as portrayals of morally injured warriors and thus as allegories of the postwar experiences of real veterans. Shay's *Shay* groundbreaking works within psychology and trauma study provided the initial and most extensive examples of this practice by interpreting the Greek mythological heroes Achilles and Odysseus, in Homer's *Iliad* and *Odyssey*, as metaphors for the experiences of contemporary soldiers both in warfare and homecoming. For example, Shay explored the portrayal of Achilles in the *Iliad* by viewing Achilles as having suffered moral injury because of the betrayal of "what's right" in wartime by his commander Agamemnon.[5] Shay concluded that healing from moral injury requires the soldier to be able to tell her or his story to someone who can be trusted to relay it truthfully to the community, and this reading of Achilles's story provides soldiers with language and allegories for expressing their own stories.[6] Likewise, Shay reread the story of Odysseus in books 9–12 of the *Odyssey* as a "detailed allegory" of the difficulties of homecoming after war.[7] He used soldiers' and veterans' testimonies about their experiences as an "added source of interpretive insight" into the Greek epic that reveals it as "the story of a soldier's wanderings and troubles as he tries to make it home."[8]

Several other works on moral injury from within psychology have given similar consideration to various characters from ancient Greek literature. These works explore several questions, and seem to answer each in the affirmative: (1) Do ancient Greek writings reflect universal aspects of warfare and its effects? (2) Were the ancient Greeks aware of what we now call combat trauma and related consequences? and (3) Does Greek culture reveal any particular responses that try to address or prevent these effects?[9] Some works have examined the portrayal of Heracles by Euripides as a representation of how the madness of war leads the hero to violence even after the war has ended.[10] Similarly, a number of moral injury studies have worked with the title character of Sophocles's fifth-century BCE play *Ajax* as an example of a warrior suffering from moral distress and struggling with homecoming after war.[11] Ajax became possessed by a sudden madness due to a perceived betrayal in which Achilles's armor was awarded to Odysseus instead of him. He sought revenge, but ended up slaughtering a herd of animals, suffering humiliation, and committing suicide. Another of Sophocles's plays, *Philoctetes*, has served some researchers as a representation of the moral damage and ambiguity caused by the betrayal of trust, especially in the depiction of the relationship between Philoctetes and Neoptolemus.[12] Sherman suggests that Sophocles, himself a Greek general, had his plays such as *Ajax* and *Philoctetes* function as "reentry rituals of sorts performed before returning veterans."[13]

A second avenue that leads to this reading of the Saul story is the way that some moral injury works, both inside and outside of Christian approaches, have engaged biblical characters as the same kinds of possible allegories for the experiences of soldiers and the dynamics of moral injury. These engagements in nonreligious works usually approach the Bible as a cultural artifact in touch with the realities of war. For example, Tick claims, "Western civilization's founding epics—the *Iliad* and the Old Testament—are 'war bibles' of utmost brutality."[14] More specifically, some works read the Joseph story (Gen 37–50) as the tale of a person morally wounded by experiences other than warfare and as an example of the importance of memory and forgiveness in moral healing.[15] Other Old Testament characters that have been engaged, although sometimes only in cursory ways, include Job (especially around issues of betrayal), Saul, and David.[16]

The final and most relevant avenue that leads to this reading of the Saul story is the way that some very recent works within biblical scholarship have undertaken creative rereadings of biblical narratives and characters through the lens of moral injury. For example, as part of a larger examination of storytelling, Frank reconsiders Jacob's wrestling (Gen 32:22-32) as his struggle with the moral injury he suffered in a series of betrayals that started with his birth family.[17] As chapter 2 mentioned, the volume of essays entitled *Exploring Moral Injury in Sacred Texts* provides several examples in which biblical scholars offer extended interpretations of stories and characters such as Abraham, Lot, Sodom and Gomorrah, David, Peter, Judas, and the Gerasene Demoniac in dialogue with the experiences of moral injury.[18]

In keeping with the dynamics of these previous engagements with characters of ancient Greek tragedies and biblical texts, the story of King Saul (1 Sam 9–31), with its often-cited tragic dimensions, might be read as the tale of a morally wounded warrior and might, in turn, contribute to the understanding of moral injury.

King Saul, the Morally Wounded Warrior

The character, motivations, and actions of Israel's first king, Saul, depicted in 1 Samuel 9–31, have occupied the attention of both ancient and contemporary interpreters.[19] These interpreters have often viewed Saul in a negative light, as having a less-than-admirable, even deeply problematic, character and personality—a virtual madman perhaps suffering some sort of psychological disorder and steadily descending into deep existential darkness and violent rage.[20] The majority of interpreters simply reiterate the biblical text's negative image of Saul, which identifies his flawed character and questionable deeds as part of the divine punishment for his unfaithfulness to the Israelite God, Yhwh.[21] Although these opinions of Saul seem firmly established, what happens if one considers the figure of Saul in the stories of 1 Samuel in the ways that moral injury literature has done with various figures from Greek mythological texts? Perhaps the Saul texts, like those describing Odysseus, point not to psychological illness but to the effects of moral trauma on character, social trust, and personal survival.

The composition and literary history of the Saul narratives in 1 Samuel 9–31 remain debated, and the text is clearly a collection of diverse materials and different traditions with a complex editorial history. For instance, 1 Samuel 9–11 appear to contain at least three different stories of how Saul became king, and many of the remaining Saul stories are embedded in what biblical scholars have called the "History of David's Rise" in 1 Samuel 16 and beyond.[22] Notwithstanding these issues, our purposes are served by treating the Saul narrative as it stands in its present form, beginning with Saul's appearance in chapter 9 and ending with his death in chapter 31. The Israelites request a king and Saul is chosen and subsequently proves himself in battle. Yet both Samuel and Yhwh have allowed kingship only as a sufferance, and soon Saul seems to fail several tests, which prompts Yhwh to abandon him in favor of his replacement, David. The remainder of the stories depict Saul's struggle for political, theological, and personal survival, witnessing the loss of his family and friends and ending with his suicide.

The Experiences of Moral Injury

If we reread the Saul texts as the story of a morally wounded warrior, where and how might Saul have experienced moral injury in the narrative? The process of answering that question begins with some observations about the initial chapters of Saul's story. The opening section of the account of Saul's kingship appears in 1 Samuel 9–15, prior to the introduction of David as his divinely ordained replacement in chapter 16. This opening section divides into two parts: chapters 9–11 give the traditions of Saul's establishment as king, and chapters 13–15 relate three episodes of Saul's initial activities as king. These parts are separated, however, by a decisive theological discourse by Samuel in chapter 12. From Saul's first public appearance (1 Sam 11) after his anointing and proclamation as king, he is placed in a battle against the Ammonites at Jabesh-Gilead. Moreover, even the text's first description of Saul in 9:2 emphasizes his warrior-like physical characteristics, and other texts associate his tribe of Benjamin with particular prowess in warfare (e.g., Judg 3:15-30; 19:1–20:48).

In the battle story of 1 Samuel 11, Saul's combat actions serve only to defend the people of Jabesh against the violent incursions of Nahash the Ammonite (vv. 1-4), and the "spirit of God" equips Saul with power through which his forces rout the people's oppressors (v. 6). There is no episode in chapters 9–11 that explicitly depicts Saul perpetrating an act in a warfare context that transgresses his moral beliefs. In fact, at the conclusion of chapter 11, he goes out of his way to avoid a morally questionable act. In the wake of his victory, Saul refuses his supporters' wishes to execute those who had earlier expressed reservations about his rule, sparing his own detractors and resisting the use of his power for personal vengeance (vv. 12-13). While some of the traditions that make up the story of Saul's rise in chapters 9–11 contain hesitations and negative evaluations, readers may imagine that the experiences depicted across these chapters left Saul with a positive sense of his person and position.[23]

Suddenly, however, the positive depiction of Saul as Yhwh's appointed saving agent in chapter 11 gives way to a speech by the prophet Samuel in chapter 12 that recasts this new kingship in a most negative light. Often labeled Samuel's "farewell speech," this chapter's present connection with the preceding episode is jarring. At the close of Saul's victory over the Ammonites, Samuel calls the people back to Gilgal to reaffirm the kingship (11:14-15). What follows in chapter 12, however, is an extended theological discourse in the form of a prophetic judgment speech in which the prophet says the establishment of kingship—previously endorsed as Yhwh's will and guided by divine providence—was a rebellious act by the people outside of the covenant.[24] Samuel uses the pattern of the Judges' era to claim that the appropriate response to the Ammonite oppression should have been to repent and cry to Yhwh for deliverance, but the people chose to demand a human king (vv. 11-18). As Brueggemann explains, Samuel asserts that "monarchy threatened the very character of Israel as a covenant community" and violated the established moral character of the people in relationship to Yhwh.[25] By the end of the discourse, Saul's own Israelite people follow Samuel's reassessment and describe their demand for a king as "evil" (v. 19).

Although the prophet's speech in chapter 12 doesn't mention Saul by name, readers viewing the text through the lens of moral injury may imagine the morally injurious effects that Samuel's reassessment had on Saul's character. The language and force of the prophet's judgment speech remind readers that the potential causes of moral injury include the transgression of moral convictions by self or others and betrayals of trust. Saul stands offstage in this scene, yet he stands as one who has been depicted from the beginning as a consistent Yhwh follower and one who to his knowledge had been appointed as king at the direction of Yhwh (10:1)— an appointment subsequently confirmed by the evidence of Yhwh's spirit (10:5-13) and victory in battle (11:1-11). Now, however, he hears from Yhwh's authoritative prophet that the monarchy is an abandonment of Israel's long-established, covenantal way with Yhwh and that he himself is the embodiment of this violation of the very moral identity of Israel as a people.[26] Saul now learns that by his very act of being king he has, even if unwittingly, violated part of his own moral character and identity as part of Yhwh's covenant people and served as the means for the community to do so as well. Additionally, in what is perhaps the most injurious element for Saul, the text solidifies the impression given by some passages across chapters 9–11 that Saul's own deity has a deep ambivalence and even hostility toward him.[27] Readers will soon see this divine disposition manifest itself when Yhwh afflicts Saul with evil spirits and seems determined to thwart his every move.

Saul subsequently experiences two more betrayals of trust in the stories of his reign before the introduction of David (chs. 13–15). These episodes (13:1-15; 15:1-35) stand on either side of a battle account in chapter 14. They depict Saul's failure in the eyes of the ancient Israelite writers who composed the books of Samuel as part of a larger literary work (the so-called deuteronomistic historians) and his rejection by Samuel.[28] In the context of battle against the Philistines, Saul in chapter 13 proceeded to Gilgal and waited seven days for Samuel to arrive, as the prophet had commanded him (see 10:8). Not wanting to begin the battle without offering the proper sacrifice but witnessing the continued absence of Samuel and the desertion of his soldiers, Saul went ahead and offered the burnt offering in Samuel's absence (v. 9). Immediately after this act, Samuel appeared and delivered a condemnatory and sweeping theological verdict on Saul (vv. 10-15), declaring that Saul had disobeyed the divine command and Yhwh would thus not give Saul a dynasty.[29]

Several commentators have proposed a sympathetic reading of Saul's actions here, suggesting that Saul acted in good faith after being placed in a high-stakes but no-win situation by a prophet who was already convinced of his ultimate illegitimacy.[30] Caught between Samuel's demand to wait and the needs of his army and people, Saul remained committed to having the proper ritual act completed before battle. He waited precisely the required seven days that Samuel had commanded, even though that order (10:8) was, in fact, ambiguous and never connected to a divine commandment, as Samuel later implied (v. 13).[31] Saul's defense of his actions to Samuel (vv. 11-12) seems reasoned and legitimate, even stressing that he reluctantly "forced himself" (v. 12) to make the offering and did not act out of greed or in an attempt to preempt priestly authority. From this perspective, Samuel's harsh accusations (vv. 13-15) rest on only the flimsiest grounds and a self-serving, prejudged notion of Saul's unworthiness.[32] Moreover, Samuel implied that Saul's fate had been a set-up, since Yhwh had already chosen a new ruler who enjoyed the deity's favor. It is hard to resist the sense that Samuel has betrayed Saul's trust, placing him in an untenable position within a high-stakes battle situation. From the prophet's perspective, however, Saul's motives were irrelevant because he had already been identified as the embodiment of the people's unfaithfulness (ch. 12). Samuel's posturing resembles a brutal game in which Saul's real failure was failing to follow *Samuel's* personal orders and colliding with the prophet's apparent resentment of the king and unwillingness to surrender his priestly power.[33]

Much the same evaluation could be given for the story of Saul's encounter with the Amalekites in 1 Samuel 15, which is the climactic portrayal of Saul's rejection by Yhwh. After the battle with the Philistines in chapter 14,[34] Samuel ordered Saul to "utterly destroy" (15:3) the Amalekites, leaving no persons or animals alive. Saul captured King Agag of the Amalekites, as well as the best of the sheep and cattle (vv. 4-9), taking them to Gilgal before being confronted by Samuel. As in chapter 13, Samuel immediately adopted an accusatory tone toward Saul, claiming that he disobeyed the divine voice and did evil in Yhwh's sight (v. 19). In spite of Saul's attempts to explain his actions as obedient to Yhwh, Samuel declared that Yhwh had now rejected Saul as king (and not just the promise of his dynasty as in ch. 13). Samuel also slaughtered King Agag and parted ways with Saul (vv. 22-35).

It isn't difficult to read Saul's actions here in a more sympathetic, perhaps even well-intentioned, light. Commentators divide, for instance, over whether Samuel's demand that Saul carry out the wholesale slaughter of the Amalekites made any military or strategic sense or simply represented Samuel's idiosyncratic and self-interested interpretation of the lingering exclusivism of covenant theology.[35] Additionally, the text states that Yhwh had already declared to Samuel beforehand that Saul's kingship was the object of divine regret and that Saul's actions constituted disobedience to divine commands (vv. 10-11). Samuel's stringent requirements and Yhwh's predetermined evaluations of Saul seemingly made it inevitable that he would fail.[36] Readers might once more imagine a betrayal of trust, as Yhwh and his prophet placed the warrior-turned-king into an untenable position in a high-stakes battle situation, having issued an ambiguous command and prejudged Saul's guilt.

The dismissal of Saul's response (vv. 15-21) confirms this impression. One may read this response as an expression of Saul's attempt to follow the spirit (if not the letter) of Samuel's command with genuine intent and in good faith.[37] Picking up on the reference to "Saul *and the people*" acting together to spare Agag in verse 9, Saul told Samuel that it was the army who spared the animals and that he, in fact, intended to fulfill Samuel's demand to slaughter them but to do so as a more pious act in the form of a sacrifice to Yhwh (v. 15). Samuel had not specified that the captives and spoil had to be killed on the spot and, contrary to the self-glorification motives suggested by the prophet, Saul took the spoil to Gilgal (vv. 12, 21), where he had sacrificed previously in chapter 13, and not to his home in Gibeah.[38] Saul's second assertion of his obedience (vv. 20-21) made this sacrificial intention even more explicit. Even so, Samuel, perhaps based on the divine predetermination of Saul's disobedience (vv. 10-11), interpreted Saul's actions in the most uncharitable way possible and rejected the explanations out of hand. In the final interchange, Saul seemed willing to admit that he had misinterpreted the prophet's instructions and asked for pardon (vv. 24-25). Still, Yhwh and his prophet refused to have compassion on Saul and doled out the maximum punishment of full and final rejection. Given the ambiguous nature of the motives and actions involved, it isn't even clear whether Saul sinned, but it's even less clear whether the punishment was fair or proportionate to the wrongdoing.[39]

These ways of reading chapters 13 and 15 connect to an interpretive trend within biblical scholarship that has emerged in earnest since the 1980s. Recent interpreters have increasingly identified Saul as a tragic figure and explored the story of the rise and fall of his kingdom in the literary category of tragedy.[40] Gunn, for example, identifies Saul as a "figure of tragedy" who is subject to forces beyond his control and not solely responsible for his fate.[41] Gunn distinguishes between two types of tragedy known from Greek literature, noting that most interpreters see Saul's story as a "tragedy of Flaw"—"that in which the tragic hero is 'flawed' in some way."[42] By contrast, Gunn reads Saul's story as a "tragedy of Fate," in which the hero falls victim to an "irresistible, cruel, overruling Fate."[43] Overall, this interpretive trend highlights that although the biblical text portrays Saul as guilty, his exact wrongdoing is ambiguous in the early stories of his reign and he seems to receive uncharitable treatment and have little chance in untenable situations.[44] More specifically, these tragic interpretations often rely on comparisons to Greek tragedy, drama, and mythology in the same way that the examination of characters such as Achilles and Odysseus has provided one mechanism for studying the experiences of modern soldiers in military and clinical literature.[45] Exum, for instance, has embedded a reading of the Saul narrative as a biblical tragedy within a larger discussion that relies on comparisons with Greek, Shakespearean, and modern tragedy to identify the presence of a "tragic vision" in the Old Testament that is characterized by a hostile transcendent power and human struggle against fate.[46]

Overall, then, how do the opening stories of Saul's rule in 1 Samuel 12–15 present Saul as morally wounded, especially in his encounters with the authority figure, Samuel? From Samuel's initial prophetic condemnation in chapter 12, Saul seems awash in the moral and ethical ambiguities of war, regularly experiencing the transgression of moral convictions about God and the world by himself and others. He attempted what he thought to be the proper actions under the circumstances—whether refusing to neglect the needed prebattle sacrifice (ch. 13) or waiting to carry out the commanded elimination of King Agag and the spoils until it could be a sacrificial act to Yhwh (ch. 15)—only to be told repeatedly that the actions were inadequate and improper for reasons that weren't always fair or coherent. Saul often learned after the fact (and in the harshest way) that many of his well-intentioned deeds actually violated the moral and ethical demands at the core of his identity as Yhwh's anointed. Although one could view Saul as rebellious, selfish, and sinful, it isn't difficult to see here moral injury's element of a soldier who experiences a wrecked sense of what is right and how the world should work, as Saul continually found his moral world to be unreliable in its responses to his actions in warfare.

All in all, Saul betrayed the trust placed in him by Yhwh and the prophet; yet he also experienced a sense of the betrayal of trust by his prophetic and divine authorities, as they issued ambiguous commands, prejudged his guilt regardless of his motives, and interpreted his actions in the most un-charitable ways possible. One can imagine the following comment about ✷ Saul being spoken about a morally injured veteran today:

> Here is a man caught between opposing forces, forces that he incompletely understands and insufficiently controls, forces that are partly external in origin, partly deriving from his own nature, forces that render him increas-ingly desperate and that, ultimately, will destroy him psychologically and physically.[47]

The biblical writers, however, perhaps due to their ideological per-spectives concerning the chosenness of David, portray Saul's early (mis)deeds in 1 Samuel 12–15 in precisely the way that clinicians say pro-duces moral injury—namely, the biblical writers present Saul's actions as being global, internal, and stable.[48] According to the text, whatever Saul's intentions might have been, Samuel, Yhwh, and others see the king's ac-tions as the result of some internal character flaw that isn't produced by or limited to a particular circumstance but will unavoidably remain part of his person. Hence, he is condemned. By contrast, a moral injury interpre-tation suggests that Saul was morally wounded in the opening episodes of his story and thus provides a new perspective not only on those episodes but also on the king's problematic dispositions and actions that follow in 1 Samuel 17–31. Perhaps readers may conclude that if Saul later emerged as an unstable and violent personality, this was at least partially the conse-quence of moral injury from his experiences with Samuel.[49]

The Consequences of Moral Injury

If we identify elements of moral injury in the stories of Saul's early experiences as king, we can reconsider his increasingly unstable and vio-lent actions in the remainder of 1 Samuel as consequences of moral injury rather than evidence of treacherous disobedience, divine manipulation, or psychological illness. Certainly this approach reads against the grain of the text's dominant portrayal of Saul, and we need not exonerate Saul of all wrongdoing or failure of character. As the research on moral injury indicates, however, the transgression of moral codes and the betrayal of trust can produce emotional, psychological, social, and spiritual effects that include negative changes in ethical behavior and attitudes, changes in or loss of spirituality, reduced trust in others and social contracts, and feelings of guilt and shame—nearly all of which appear in the remainder of Saul's story.[50] Shay's analysis of Odysseus identifies the primary symptoms of moral injury that can deny soldiers a healthy homecoming, and many of these accurately describe problematic elements of Saul's behavior.[51] These symptoms include an inability to move out of combat mode, irresponsible thrill seeking with boasting and taunting, a sense of unremitting danger, suspicion and fear of women, the need and effort to place blame, emotional numbness and loss of trust in relationships, violent rage and desire for revenge, and the potential for despair and self-harm. In Saul's story, these consequences manifest themselves as failed relationships with his daughters and son, distrust of his own men, suspicion of and violent rage against innocent bystanders, persecution of a presumed usurper, and a descent into despair and isolation.

What follows is a suggestive sketch that outlines some of the episodes in the remaining chapters of 1 Samuel that might fruitfully be examined from the perspective of the consequences of moral injury. Although there may be flashes of such consequences already in Saul's rash vow and acts with Jonathan in 1 Samuel 14, the main accounts of Saul's actions for consideration begin after the narrative's introduction of David in chapter 16.[52] First is Saul's initial meeting with David in 1 Samuel 16:14-23. The text announces that Yhwh's spirit has come upon David (v. 13) and has departed from Saul (v. 14). Simultaneously, the episode introduces some emotional or other type of affliction from which Saul suffered repeatedly, as well as the treatment provided by David's soothing music. Predictably, the text attributes Saul's condition to an "evil spirit from the LORD" (v. 14), reflecting ancient ways of thinking theologically about the divine cause of all things. The larger context of Saul's experiences with Yhwh and Samuel in chapters 12–15, however, brings Saul's condition into a new frame of reference. Against the backdrop of these experiences, Saul's seemingly manic-depressive distress here reminds one of the emotional numbness, alienation, and despair that can emerge from the moral ambiguity, rejection, and loss of social trust that Saul has already endured.[53]

This element of Saul's story forms an intriguing parallel with accounts of moral injury experience. Some sufferers of moral injury have described feeling like they had absorbed some kind of "personal form of evil" from the act of killing another person.[54] Shay, for example, mentions a soldier who described feeling like a "monster" had entered him and remained even after combat.[55] Moral injury work, especially within clinical psychology, has generally refrained from engaging with this kind of feeling, perhaps because of uncertainty over how to name or account for some soldiers' sense that part of their moral loss is caused by a force greater than themselves, whose effects seem to transcend natural explanations and dimensions. Contemporary readers of scripture should certainly acknowledge the ancient cultural understandings that result in the Bible's attribution of these feelings to evil spirits; however, the presence of such references within the biblical account may provide a way for soldiers and caregivers to acknowledge and discuss the feelings of some morally injured persons that a powerful and personal evil has come upon them as a result of their war experiences.[56]

On the other side of the story of David's triumph over Goliath, 1 Samuel 18 contains three scenes that portray Saul with an escalating suspicion, fear, and hostility toward his family, the people, and David. Although often interpreted merely as manifestations of Saul's evil character and treacherous pride, the actions here could perhaps also be considered in light of the dynamics of moral injury, especially negative changes in ethical behaviors and attitudes and reduced trust in others. The victory song sung about Saul and David by the women of the towns of Israel after the battle with the Philistines (vv. 6-9) marks a turning point after which Saul increasingly manifests these kinds of behaviors and attitudes. Even the king's angry reaction to the song, however, seems shaped by his previous experiences. As many commentators observe, the Hebrew poetic structure (or "parallelism") and terminology in verse 7 don't necessarily indicate a comparison at Saul's expense, and the terms could simply function synonymously to proclaim that both the heroes have killed many enemies (see also Ps 91:7).[57] But in Saul's mind, there is no ambiguity. His growing suspicion, jealousy, and fear lead him to interpret a possibly neutral statement as a slight and threat that propels him to violence.

Throughout the remainder of chapter 18, Saul acts out of fearful suspicion and violent rage, reflecting an eroding sense of moral order and stability alongside negative ethical behaviors. The most dramatic act occurs when Saul's state of torment ("an evil spirit from God," v. 10) returns and he hurls a spear to try to kill David (vv. 10-11). But this is surrounded throughout the chapter by expressions of Saul's suspicion and fear: "So Saul eyed David from that day on" (v. 9); "Saul was afraid of David" (v. 12); "So Saul was David's enemy from that time forward" (v. 29). In the chapter's final scene (vv. 17-30), Saul's suspicion of David takes the form of two unsuccessful attempts to get him killed by the Philistines. In both cases, Saul manipulates his daughters and their potential marriages for his own self-interest. For readers familiar with the effects of moral injury, these actions show the breakdown of social trust and family relationships that flow from the loss of moral stability. Moreover, Saul's responses to the actions of women in this chapter introduce the theme of Saul's suspicion of women as agents of danger and betrayal that will appear throughout the remainder of his narrative. He heard the women singers' lyrics as slights to his authority, and his daughter, Michal, whose marital status he planned to use for his own purposes, took the initiative and attached her love and loyalty to David (vv. 20, 28).

The disruption of trust-based relationships with a sense of betrayal comes to the fore in the next two chapters (1 Sam 19–20). At one level, these chapters highlight Saul's growing fear and attempts to kill David, with Saul now moving from merely inward suspicion and indirect attempts to an openness and desperation unconcerned with keeping his desire secret (19:1). Even in this aspect, one recognizes some dynamics of moral injury, as Saul continues to lose not only the ability to trust others but also his own trustworthiness. After Jonathan's intercession in verse 6, Saul pledged not to kill David; yet, at David's next military success, an "evil spirit from the LORD" came upon Saul, and he once again attempted to kill David with a spear (vv. 8-10). In what follows across chapters 19–20, as Saul repeatedly attempts to take David's life and commits to do so in the future, the king's "descent into degenerate violence and madness becomes complete."[58]

The episodes in chapters 19–20 also bring to the fore the often-cited consequence of moral injury in which injured warriors lose the ability to trust even the closest relationships within their family—a loss sometimes interpreted as betrayal. In three consecutive scenes, people close to Saul help David escape his grasp and choose loyalty to David over Saul. Michal, Saul's daughter and David's wife, foils Saul's attempt to capture David at his home, even placing an idol in his bed to fool the captors and deceiving her father by claiming that David forced her to aid him (19:8-17). When Saul then pursues David to Samuel's residence in Ramah, the very prophet who had previously championed him shelters his enemy, and Saul ends up stricken by the spirit, lying prostrate, naked, and raving in a frenzy (19:18-24). Finally, Jonathan, Saul's firstborn son and heir, solidifies his devotion to David, which appeared first in 18:1-5, executing a plan to save David from Saul once again, establishing a covenant that looks toward David's future reign, and seemingly ceding to David his status as heir to the throne (20:1-42).[59] Readers attuned to the dynamics of moral injury can sense the experience and perception of family betrayal and the loss of trust in the correct moral working of the world. These elements come to a head near the end of the final scene (20:30-34), when Saul succumbs to rage and hurls his spear at his own son, attempting to kill him in the same way he had tried to kill David (see 18:11; 19:10).

Following some intervening scenes describing David's movements, the episode in 1 Samuel 22:6-23 provides one of the most troubling portrayals of the negative changes in Saul's behavior. Saul's actions in the preceding scenes have especially highlighted his increasing fear, paranoia, rage, and violence, and those elements now surface with particularly destructive force. In the midst of Saul's continually frustrated efforts to find David, the opening scene (vv. 6-10) shows a king whose ability to trust is shrinking and whose paranoia is growing. Saul finds himself accompanied only by a small group, namely, his own Benjaminite tribesmen and his closest officers and advisors. Saul is unable to trust even these, however, being haunted by the desperate sense that even they have conspired against him with David (vv. 7-8). In moral injury terms, Saul has lost any conviction that the world around him can be trusted. In the next section (vv. 11-19), this paranoia gives way to a violent and unreasonable rage based on a sense that no one—not even a priest of Yhwh—can be trusted. After learning of David's previous visit to the priests at Nob (see 21:1-9), Saul demands an account from the priest Ahimelech. The priest's explanation for having aided David (vv. 14-15) is convincing and reasonable, making clear his innocence in having trusted David's false statements to him. Nonetheless, Saul declares that Ahimelech and his whole household should be slaughtered. In chapters 13 and 15, Saul gave what appeared to be similarly reasonable and genuine explanations for his actions, yet Samuel rejected these as untrustworthy and declared the elimination of Saul's kingship and dynasty. Saul now commits the very action with Ahimelech that contributed to his own earlier experience of moral injury. Perhaps out of a sense of moral uneasiness, Saul's Benjaminite men refuse to carry out the slaughter (v. 17), and he turns to the foreigner, Doeg the Edomite, to do what no Israelite would.

Ironically, the king who has been morally wounded himself commits precisely the kind of atrocity that might generate moral injury for those forced to participate in or witness the event. Saul has reached a new level as a leader who not only commits unwarranted violence but orders others to do so as well. This element resonates with a dimension of moral injury that often appears in both theoretical analyses and illustrative readings of figures from ancient literature. Shay in particular notes that moral injury can result from untrustworthy leadership in high-stakes situations in which those who yield official power violate the trust that they will act in accordance with what is right.[60] He observes, "Epic heroes of the Homeric poems, Odysseus and Achilles, were both 'men of pain,' suffering greatly, but also causing great pain and destruction to others."[61] Readers may find in Saul a morally ambiguous figure who, like Odysseus, stands for veterans who have suffered moral injury but also for flawed military leaders who have become "destroyers of trust" themselves.[62]

Over the next episodes, the narrative focuses on Saul's pursuit of David (esp. 1 Sam 23–26).[63] In light of the dynamics of moral injury, readers may see in these chapters, on the one hand, a king who is now completely overcome by fear, paranoia, suspicion, and rage. On the other hand, mixed throughout these episodes is a growing level of grief and remorse within Saul, which reflects the often-noted emotional consequence of moral injury in the form of guilt and shame. The text expresses this element most noticeably in the encounters with David that end with Saul weeping or confessing his wrongdoing (e.g., 24:16; 26:21). Here one finds the unstable vacillation between trust and mistrust, suspicion and hope that often marks the character of a person whose moral stability has been shaken. The spiral toward grief and despair reaches its nadir in chapter 28, as Saul consults a female medium to summon the now-deceased Samuel from Sheol (the place of the dead in ancient Israelite thinking). Everything in the story points to a final act of desperation by one who grasps at an attempt to reestablish some kind of moral reliability.

At the beginning of the scene, Saul once more finds himself rejected by the divine authority who established him as king, as Yhwh refuses to answer Saul's inquiries through any means (vv. 3-6). Saul disguises himself, violates his own ban on necromancy, and implores a medium to contact Samuel (vv. 7-14). Readers sense that Saul's moral world has descended into chaos: "Saul becomes more desperate. He acts finally like a person diagnosed with a terminal illness. . . . The fearful one may turn to any possible treatment, any available quack. . . . He is simply a frantic man with no resources."[64] In pitiful fashion, however, Saul's pleas of distress meet with a divine rejection and death sentence, as the conjured prophet proclaims that Yhwh has preordained Saul and his sons to die the next day, even as his army will fall to the Philistines in battle (vv. 15-19). Although the text presents this pronouncement as the concluding judgment for Saul's disobedience, readers might also recognize here the final manifestations of Saul's wrecked moral world in rejection and isolation. At the end of chapter 28, Saul stands as a warrior who has been morally wounded by authorities, situations, and his own deeds, and has descended into a wrecked morality and despair. The tragedy reaches its ultimate point with the succinct and understated recounting of Saul's battlefield suicide in 1 Samuel 31.[65] As Klein notes, mortally wounded, Saul's death is "reported in almost heroic fashion, with touches of final courage."[66] Despite his divinely preordained failure, Saul dies trying to do his duty as king. Although the biblical writers' construction of Saul's narrative casts his death as judgment for disobedience, it isn't difficult to feel pity for Saul as one who dies amid the ruins of a morally wrecked world, stripped of his family, troops, prophet, and deity.

Overall, then, with an eye to today's emerging insights into moral injury, the biblical figure King Saul, who was first introduced as a warrior in the midst of armed conflict and who many have identified as a tragic hero, came to represent one who suffered moral injury at the hands of authorities seemingly set against him and through his own, perhaps sincere but misguided, actions. The remainder of his story, which interpreters have

often viewed as a downward spiral of disobedient deeds and selfish violence, revealed the complex personal, psychological, social, and religious
consequences of struggling with a moral world that no longer seemed reliable. In moral injury's theoretical terms, Saul experienced acts that trans-
gressed his moral sense and created moral and ethical dissonance. Rather
than being given means by which he could reconstruct a moral identity
and reconceive of a just world, the text asserts that for Saul these acts
became "global" (i.e. not context dependent), "internal" (i.e. the result of
flawed character), and "stable" (i.e. enduring without possible change).[67]
The kind of intertextual reading represented here doesn't need to claim
authorial intentionality, seek to justify the actions attributed to Saul, or
ignore the interpretation that the biblical writers give to these events in
keeping with larger theological purposes. The reading may, however, illustrate how biblical interpretation might learn from and contribute to the
attempt to offer creative readings of literary figures as metaphors for the
postwar moral experiences of real soldiers.

Moral Injury Connections

The seemingly tragic tale of Israel's first king in 1 Samuel 9–31 operates within the first of the two primary trajectories noted in chapter 2 that
have emerged concerning how ancient texts (including the biblical writings) have been and might be fruitfully used within work on moral injury.
The interpretation of the story of King Saul here represents the trajectory
that undertakes creative rereadings of literary figures as portrayals of morally injured warriors and thus as instructive and illuminating metaphors
for the postwar experiences of real soldiers—a trajectory that has appeared
in Shay's and other researchers' use of Greek mythological figures, as well
as in some biblical scholars' recent interpretations of certain biblical characters and stories. Additionally, the story of King Saul provides an Old
Testament case study for my thesis that the engagement between the Bible
and moral injury generates a two-way conversation in which moral injury

can be an interpretive lens that brings new meanings out of biblical texts (especially those associated with war and violence), and the critical study of the Bible can make substantive contributions to the ongoing attempt to understand, identify, and heal moral injury.

This first case study concludes with some summarizing reflections on the connections between the story of King Saul and the ongoing work on moral injury. We begin, however, with some general comments about the contributions that engaging biblical narratives can make to those who seek to understand, articulate, and address moral injury, or to help others do so. This kind of engagement with biblical stories fits into the long-standing trend in moral injury work that has looked for analogous experiences in ancient Greek myths and tragedies. This effort has come both from the conviction that a key element of moral injury work is helping morally injured persons gain the ability to tell their story and express their feelings, and from the realization that such persons need concrete ways, even models, to help them articulate and share these things. When victims of moral injury construct their own war narratives and honestly tell their stories, they are better able to see clearly their ideals and perceptions, the nature of events that took place, the unrecognized effects of those events, and the otherwise invisible injuries that have been inflicted on their sense of morality, character, self, and the world.[68] Yet creative resources are needed to accompany soldiers and veterans through the task of narrating their story and reflecting insightfully on their experiences.

Perhaps understandably, many contemporary Christian readers avoid the biblical stories that feature warfare and violence (see ch. 6). These very stories, however, offer important resources for conversations about moral injury in just the ways mentioned above, especially for those who seek to understand and address moral injury within contexts that look to the Bible as Christian scripture for moral guidance, faith formation, and character development. Biblical stories like that of King Saul can provide models and language to help morally injured persons name their experiences, tell their stories, and gain honest insight into the effects that come

from them. Engaging the Bible's war stories though the lens of moral injury can help soldiers and veterans (and their family members) see their
experiences more clearly and find ways to express those experiences and
their effects in their own voice. The stories of biblical characters such as
Saul can become accompanying diagnostic guides and reference points
that stand alongside morally injured persons and provide resources for
new self-understanding and self-expression as the soldier or veteran inter-
acts creatively with the various elements of the stories. As Larson and Zust
note, "Thus, war narratives are the most accessible way of learning about
the hidden effects of combat upon soldiers and their family members.
These narratives also reveal 'touch points' by which veterans can reconcile
their experiences with their identities in order truly to return 'home.'"[69]

Additionally, the fact that the Bible itself contains stories with the
kinds of war-related moral and tragic dimensions like those found in the
story of King Saul carries special significance. The presence of these stories
in the Bible underscores the discussion in chapter 1 of what it means to
view these ancient Israelite writings as canonical scripture for believing
communities and how they function in that capacity. As noted earlier, this
view reads the Old Testament as part of a larger, inspired canon, which
can shape the imagination and practice of its readers toward the character
and ways of God's intentions for human life and all creation. Far from being a set of moralistic answers or a collection of outmoded ancient cultural
expressions, the biblical texts—viewed as Christian scripture—fund new
and authoritative ways of imagining who God is, who we are as human
beings created in God's image, and how we should live together in God's
world. Seen in this way, scripture's narratives such as the tale of King Saul
serve as human-centered, realistic portrayals that can illuminate and express our experiences of moral and ethical struggle. The fact that depictions of morally wounded figures even appear in the sacred scriptures of
Judaism and Christianity validates the moral and ethical struggles of many
soldiers and veterans. Implicitly, these sacred writings resist any attempt to
say that experiences of moral injury are illegitimate or imagined. Instead,

they affirm that any person, even those remembered as seminal figures in the story of God's chosen people, can suffer the kinds of morally injurious effects caused by the actions and environment of war, killing, and betrayal.

In addition to these more general reflections on biblical narratives, two specific connections between the story of King Saul and elements of moral injury work provide further insight. First, the overview in chapter 2 mentioned that the original formulations of moral injury (especially in Shay's works) identified it as the deleterious effects experienced by soldiers because of the betrayal of what is morally and ethically right by leaders and organizations in authority over them. Thus, moral injury's initial formulations included a significant element of social criticism directed at war practices, military operations, and the treatment of soldiers. This dimension was largely lost, however, in the subsequent clinical studies that focused primarily on acts done by individual soldiers that violated their moral convictions. The engagement with Saul's story provides a means to recapture and express some of moral injury's initial critique of war and leadership. As the preceding interpretation noted, the story of King Saul transparently and tragically depicts the devastating personal effects not only of morally questionable acts done by an individual, but also of the feeling that one has been betrayed by persons (or even deities) in authority. The interpretation of Saul as a morally wounded warrior provides a way to express forthrightly the painful realities that accompany participation in war by individuals and communities, especially the experience of betrayal and loss.

A second specific connection between the story of King Saul and elements of moral injury work relates to the theological conception of moral injury described in chapter 2. The work of Powers in particular used Augustinian theology to argue that moral injury occurs when a person's will has been reoriented to pursue a new set of goals identified as "goods," but then she or he comes to realize that the new goods toward which the will had been directed were only false goods—not virtuous, loving, or life-giving in keeping with the image of God.[70] The moral wound that emerges from this experience isn't just the confusion or loss of any sense of a moral order to the world; it's also the "deformation" of the person's own moral character so that her or his internal sense of what is good and right is distorted.[71] Saul's actions, especially his decline into self-protective violence, loss of trusting relationships, and ultimately self-harm, constitute a striking portrayal of the results that can come from this wounding and deformation of a person's deepest internal moral understanding. Saul tragically shows us how morally injurious events, such as a sense of betrayal or the perpetration of unethical violence, can lead a person into a moral and ethical confusion that results in distrust, isolation, violence, and even suicide. His story stands as a cautionary tale, a warning, and a call to action.

Chapter 4
Moral Injury and the Bible's Postwar Rituals

I wish I had been untrained afterward...reintegrated and included. My regret is wasting the whole of my productive adult life as a lone wolf.

—*Jim Shelby, Vietnam veteran* [1]

There is a boot camp to prepare for war, but there is no boot camp to reintegrate veterans to civilian life. They were taught reflexive fire shooting, but not how to recover a shredded moral identity.

—*Rita Nakashima Brock and Gabriella Lettini* [2]

The Old Testament case study in this chapter is the second attempt to explore how the engagement between the Bible and moral injury generates a two-way conversation. The interpretations of some of the Bible's war-related texts undertaken here and in the other chapters illuminate how moral injury can be an interpretive lens that brings new meanings out of the biblical writings, and how the critical study of the Bible can make substantive contributions to the ongoing attempt to understand, identify, and heal moral injury.

Toward that end, this chapter and the next will put the Old Testament's rituals and symbolic practices related to the return and reintegration of soldiers after war in dialogue with perspectives from moral injury study.[3] The relevant textual descriptions appear in various, largely unconnected, places throughout the Old Testament, but five postbattle rituals and practices are apparent overall: (1) purification of warriors, captives, and objects; (2) appropriation of booty; (3) construction of memorials and monuments; (4) celebration and procession; and (5) lament. This chapter will discuss the first three, and the following chapter will treat the final two, with a special emphasis on the significance of lament. The goal is twofold. First is to offer something akin to a mapping survey that sets out the Old Testament texts that present postwar rituals and practices of return and reintegration and considers those texts against the social and cultural backdrop of similar rituals from the ancient Near East and elsewhere. Second is to explore the possible connections between those ancient practices and moral injury, especially how perspectives from recent moral injury study may illuminate the possible symbolic functions of these ritual acts and their potential import for helping those dealing with the effects of war today.

In this way, the discussion below represents an example of the second of the two primary trajectories noted in chapter 2 that have emerged concerning how ancient texts (including the biblical writings) can be used fruitfully within work on moral injury. As mentioned previously, these trajectories offer the most immediate entry points for chaplains, ministers, psychologists, biblical scholars, and other interested persons to consider creatively what moral injury research can contribute to the interpretation of biblical texts (especially warfare and violence texts) and what the study of the Bible (both academically and devotionally/pastorally) can contribute to the ongoing efforts to understand and address moral injury. This second established trajectory within moral injury study has looked to ancient cultures and traditional societies to identify rituals and symbolic acts that might be used to address the felt needs of morally injured persons for forgiveness, purification, communalization, and hope.

What follows is an exploratory venture that illustrates how readers of the Bible might look for textual descriptions of war-related ritual practices that suggest attempts to deal with or even prevent the kinds of negative effects now identified with moral injury. The goal isn't to argue that the Old Testament materials cited here actually functioned as a kind of moral injury therapy for ancient Israel. Rather, it is to suggest that the Old Testament postwar rituals and practices performed a function for Israelite society comparable to what is attempted in moral repair work today and thus can serve as a resource for such present-day work, especially in ministerial and chaplaincy contexts. The first part of the chapter will survey the background of the discussion of postwar rituals of return and reintegration that has occurred within moral injury work in general. The second part of the chapter will work through the various postwar rituals and symbolic practices in the Old Testament with an eye to moral injury's dynamics, experiences, and consequences. The chapter will conclude by considering the potential insights that emerge from this encounter between the Bible's postbattle performances and moral injury.

Background: Postwar Rituals, Symbolic Practices, and Moral Injury

Moral injury research from its beginnings in psychology and veterans' care to its present formulations in chaplaincy and Christian ministry has emphasized the need for returning soldiers (and noncombatants who've been affected by the experiences of war) to make a healthy and marked transition from combat contexts to civilian environments. In clinical terms, the need is to provide soldiers with "meaning-oriented interventions" that help them "regain a sense of purpose and direction" for heading into life away from war.[4] The need is to provide parallel experiences to the boot camp whose practices and performances first integrated soldiers into a military culture and prepared them for combat contexts. As Bica asserts, "Returning warriors must be deprogrammed, that is, prepared to reintegrate into a non-martial environment."[5] This kind of postwar transition should help soldiers reengage with social, communal, and family relationships and find balance in daily life on the other side of combat. But the transition also needs to help soldiers to deal with grief and loss, or even to accept responsibility and experience forgiveness where needed.[6] On this last point, psychologists, chaplains, and other caregivers have expressed the need to provide postwar transitions that don't cover over the hurt, disillusionment, guilt, and self-doubt that can result from participation in combat, but rather help soldiers acknowledge and face war's wounding effects.[7]

Studies on moral injury have consistently proposed that this goal of providing concrete and healthy transitions is best accomplished by the performance of rituals and other symbolic practices that serve the kinds of postbattle functions noted above. Furthermore, moral injury research over the last decade has increasingly looked to rituals and practices from ancient cultures and traditional societies (and their surviving writings) for models.[8] The sought-after rituals and practices have most frequently centered on the goals of providing returning soldiers with a sense of purification or communalization. Concerning purification, for example, Shay advocated for the development of a communal, religious-like ritual that "recognizes that *everyone* who has shed blood, no matter how blamelessly, is in need of purification" to deal with a sense of guilt and shame. He argues this kind of purification ritual should be done by the community with the returning veterans because "the community as a whole, which sent these young people to train in the profession of arms and to use those arms, is no less in need of purification."[9]

Concerning communalization, Sherman has similarly emphasized the importance of giving returning soldiers a sense of a wider moral community that includes service members and civilians who together shoulder the moral burdens of war.[10] The healthy reintegration of soldiers depends on their ability to reframe the warfare as communally, rather than individually or personally, owned and executed. Returning soldiers need practices that distribute the moral burden and responsibility equally among service members, leaders, and their community, even those who remained outside of the direct conflict.[11]

Examples of postwar rituals and practices that have appeared in moral injury works cover a wide range of types from general to specific, communal to individual, religious to nonreligious. Some of the symbolic acts proposed in moral injury discussions involve positive, redemptive actions of well-being designed to counter involvement in war's destructiveness. These include formal participation in community service projects, disaster relief, or other acts of kindness.[12] Most the of the discussed rituals, however, involve acts that symbolize cleansing or forgiveness for the sake of transitioning out of combat. For instance, Lynd and Lynd describe a chaplain's end-of-deployment "ritual of forgiveness" in which soldiers write down things for which they feel shame, anger, regret, or grief, and the papers are burned in a baptismal font.[13] Others also reference religious-type rituals such as Catholicism's confession, Judaism's "Ten Days of Repentance," and Native American purification lodges.[14] Brock and Lettini point to a Navajo ceremony called "the Enemy Way" meant to purify from the sickness that comes from participation in war, contact with corpses, and other experiences.[15] In specifically Christian terms, recent literature on chaplaincy stresses the use of rituals and rhythms related to the seasons of the liturgical year (e.g., Lent), practices of penance and absolution, and the telling of sacred stories.[16] For instance, Liebert identifies the "classic" spiritual practices of the use of lament psalms and the "examen" (self-introspection), as well as the newer practices of deep listening and the circle process, as aids to moral repair.[17]

Some moral injury works have specifically referenced—albeit only in cursory ways—the Old Testament as a potential source for the needed postwar rituals and practices, especially the purification acts described in Numbers 31 (see discussion below).[18] The most extensive references, however, have pointed to the practices of the early and medieval Christian church concerning returning soldiers.[19] The book-length study by Verkamp, for example, demonstrated how church writings from this era frequently required soldiers to do various kinds of penance as a means of purification, expiation, and return to the community, even when the war had been seen as morally justified and ethically prosecuted.[20] The prescriptions varied, but generally involved requirements such as abstaining from communion, church gatherings, or eating only designated foods for a certain period. For example, a canon of Basil the Great (died 379 CE) stipulated that returning warriors were prohibited from taking communion for three years, and a penitential ascribed to Theodore of Tarsus (archbishop of Canterbury, 668–690 CE) declared that those who had killed in war should abstain from church gatherings for forty days.[21]

The assumption seems to be that returning soldiers, no matter the justness of the cause and the rightness of their actions, would have felt the need for resolution and forgiveness. Scholars have cautioned that such penance acts weren't necessarily a universal church practice and might have reflected only local or regional perspectives. Additionally, the practice of postwar penance began to lose ground under the influence of Thomas Aquinas and others by the time of the high Middle Ages, although the practice continued to appear in some Christian writings through the centuries following the Protestant Reformation.[22] While modern ministers, chaplains, and counselors may want to rethink the helpfulness of prescribed exclusion from the church and its practices today, references to these historical Christian practices in moral injury work highlight the belief that postwar rituals play a crucial role in the healthy return and reintegration of soldiers.[23]

Within the trajectory of moral injury study that has looked to ancient cultures and traditional societies to identify rituals and symbolic acts that might be used to address the felt needs of morally injured persons, these examples provide the background for this work with the Old Testament texts. And among these moral injury works, psychologists and other writers have called for the identification of more models from wide-ranging sources.[24] Perhaps the Old Testament texts examined below can provide some of those sought-after sources for further considering postwar rituals and symbolic practices for today, even as insights from moral injury offer new perspectives on the biblical depictions.

Postwar Rituals of Return and Reintegration in the Old Testament and Its Context

In spite of the recent attention to postbattle practices within moral injury works specifically, and the longstanding interest in the effects of war upon returning soldiers more generally, the academic study of warfare in the biblical texts and the ancient world hasn't examined the aspect of postwar return and reintegration for warriors in any substantial way. Certain elements connected to the conclusion of military conflict, including rituals and symbolic practices, appear consistently throughout the historical sources related to ancient warfare.[25] Yet the classic work by von Clausewitz, for instance, which set the agenda for much of the modern study of warfare, doesn't even mention the practices involved in the conclusion of hostilities.[26] Likewise, the classic study within biblical scholarship, von Rad's *Holy War in Ancient Israel*, assumed that holy war arose out of a well-formed social and cultic community (the so-called *amphictyony*) to which warriors would've returned, but identified only rituals concerned with the preparation for and conduct of battle.[27]

A preliminary consideration for the inquiry into the Old Testament's postwar rituals of return and reintegration concerns the nature of the available sources. The biblical writings don't allow any comprehensive picture of postwar rituals within ancient Israel. The Old Testament as a whole contains very few detailed accounts of military activity and even fewer explicit and reflective accounts of postwar rituals devoted to the subsequent status and actions of the warriors who fought in the conflict.[28] The texts that do contain elements that are at least suggestive of rituals for return and reintegration appear in various books, with predictably high concentrations in the Pentateuch (Genesis–Deuteronomy) and Historical Books (Joshua–2 Kings). They reflect different historical backgrounds, compositional histories, and literary genres, with no explicit connections among them other than the shared subject of postbattle activities. As the following discussion will show, there is perhaps only one Old Testament text that explicitly depicts ritual acts associated with the reintegration of warriors (Num 31:13-54). Even this text, however, doesn't provide any sustained reflection on the significance of the post-battle activities described or on what they might have meant to those who participated in them. While the following analysis attempts to map the postwar rituals that appear in various biblical texts and consider them in their comparative social and cultural contexts, the nature of the available sources doesn't allow the formulation of a standard practice of postwar rituals, even for specifically defined time periods or traditions within ancient Israel and Judah.

Additionally, the discussion below assumes several things worthy of more examination concerning the definition of ritual, including what counts as ritual behavior and how one identifies such behavior within the Old Testament. The effort to define ritual behavior remains contested, and this is one of the perspectives that critical academic biblical scholarship adds to the broader consideration of ritual and moral injury.[29] We may assume that a number of routine activities such as the burial of the dead (e.g., 2 Sam 2:24-32; Ezek 39:11-12) occurred at the conclusion of battle, many of which likely go undescribed in biblical texts and may or may not have constituted ritual behavior. Nonetheless, the textual map given here will use the category of ritual in the most general sense—a set of prescribed or stylized actions performed for their symbolic function in certain contexts. More specifically, activities may be considered to be ritual in nature when they are symbolic as well as "repeated and/or formalized; of social and cultural significance and giving rise to social and cultural effects; and/or for the purpose of shaping power relations."[30]

Return and Reintegration in the Old Testament

The Old Testament texts that are suggestive of postwar rituals of return and reintegration fall into five categories, with some overlap among them:[31]

1. Purification of Warriors, Captives, and Objects: Num 31:13-24

2. Appropriation of Booty

    a. Simple taking of booty: Deut 20:10-18; Josh 7:1; 8:24-29; 11:14; 1 Sam 14:31-35; 15:1-9; 23:1-5; 27:8-12; 2 Chr 28:8-15

    b. Redistribution of booty among combatants, noncombatants, and sanctuaries: Gen 14:17-24; Num 31:25-47; Josh 6:24; 22:7-9; Judg 5:28-30; 1 Sam 5:1-8; 30:21-31; 2 Sam 8:9-12; 1 Chr 26:26-28; 2 Chr 15:11; Ps 68:11-14

3. Construction of Memorials and Monuments: Exod 17:14-16; Num 31:48-54; Josh 6:24; 1 Sam 5:1-8; 31:8-10; 2 Sam 8:9-12; 1 Chr 18:7-8, 10-11; 26:26-28; Dan 1:1-2; 5:2-3

4. Celebration or Procession: Exod 15:1-18, 20-21; 1 Sam 18:6-9; 2 Sam 19:1-8 (implied by opposite); 2 Chr 20:24-30; Esther 9:16-17; Ps 68:21-27; Isa 25:6

5. Lament (often corporate): 2 Sam 1:19-27; Pss 44; 60; 74; 79; 80; 89; Isa 14:3-20 (ironic); 15–16 (ironic); Jer 48 (ironic); Lam 5; Ezek 32:1-16 (ironic); Joel 1:2–2:17

The following discussion will highlight representative texts from each category to identify some of the central elements that appear across the depictions (before the following section sets them against their ancient cultural backdrop). As noted above, this chapter will discuss the first three categories, and the following chapter will discuss the remaining two.

Purification of Warriors, Captives, and Objects

The texts in the first category depict purification rites for returning warriors, captives, and objects. Numbers 31:13-24 is the only explicit example of this category within the Old Testament. The larger unit of Numbers 31:13-54 is the most, and perhaps only, explicit depiction of postbattle rituals for returning warriors, and the unit as a whole devotes much more space to the postwar activities than to the battle itself, bringing together several elements found individually elsewhere. The passage describes an encounter among Moses, Eleazar the priest, and Israelite warriors returning to the congregation at the camp in the plains of Moab after a victorious battle with the Midianites. Having slaughtered all the Midianite men, the returning warriors bring with them "the women of Midian and their little ones," as well as "their cattle, their flocks, and all their goods as booty" (Num 31:9). In this context, Moses's first instructions are to kill all the male children and nonvirgin women. In the following verses, the instructions turn to activities to be carried out by the warriors prior to their reintegration into the camp.

The first section (vv. 19-24) prescribes the ceremonial (and literal) purification (and washing) of the warriors, captives, and booty. Moses commands the returning warriors who killed a person or touched a corpse to remain outside the camp seven days, purify themselves and their captive virgin women on the third and seventh day, and purify the captured garments and articles. Eleazar then stipulates (vv. 21-24) that any objects that will not burn (gold, silver, bronze, iron, tin, lead)—presumably both booty and weapons—must be passed through the fire and perhaps also purified with water. Objects that cannot withstand fire are simply passed through the water. Additionally, the warriors must wash their clothes on the seventh day.

The actions depicted in Numbers 31:13-24 reflect the ideas and concerns of the Old Testament's so-called priestly tradition. The chapter has generated a large amount of commentary that tries to understand the postbattle prescriptions within the origin, development, and expressions of priestly notions of purity and impurity.[32] Much more could be said about issues of compositional history, yet no other Old Testament text contains this ritual prescription of postbattle purification or explicit examples of such purification taking place. The purification ritual here seems to depend most directly upon priestly laws concerning ceremonial defilement caused by corpse contamination (especially Num 5:1-4 and 19:1-22).[33] The underlying conviction in these laws is that death defiles the person and the camp. Numbers 5 provides the initial statement that contact with a corpse defiles a person, and Numbers 19 stipulates the procedures for ritual purification from corpse contamination. In the latter, the priests involved in the disposal of the animal (a red heifer) that was ritually slaughtered in the ceremony must wash their clothes and bathe before returning to the camp (vv. 5-6), the one touching a human corpse is unclean for seven days and must wash on the third and seventh day (vv. 11-13), and the one touching a corpse that was "killed by a sword" in an open field is unclean for seven days (v. 16).[34] A possibly additional background text is the legislation concerning the transition of a captive woman taken in battle in Deuteronomy 21:10-14. Before an Israelite can marry the woman, she must shave her head, cut her nails, change her clothing, and remain for a month in the man's house—acts probably meant to symbolize a new birth and forced transition into a new identity.

The ritual in Numbers 31 uniquely applies these background provisions to the practice of war and demands the purification of warriors who have killed someone, enemy captives, and even objects.[35] Perhaps the most distinctive aspect of the Numbers construction, however, is how the priestly notion of warfare as a ritually defiling activity departs from the Old Testament's other war traditions. No other traditions make (at least explicitly) this connection between warfare and corpse contamination.[36] It seems likely that the underlying notion of death being the "utmost desacralization" is what leads to warfare being considered a defiling activity.[37] In the conceptions represented by biblical and extrabiblical texts, defilement most essentially represents estrangement from the divine presence and death constitutes the ultimate form of such separation.[38] Hence, often the determining factor of whether something causes defilement is whether it represents death in some manner.[39] In the view of warfare represented by Numbers 31, war defiles because it leads to contact with death.[40]

Appropriation of Booty

The next section of the story in Numbers 31 (vv. 25-47) moves the narrative focus away from the purification of the warriors and onto the second category of postwar rituals listed above—the appropriation of booty after battle. The actions in this category are not as obviously or explicitly oriented toward return and reintegration as those in the other categories. Yet they often involve things done with the spoils upon return or in relation to those who remained at home during the battle.

In Numbers 31, notwithstanding the uniqueness of the preceding purification ritual, the handling of the booty occupies the central place in the narrative. In verses 25-47, the people are to divide the booty (presumably equally) between "the warriors who went out to battle" and "all the congregation" (v. 27). From the warriors' share, items are set aside as a levy to the priests and offering to God at the rate of one per five hundred, while from the congregation's share items are set aside for the Levites at the rate of one per fifty.[41] The background for the legislation concerning booty is the general principle in Deuteronomy 20 that the army must kill every living thing in cities within the land but can take women, children, and animals as plunder from cities outside the land. Similarly, Deuteronomy 21:10-14 allows for an Israelite to marry a woman taken as booty in war after she undergoes a process signifying her forced transition to a new identity. Numbers 31 develops these principles by restricting the human booty to virgin women and including a levy for the priests.

Although the levy for the priests in Numbers 31 is unique in the Old Testament, this practice of the redistribution of the spoils features prominently in both biblical and extrabiblical texts.[42] In fact, the postbattle activity of handling spoils dominates all others in Old Testament texts. Scattered across various books within the Old Testament are nearly two dozen references to the appropriation, use, and division of spoils after battle. There are two main Hebrew terms (alongside a few less prominent ones) used to designate *spoil/plunder/booty* within the Old Testament (*šālāl*; *baz*), both of which are linked to the basic notion of the confiscating of persons, animals, and property by a victorious army. The first term (*šālāl*), usually in noun form, typically denotes the *goods* confiscated, while the second term (*baz*), usually a verb, typically denotes the *act* of taking by soldiers.

Many Old Testament texts that use these terms simply report the taking of plunder by the victorious warriors and don't allude to any kind of practices for return or reentry (e.g., Deut 20:14-15; Josh 8:24-29; 11:14; 1 Sam 14:31-35; 15:1-9; 23:1-5; 27:8-10; 2 Chr 28:8-15).[43] Beyond these general references, however, Numbers 31:25-47 represents the first of two specific kinds of descriptions that appear especially in the Pentateuch and Historical Books and that reflect two somewhat distinct postbattle practices of appropriating and dividing spoils. First, as Numbers 31:25-47 exemplifies, several texts describe the act of redistributing the spoils after battle among both combatants and noncombatants upon the warriors' return. Numbers 31:25-47 provides one of the earliest instances of this first practice. First Samuel 30:21-25 also provides a clear example. Here, David redistributes the spoils from his victory against the Amalekites among the four hundred men who went to battle and the two hundred who stayed behind, specifically countering the objection that only the warriors should receive the spoils. He also sends other portions of the booty to his supporters among the elders of Judah. The biblical writer includes the claim that this practice became a "statute and an ordinance for Israel" that continued to the "present day" (v. 25). Likewise, Genesis 14:17-24 notes Abram's division of the remainder of the spoils after his gift to Melchizedek between the warriors and the king of Sodom. Joshua 22:7-9 instructs the tribal warriors from the Transjordan returning home after the conquest of Canaan to share the booty with their kindred who had remained outside the land. Psalm 68:11-14 alludes to the women who remained home "among the sheepfolds" (v. 13) dividing the plunder captured from the defeated foe. In the most poetic depiction, the conclusion of Deborah's song in Judges 5:28-30 personifies the general Sisera's mother gazing out the window and imagining the victorious Canaanite warriors lingering to divide their booty—human and otherwise.[44]

Construction of Memorials and Monuments

The third category of postwar rituals of return and reintegration in the Old Testament appears explicitly in the final portion of the story in Numbers 31 (vv. 48-54), with a few suggestive texts elsewhere. This category also represents the second way that Old Testament texts portray the appropriation of spoils after conflict. The postbattle texts in this category describe the practice of redistributing and dedicating spoils into sanctuaries or temples, and, sometimes, using a portion of the booty to construct memorials on the battlefield or in the holy place. In Numbers 31, for example, the army's commanders voluntarily bring to Moses an "offering" to Yhwh consisting of gold articles of booty and serving to "make atonement" (v. 50) for themselves. Moses and Eleazar bring this gold into the tent of meeting and set it up as a "memorial" (or "remembrance" v. 54) before Yhwh. The atonement offering and subsequent memorial appear in this precise form only here, and debate continues over how to interpret the motivation of the warriors and the significance of the acts.[45]

Notwithstanding the unique formulation in Numbers 31, comparable postwar actions occur elsewhere in the Old Testament. Concerning the erecting of battlefield memorials, Exodus 17:14-16 is merely suggestive, as it describes Moses's building of an altar with a militaristic name ("the LORD is my banner" v. 15) in the aftermath of Israel's defeat of the Amalekites. Concerning the use of booty for memorials in sanctuaries and temples, the ending of the Jericho story in Joshua 6:24 reports that the Israelites took the material booty of precious metals and placed it into the "treasury of the house of the LORD." Similarly, 2 Samuel 8:9-12 indicates that David dedicated the spoils from the defeat of Hadadezer to Yhwh (presumably via the priests), and 1 Chronicles 26:26-28 reports that the booty was allocated for the maintenance of the temple. See also David's action of bringing spoils to Jerusalem and dedicating them to Yhwh in 1 Chronicles 18:7-8, 10-11, and Asa's use of war booty as a sacrifice to Yhwh in 2 Chronicles 15:11.[46]

Similar acts of temple dedication from the opposite perspective appear in the stories of Israel's defeat at the hands of the Philistines in 1 Samuel. In 1 Samuel 5:1-8, the Philistines place the captured ark of the covenant into the temple of Dagon as a victory memorial. In 1 Samuel 31:8-10, they place Saul's armor into the temple of Astarte and hang his body on the wall of Beth-shan. One might also note the reference in Daniel 1:1-2 to Nebuchadnezzar's placement of vessels from Jerusalem's temple into the "treasury of his gods" (see also Dan 5:2-3).[47]

Return and Reintegration Outside the Old Testament

The practices represented by the categories discussed above—purification of warriors, captives, and objects, appropriation of booty, and trophy/monument construction (as well as celebration or procession and lament to be discussed in the next chapter)—are the most suggestive postwar rituals of return and reintegration in the Old Testament, with various levels of overlap among them. The next step in considering these texts and practices is to place them against the backdrop of comparable texts and practices from other sources in ancient and modern contexts. This interpretive move represents the kind of perspective provided by a sophisticated engagement informed by biblical scholarship rather than a cursory reference or a simple listing of passages.

There are two lingering questions for the sources under consideration here that place ongoing limitations on the analysis. First, as noted above, all of the relevant biblical texts remain only suggestive, so we can't be certain to what extent the depictions in these texts reflect actual practices or recurring rituals. Second, it remains unclear whether one should (or could) distinguish among the practices described above those that are truly postwar rituals and those that are more immediate postbattle rituals. In other words, do some (most?) of these practices envision activities that took place to mark the homecoming at the completion of a campaign ("war") or simply the end of one particular battle? This question likely bears on the possible symbolic functions fulfilled by the acts themselves, but the available evidence suggests a high level of overlap among the different kinds of practices and permits few clear-cut distinctions. As the following discussion shows, these same two questions also bear upon the evidence for postwar practices in sources outside the Old Testament.

The potential evidence for postwar rituals from Israel's broader social and cultural context in the ancient Near East is diverse and widespread, with significant source material coming from ancient Mesopotamia, Egypt, Greece, and Rome, as well as modern, especially tribal, cultures and early and medieval Christianity. What follows is a representative survey that doesn't claim comprehensiveness. As with the Old Testament, a lack of clear textual evidence for certain areas, most notably ancient Syria-Palestine, makes it difficult to describe the various elements of warfare practice in any systematic or detailed manner. Additionally, Kang observes that the overall framework for many of the ancient Near Eastern war texts, just as for the Old Testament, is the notion of divine war, which includes both a divine command to execute the war and the belief that the gods fight alongside the armies (mainly through natural phenomena).[48] This larger framework shapes the ancient texts' descriptions of activities before, during, and after battle. Even so, while the relevant practices can vary greatly in different cultures and societies, the efforts to handle booty, celebrate victory, and help warriors transition back to life in the community correspond in general terms to the categories found in the Old Testament.

The first category of the ritual purification of warriors returning from battle appears explicitly in only one Old Testament passage (Num 31), but it is extensively attested in several comparative contexts. Sources from Mesopotamia and the wider ancient Near East, including Hittite, Egyptian, Ugaritic, and Akkadian texts, refer to a variety of practices involving ceremonial purification after battle, especially washing the body or the weapons used in battle. In some cases, the texts seem to imply that deities themselves became defiled through warfare or bloodshed and underwent ritual acts of purification following the conflict. For the purposes of this study, however, it is important to note that postbattle purification rituals for human warriors in particular appear in a number of Mesopotamian texts. An early representative example appears in an inscription of Yahdum-Lim from Mari that reports that the king marched to the Mediterranean Sea and offered sacrifices while "his troops washed themselves in the Ocean."[49] Likewise, the Babylonian Gilgamesh Epic features Gilgamesh washing himself and his equipment after battle.[50] The Assyrian royal inscriptions contain numerous similar examples of postbattle ritual washings, usually of the soldiers' weapons, not bodies, and typically featuring some form of the common expression that "I washed my weapon in the sea." Inscriptions from the Assyrian kings Sargon, Ashurnasirpal II, Shalmaneser III, and Ashurbanipal, for instance, record washing their weapons in the Mediterranean Sea and offering sacrifices.[51] Admittedly, these rituals take place while the army is still abroad and whether they imply ritual impurity remains debated. Yet the connection of the washings with offering sacrifice in the Mari and Assyrian texts suggests a cultic and ritual dimension.

Most historians of Greek warfare have concluded that the evidence for postwar purification rituals is limited at best.[52] There may be sporadic indications that a soldier required ceremonial atonement before participation in the temple, but only one seventh-century BCE passage seems to suggest that soldiers had a formal postwar purification ritual.[53] The Greek texts that most explicitly indicate a purification ritual for the army occur under particular circumstances and don't seem to reflect a mandated ceremony upon return from battle.[54] Roman sources, however, provide more indication of ceremonies of purification for returning armies, largely revolving around lustrations to remove the blood from battle and other evil contagions.[55] The most famous Roman victory ritual, the "Triumph," includes a ritual of purification and thanksgiving for the army before it begins a celebratory procession.[56] Other Roman practices are suggestive but their exact meaning remains uncertain. For instance, Roman soldiers from some eras were prohibited from wearing their red capes into the city or from marching past the Rubicon into the city of Rome. These prohibitions may connote a sense of defilement associated with combat.[57]

Anthropological research into tribal societies from various periods, including modern peoples such as the African Zulus, Eskimos, and Native Americans, has also produced evidence of postbattle rituals for returning warriors that include the removal of blood-stained clothes and equipment, washing, and isolation.[58] Among the practices of the ethnic Meru people of Kenya, for instance, return required the sacrifice of a ram and the placing of a portion of the sacrifice on the warrior's spear.[59] Similarly, the early Irish/Celtic literary epic the *Táin* describes a multistep purification process for the hero's return from combat that includes women baring their breasts to the warrior—likely a symbol of the nurture provided by children, family, and community—the warrior being placed into successive baths of water that symbolize a "cooling down," and the changing of the soldier's clothes.[60] The first section of this chapter noted that these kinds of postwar rituals for returning warriors received their fullest and most explicit articulations in the formulations of the early and medieval Christian church. As described above, writings from the church in this era frequently required soldiers to do various kinds of penance as a means of purification, expiation, and return to the community, even when the war itself was considered just.[61]

The second category observed in Old Testament texts—the appropriation of booty—features prominently in postwar rituals found in texts from the ancient world, often being the most fully described postbattle element. Mesopotamian sources attest the postwar redistribution of booty among the king, military officers, and other persons in a manner not unlike the distribution between combatants and noncombatants in Numbers 31 and other Old Testament passages. The practice appears in Mari and Hittite texts, with clear examples in other Akkadian inscriptions.[62] Several texts from ancient Mari, for example, show spoils being distributed in various ways, including some booty being divided on the spot among leaders, soldiers, and allies, and other booty being sent to the king in the capital.[63] The Akkadian inscription of Idrimi includes the ruler's claim that he distributed captured booty to his servants, family, and friends,[64] and Esarhaddon's inscriptions for his sixth campaign report, "From the booty of the lands...I selected from among them, and added to my royal equipment. From the great spoils of enemy-(captives), I apportioned (men) like sheep to all of my camp, to my governors, and to the people of my (large) cities."[65] Greek postwar texts focus on memorials in temples (see below) but also attest that the military commander was free to distribute booty or proceeds from its sale according to his discretion while the army remained in the field.[66]

The third category observed in the Old Testament writings—the construction of memorials and monuments, with the dedication of portions of spoils into sanctuaries—also appears prominently among ancient postwar rituals in Hittite, Assyrian, Egyptian, and Greek sources. Late Bronze Age Canaanite texts from Ugarit describing the god Baal mention weapons from defeated armies being given to temples as trophies and dedicatory offerings.[67] Many Mesopotamian texts also feature the giving of some or all of the booty to the gods, presumably through dedication to the temple. The practice reminds biblical readers of the military officers' donation to the sanctuary in Numbers 31 and may derive from the ancient Near Eastern conviction that the battles were a form of divine war.[68] The Assyrian king Ashurbanipal's inscriptions state, "The people and spoil of Elam, which at the command of Ashur, Sin, Shamash, Adad...I had carried off, the choicest I presented unto my gods."[69] Likewise, the Babylonian ruler Nebuchadnezzar claims, "I had them brought into Esagila and Ezida before Marduk the great lord of the gods and before Nabu his beautiful son who loves my royalty."[70] Greek postwar texts frequently refer to the dedication of portions of booty to the gods, especially in the form of a "tithe" set aside from the spoils and given to the temple.[71] This *dekate* could consist of various items such as money, captured armor, land, and slaves, and could be offered by military leaders, as well as ordinary soldiers.[72]

A significant subdivision of this postbattle category is the practice of taking divine trophies from the defeated enemy.[73] Although trophies taken at the conclusion of battle included statues of kings and other public monuments, the primary trophies were images of gods, which were subsequently exhibited in ceremonies for the public when the army returned home. The practice appears most prominently in Assyrian royal inscriptions, primarily from the time of Tiglath-pileser I in the late Middle Assyrian period and the Sargonids in the eighth and seventh centuries BCE.[74] The precise function of this postwar practice remains debated and likely varied in different periods and areas, probably serving to legitimate the newly expanded kingship of the conqueror and reframe the soldiers' actions as part of the divine world and its orchestration of human, especially royal, affairs.[75]

In addition to the dedication of portions of booty for memorials in temples, the postwar rituals in this third category also take the form of erecting a monument or boundary stone (often on the battlefield) to commemorate the victory and offer praise to a deity.[76] The Zakkur Stela, for instance, mentions the king's establishment of a stela before the god Ilu-wer, Esarhaddon's inscriptions refer to erecting a victory stela recording the praise of the god Ashur, and Egyptian texts record Thutmose III's carving of a stela into a rock following a campaign to the Euphrates.[77] Although Greek sources highlight the giving of a tithe of the booty to temples, they also include the ritual of erecting a monument or "trophy" on the battlefield as one of the primary postbattle rituals.[78] These monuments often consisted of captured armor, shields, and weapons, among other items, which were placed around a pole or tree, often at the place where the battle turned.[79]

Summary

The preceding survey of the first three Old Testament examples of postwar rituals and their extrabiblical parallels (see ch. 5 for discussion of the final two categories) leads to two preliminary observations. First, the texts don't explicitly state that the practices mentioned were intended to fulfill certain functions for returning soldiers, and they certainly aren't systematized in a coherent or comprehensive way. Second, the available texts only describe the practices and rarely, if ever, offer insight into what possible meanings the various postwar rituals may have had. The biblical writers provide no sustained reflection on the significance of these post-battle activities or what they might have meant to those who engaged in them or preserved their memory. Even so, the identification of these rituals invites the question of their possible meanings and functions. The function of ritual is determined by a sociohistorical context in which the inherent relationship between an act and its meaning was understood, even if, over time and distance, this connection becomes obscured and not always explicitly expressed.

Clearly, at the most basic level, the postwar rituals depicted in these texts deal with pragmatic issues. They are concerned with handling the material objects used in and gained from combat, compensating and sustaining those involved and affected, and bringing the soldiers back to their local and domestic responsibilities. Considered as a whole, however, the postwar rituals suggest that they weren't merely pragmatic but had larger symbolic functions unidentified in the available sources. The question of interest for the exploration here is whether an interdisciplinary engagement between these biblical depictions and moral injury's work with how soldiers conceive, experience, and respond to return and reintegration might allow us to recognize symbolic functions that remain unacknowledged in the sources themselves, even as we consider what these biblical references might contribute to the nature and role of rituals and practices in the healing of moral injury today. Put differently, taking a cue from Bahrani's study of rituals, art, and monuments related to war and the body, we might consider whether the postwar rituals under consideration here constitute a "semiotics" of war designed for the warriors themselves and, to a lesser extent, the community as a whole.[80] Perhaps the postwar rituals concerning purification, booty, and memorials (as well as celebration and lamentation; see ch. 5) form a set of signs related to the representation of war that functions to reframe the way warriors and communities conceive, experience, and respond to the realities of combat. And perhaps engagement with moral injury unlocks this function.

Moral Injury Connections

The collection of postwar rituals and symbolic practices in Old Testament texts operates within the trajectory within moral injury study that emphasizes the role of rituals and practices related to the return and reintegration of soldiers after battle and looks for models among ancient and traditional cultures that could be adapted for today. The engagement between the Bible and moral injury generates a two-way conversation in which moral injury can be an interpretive lens that brings new meanings out of biblical texts (especially those associated with war and violence), and the critical study of the Bible can make substantive contributions to the ongoing attempts to understand, identify, and heal moral injury.

First, at a general level, engaging in postbattle activities such as purification ceremonies, service projects, or acts of repair can accomplish the very things that initial explanations of moral injury said were needed for those affected. For example, dealing with the fundamental disruptions in beliefs about self and the world that are caused by morally injurious experiences requires helping soldiers see those experiences as confined to specific, time-bound contexts, and as the result of outside exigencies and demands.[81] The concrete actions performed in postwar rituals, especially those undertaken in the war context and those that mark the transition from combat settings, communicate that the events and experiences of war are context dependent and shared by a group. The rituals acknowledge that morally injurious acts have been committed, witnessed, or experienced, but they also signify that these things were at least partially caused by certain circumstances, were connected to the group rather than just an individual, and were not a sign of a permanently tainted internal character.

Similarly, at the general level, postwar rituals and symbolic actions relate to an emerging trend within moral injury work that stresses communal experience and healing. For example, most work has focused on moral injury as an individual experience, but caregivers should consider the possibility that moral injury may be experienced by a group—and that the group may seek collective means of healing together.[82] Since many of the postbattle activities cited from ancient texts and proposed for contemporary settings are undertaken by groups, they offer a resource for attending more fully to the possible communal dimensions of moral injury and repair. More particularly, when modern soldiers use or adapt ancient postwar rituals, they have the opportunity to feel connected across time with those who've had similar experiences and perhaps to regain the sense of a "humanity shared across the ages."[83]

Along with the preceding more general observations, insights from moral injury enhance our understanding of the specific Old Testament rituals and symbolic actions surveyed in this chapter and their possible functions within ancient Israel. As mentioned previously, the relevant biblical texts only describe the practices and rarely, if ever, offer insight into what possible meanings the various rituals may have had. The engagement with moral injury addresses this lack but also allows for the biblical depictions to contribute to today's efforts to resource moral healing through rituals and symbols.

There is a direct connection between the descriptions of rituals related to the purification of warriors, captives, and objects in the Old Testament and its context and the well-established emphasis in moral injury work that some sense of undergoing purification after battle is needed in today's practices of return and reintegration. Without practices that can serve a function of symbolic purification, soldiers may find themselves unable to shed not only any feelings of guilt or shame from killing but also social adaptations and behavioral norms that characterize warfare contexts.

Perhaps this is a symbolic function of the ancient rituals of purification that seem ceremonial and pragmatic on their surface. They mark with clarity the boundary and transition from a combat context, with its norms and behaviors, to a noncombat context, with a different set of norms and behaviors.

But purification rituals go beyond marking transitions. They also create time and space for self-reflection and honest disclosure of the actions, experiences, and effects of participation in battle. They honestly acknowledge—in concrete and active ways—that no matter how legally justified or seemingly necessary war might be, it is still a grievous and harmful reality for all participants, active or otherwise. Purification rituals are a visible and bodily demonstration of the ruinous ills that attend any and all war. They embody the conviction that a sense of having participated in something grievous and ruinous lingers over all involved, and this feeling must be addressed. Symbolic acts of purification are acts of mourning, even for those commonly judged victorious in war. As Levine says, "Mourning tells the dastardly and ugly truth of war and allows warriors to quietly acknowledge that, despite heroic behavior exhibited in war, war has no heroes and has no real victories."[84] The very presence in the biblical writings of purification rituals such as the one described in Numbers 31:13-24 suggests that there was an ethical perspective in at least some ancient Israelite traditions that saw killing in war as an abomination and expressed doubts about the practice of warfare itself as an inherently and inescapably defiling exercise, even when undertaken by necessity and in ethical ways.[85]

Seen in this manner, postwar purification rituals have the possibility of functioning in countercultural ways in both ancient and modern societies. These rituals suggest that killing in war, although sometimes judged as necessary in certain contexts, shouldn't been seen as neutral or even honorable.[86] The rituals guard against an easy, uncritical acceptance of killing in combat as right and good. And this safeguarding is particularly important in the post–9/11 context of the US, which often papers over the inherently and inescapably harmful and unjust nature of war participation with parades, military honoree nights at sporting events, and reflexive expressions of "thank you for your service." These may be well-intentioned, but they run the risk of too quickly relieving the "moral responsibility" for war participation from soldiers, as well as their governments and communities, creating "amnesia about the full extent of harm that war inflicts" instead of "building the lifelong strength to live with it."[87]

In Christian theological terms, the purification rituals in ancient Israel express a willingness to say that war is sinful, even when deemed necessary. Here is a connection to the theological conception of moral injury outlined in chapter 2. Military training, culture, and participation subtly change soldiers' morality so that they begin to view killing "no longer as a necessary moral ill, but an exemplary and perhaps even obligatory moral good."[88] In the long aftermath of war, however, soldiers can't maintain this new morality, and thus suffer the consequences of moral injury. By contrast, the use of purification rituals can be a way of preserving the notion that killing in war remains a moral ill, even when it's judged to be a necessity. This acknowledgment allows soldiers to avoid possible disillusionment and moral wounding because they never adopt the untenable view that killing is a praiseworthy moral good. They never lose the sense that they are participating, even if rightly and by necessity, in something that is evil, harmful, and contrary to God's life-giving intentions for all creation. Even so, the promise of the possibility of cleansing, honesty, and newness represented by the postwar purification practices allows soldiers to accept the moral burdens of war because they can look forward to an offer of forgiveness and reconciliation to come. Because purification and newness are on offer through meaningful rituals and symbols, a soldier "goes into such an awful reality for the sake of neighbor and country with a *humbly heroic* dependence on forgiveness."[89]

When we turn to consider the postwar rituals and symbolic practices that have to do with the appropriation, redistribution, and dedication of spoils and the construction of memorials and monuments, we can see other connections with moral injury work in ways that enhance our understanding of the nature and function of these acts within ancient Israel. As described in chapter 2, some new book-length treatments and clinical studies have emphasized the role of the community and communalization as the vital component in the prevention of and recovery from moral injury.[90] To communalize war-related acts is to identify and engage in concrete practices that reframe the acts as communally, rather than individually or personally, owned and executed, especially by allowing morally wounded warriors to reconnect with the communities from which they've been separated and to develop a sense of shared moral responsibility that suggests a more just world. These practices address service members' need for a comprehensive understanding of the events and their own level of responsibility. The goal is to find practices that give soldiers a sense that the moral burden and responsibility are equally distributed among soldiers, leaders, and their community, even those who remained outside of the direct conflict. Additionally, practices related to communalization aim to help returning soldiers reframe the local and specific encounters of combat within a larger perspective that gives them a broader and more meaningful significance, placing their local and limited actions within a larger framework or story that is shared by the community as a whole. Current moral injury literature describes some of these communalizing practices in modern contexts as including soldiers gathering in small groups (often in faith communities consisting of nonveterans as well), making lists of all persons and institutions involved in responsibility for war events, and performing acts of repair, re-creation, and service in the community, which represent the opposite of war's acts of destruction.[91]

Could the emerging emphasis on communalization in moral injury work provide interdisciplinary insights into the possible function and meaning of the ancient practices of the appropriation, redistribution, and use of spoils after battle described in the Old Testament and related contexts? Or, put another way, could these ancient postbattle ways of handling spoils represent the kind of concrete practices that contemporary

moral injury research has identified as aids to helping soldiers communalize war's experiences and deal with its moral impact? The first major insight may come from moral injury's emphasis that returning warriors need
the ability to reframe the warfare as a communally owned and executed
affair. Perhaps this notion points to a possible symbolic function for the
practices related to the redistribution and sharing of booty within the biblical and extrabiblical texts. The particular practice of dividing the booty
not only among the warriors but also among parts of the community
that remained at home during the conflict would seemingly reframe the
returning warriors' conceptions of the combat, resisting the sense that the
warfare had been about selfish acquisition of plunder and closing the perceived gap between the soldiers and the community that stayed behind.
Here is a connection, for instance, to the Adaptive Disclosure treatment for
moral injury, which aims to help sufferers redistribute the blame for morally injurious actions and circumstances to indicate a shared responsibility
with the local community and larger society.[92]

The redistribution of spoils in these biblical texts resembles the kinds
of actions that recent moral injury research suggests are necessary to overcome resentment, engage both combatants and noncombatants in a sense
of shared responsibility, and produce a stronger moral community.[93] Dividing the spoils with noncombatants also resembles an "act of repair"
that moral injury research identifies with helping combatants maintain a
sense of creating or restoring in the face of warfare experiences dominated
by destroying.[94] Even so, contemporary readers of the ancient Israelite
writings must acknowledge that the symbolic function of spoils division
is only one-sided. The rituals might constitute an act of repair for the
warriors, or be restorative for their communities, but the spoils are still
the former property of others (and, at least in Num 31, the spoils include
captive and trafficked human beings). The engagement with these biblical
texts in the service of moral injury must be a critically aware engagement.

The second major insight comes from moral injury research's emphasis
that returning warriors need to reframe the local and specific encounters

of combat within a larger perspective that gives them a broader and per-haps more meaningful significance. Perhaps these symbolic functions are at work in the Old Testament's postbattle practice of giving spoils over to the sanctuary or temple, especially for the construction of memorials and monuments. Given the place of the sanctuary or temple at the center of the ancient community's religious and social life, this postbattle practice would have redefined the completed military conflict in terms of larger cosmologies, theologies, and divine action, implying that local conflicts are part of divine actions in the world. The act symbolically addresses po-tential doubts about the "values, purpose, and meaning" of the warriors' war involvement—doubts that can lead to existential questions about per-sonal worth and even divine morality.[95] The deposit of spoils into sanctu-aries and temples creates a larger meaning that points to a desired sense of purpose and direction for participation in the war.

Conclusion

Many questions remain concerning the function, meaning, and virtue (or lack thereof) of postbattle practices in the Old Testament and other ancient sources. Additionally, many questions remain when modern inter-preters, psychologists, military personnel, and others look to these prac-tices from biblical texts (and other ancient sources) as potential models for understanding and addressing moral injury. Particularly in the case of rituals concerning human captives or other booty taken in war, whatever symbolic functions these practices may have had in their ancient con-texts, contemporary readers rightly worry about their moral appropriate-ness. Today's readers may worry that rituals like those described in the Old Testament and elsewhere allow the participants too easily to justify their actions without dealing with the effects their acts have "inscribed on the bodies, cities, and soil of the conquered."[96] Brock and Lettini com-pare this danger to what they call "imperialist atonement" practices such as taking veterans back to Vietnam on short-term charity trips without actually living in the culture for periods of time and forming serious relationships.[97] These kinds of practices keep the perpetrators as the focus and give them relief without really attending to the ones who were harmed or entering into new ways of living justly together with former enemies and victims. Postwar rituals used today for return and reintegration should cultivate an opportunity to face the moral wrongs of war and even challenge participants to be morally accountable for their actions. In this way, postwar rituals and practices can resist covering or justifying harmful actions and help warriors take responsibility for their own moral agency by creating some space for reflection and, perhaps, contrition.

Even so, the postwar rituals of return and reintegration in the Old Testament and related contexts, which treat pragmatic issues, aren't merely pragmatic. They potentially serve certain symbolic functions related to moral injury. Consideration of these practices pushes those working on warfare in general and moral injury in particular toward a more comprehensive study that moves beyond how war was done to how war was conceived, constructed, and experienced socially, culturally, personally, and even bodily. This final dimension, especially the physical experiences of war and the bodily performances of return rituals and reintegration practices, connects to an important insight within trauma studies more broadly. Along with the common cognitive and literary approaches to trauma, there has been a somatic turn—a movement toward emphasizing how bodies and physicality are involved in both trauma and its healing.[98] Because neurobiology and neuroscience have shown that trauma causes physiological changes and physical effects, bodies and physicality must be involved in recovery. Cognitive re-narrating of experiences and the telling of the story can't, by themselves, reverse the damage caused by trauma. Since the body itself remembers, recovery must involve bodily practices and physical performances.

As noted in chapter 2, the relationship of moral injury to trauma remains debated. Still, the physically performed rituals and actions found in Old Testament texts and moral injury studies suggest that overcoming

the shame, guilt, grief, social disconnection, self-doubt, and other consequences of moral injury must involve more than cognitive reprocessing
or talk therapy. The effort must involve physical actions that permit "the
body to have experiences that deeply and viscerally contradict that help-
lessness, rage, or collapse" that result from traumatic or morally damaging
experiences.[99] Practices such as purification, redistribution, and memorial-
izing after battle may function as collective performances or community
rituals that actually affect the mind and its processing, but also may facilitate both a "confrontation of the painful realities of life and symbolic
transformation through communal action."[100]

Chapter 5

Moral Injury, Lament, and Forgiveness

*Never think that war, no matter how necessary, nor how justified, is not a crime.
Ask the infantry and ask the dead.*

–Ernest Hemingway [1]

The Old Testament case study in this chapter is the third attempt to explore the idea that the engagement between the Bible and moral injury generates a two-way conversation. The interpretations of some of the Bible's war-related texts undertaken here and in the other chapters illuminate how moral injury can be an interpretive lens that brings new meanings out of the biblical writings, and how the critical study of the Bible can make substantive contributions to the ongoing attempt to understand, identify, and heal moral injury.

This chapter continues the examination of the Old Testament's rituals and symbolic practices related to the return and reintegration of soldiers after war in dialogue with perspectives from moral injury study. [2] The preceding chapter examined three of the five postbattle rituals and practices in the biblical writings: (1) purification of warriors, captives, and objects; (2) appropriation of booty; and (3) construction of memorials and monuments. This chapter begins with a brief survey of the fourth postwar practice of celebration and procession, but the majority of the chapter focuses on the prevalent references to lament (both individual and communal) in relationship to war and their particular significance for moral injury work. These final two practices fit together because they represent expressions of different types of human feelings and reactions—both personal and communal—to the experiences of war (notably, contrasting emotions and reactions of exuberance and grief). The goal of this chapter is once again twofold. First is to offer something akin to a mapping survey that sets out the Old Testament texts that present these postwar rituals and practices and considers those texts against the social and cultural backdrop of similar acts from the ancient Near East and elsewhere. Second is to explore the possible connections between the ancient practices and moral injury, especially how perspectives from recent moral injury study may illuminate the possible symbolic functions of these ritual acts and their potential import for helping those dealing with the effects of war.

As with the rituals examined in the preceding chapter, the discussion of celebration, procession, and lament below represents the second of the two primary trajectories noted in chapter 2 that have emerged concerning how ancient texts have been and might be fruitfully used within work on moral injury—namely, the effort in moral injury studies to identify rituals and symbolic acts from ancient and traditional cultures that might be used today to address the felt needs of morally injured persons. Both of the two primary trajectories offer the most immediate entry points for chaplains, ministers, psychologists, biblical scholars, and other interested persons to consider creatively what moral injury research can contribute to the interpretation of biblical texts (especially war and violence texts) and what the study of the Bible (both academically and devotionally/pastorally) can contribute to the ongoing efforts to understand and address moral injury. What follows here isn't a comprehensive analysis but an initial, exploratory, and suggestive venture that illustrates how readers of the Bible might look for textual descriptions of war-related ritual practices that suggest attempts to deal with or even prevent the kinds of negative effects now identified with moral injury.

The preceding chapter gave the background of modern moral injury study's appeals to postwar rituals from ancient and traditional societies. With that same background in mind, the first part of this chapter will proceed immediately to a survey of Old Testament examples of celebration and procession after war in dialogue with references to similar practices in ancient Near Eastern and other contexts. Recent moral injury works, however, have placed a special emphasis on the elements of grief, protest, honest expression, emotional processing, confession, and forgiveness—many of which are encompassed by the notion of lament. Hence, the second part of this chapter will describe the background of modern moral injury study's appeals to lament. The third section—the heart of the chapter—will then work through various Old Testament examples and expressions of lament related to war experiences within their context in ancient Israel's world, including those found in the Old Testament Historical Books and prophets, as well as those found among the so-called lament psalms. The chapter will conclude by considering the potential insights that emerge particularly from the encounter between the Bible's war-related laments and moral injury. The goal once again isn't to argue that the Old Testament materials actually functioned as a kind of moral injury therapy for ancient Israel. Rather, the lament psalms (and other Old Testament rituals and practices) performed a function for Israelite society comparable to what is attempted in moral repair work today and thus can serve as a resource for such present-day work, especially in ministerial and chaplaincy contexts.

Postwar Rituals of Celebration and Procession in the Old Testament and Its Context

Against the background of modern moral injury study's interest in rituals and symbolic acts from ancient and traditional cultures (see ch. 4), Bible readers may note the fourth category of Old Testament post-war practices, which goes along with purification (of warriors, captives, and objects), appropriation of booty, and construction of memorials and monuments. This category contains several Old Testament passages that portray the victorious returning army participating in rituals of celebration, procession, and thanksgiving (see Exod 15:1-18, 20-21; Judg 5:1-31; 1 Sam 18:6-9; 2 Sam 19:1-8 [implied by opposite]; 2 Chr 20:24-30; Esth 9:16-17; Ps 68:21-27; Isa 25:6).[3] Overall, the texts include celebratory praise songs (Exod 15:1-18; Judg 5:1-31), feasting (Esth 9:16-17; Isa 25:6), triumphal processions back to the city (Ps 68:21-27; 2 Chr 20:24-30), and women coming out to meet the returning warriors with music and dancing (Exod 15:20-21; 1 Sam 18:6-9).[4]

For example, the victory poem about Israel's God, Yhwh, attributed to Moses in Exodus 15:1-18 is one of the first postbattle, celebratory praise songs to appear in the Old Testament (see also Gen 14:17-20; Judg 5:1-31). Moses's praise song to God follows the miraculous drowning of the Egyptian army in the sea that allowed the Hebrews to escape their captivity in Egypt (Exod 13–14). The poem celebrates the victory over pharaoh's forces but also contains mythological themes, as it attributes that victory to the actions of Israel's God (v. 1) and depicts Yhwh as a warrior whose power extends not only over human enemies (vv. 3-4) but over the forces of nature, as well (see vv. 5-8, 10). The song refers to the enemy's intentions to destroy with the sword and "divide the spoil" (v. 9), but then proclaims that Yhwh thwarted these intentions to accomplish the divine purpose of leading a particular group of people to a promised land where Yhwh's "holy abode" and "sanctuary" will be found (vv. 13, 17). Although this song portrays the celebration of a divine action rather a victory won by human soldiers, its interpretation of the events of the exodus from Egypt connects to the need noted by moral injury work to help returning warriors reframe specific conflicts within a larger perspective that gives them a broader and perhaps more meaningful significance—one shared by the community as a whole. In this case, Moses's victory song describes

Yhwh as the victorious warrior whose power deploys even the forces of the natural world in the divine service, and rearticulates the completed conflict into the realm of larger cosmologies, theologies, and divine action.

Another notable example of postwar celebration and procession is 1 Samuel 18:6-9, which appears in the Saul story discussed above in chapter 3. This passage portrays the procession of Saul, David, and the other warriors returning home after a victory over the Philistines (in which David slew Goliath; see 1 Sam 17). During the return, women come out to meet the warriors with singing, dancing, and instruments. The women sing a victory song that extols Saul's and David's triumphs, "Saul has killed his thousands, and David his ten thousands" (v. 7; see my discussion of the ambiguity of this saying in its context in ch. 3). Moses's victory song in Exodus 15:1-18 has a similar element, as it's followed immediately by the ritual performance of Miriam (Aaron's sister) and "all the women," who sing with tambourines and dancing, "Sing to the LORD, for he has triumphed gloriously; horse and rider he has thrown into the sea" (Exod 15:20-21; see also Deborah's victory song in Judg 5:1-31). The story in 2 Chronicles 20:24-30 likewise depicts Judah's king Jehoshaphat leading "all the people of Judah and Jerusalem" home after a miraculous defeat of the invading Moabites, Ammonites, and others (v. 27). The Judean army spent three days collecting spoils from the dead enemies (v. 25), and then the king led a joy-filled (v. 27) procession into the capital city of Jerusalem and to the temple with "harps and lyres and trumpets" (v. 28). As a side note, the story in 2 Samuel 19:1-8 may represent the emotional distress caused by the failure to provide returning warriors with these kinds of celebratory processionals. The text reports that David's troops, although victorious over Absalom's forces, "stole into the city that day as soldiers steal in who are ashamed when they flee in battle" (v. 3). The implication is that a celebratory processional was expected, and King David later rectified the situation somewhat by gathering the troops before him (v. 8).

Psalm 68:21-27 provides a final example of this category. This passage seems to place an allusion to a postbattle procession in the context of military victory and celebration, although the reference is opaque.[5] Perhaps as a part of this procession, defeated enemies are said to be brought to Jerusalem so that the victors may "bathe" their feet in blood (v. 23; see also Ps 58:10).[6] It is tempting to see this text as an allusion to a postbattle ritual of bathing the warriors' feet with the blood of the defeated and connect it with other evidence for the shame and mutilation of enemies.[7] Yet it's unclear whether the language is literal or metaphorical, and this action doesn't appear in any subsequent or developed form elsewhere in the Old Testament.

In terms of sources from the ancient Near East and elsewhere outside the Old Testament, numerous references exist to various kinds of victory celebrations that involve processions, music, sacrifices, and other ritual activities in many ancient and modern cultures. Ancient Egyptian texts, for example, refer to the celebratory homecoming of the king and army, sometimes including a speech by a deity about the king and offerings of praise by the soldiers.[8] Greek texts associate various drink offerings and sacrifices with celebration at the end of battle.[9] Later Roman texts from the second century BCE describe what is perhaps the most famous victory celebration ritual, the "Triumph" (*triumphus*).[10] This celebration featured a public ceremony honoring victorious military leaders and included an organized procession of the troops and spoils ending at the temple of Jupiter.

Moral Injury, the Needs of Soldiers, and the Practices of Lament

The background for this discussion of war-related laments in the Old Testament is the presence of certain perspectives and emphases related to lament that have appeared in moral injury research from its beginnings in psychology and veterans' care to its present formulations in chaplaincy and Christian ministry. Overall, moral injury work has talked about these perspectives and emphases as a series of needs that returning soldiers have in order to deal with the effects of moral injury, facilitate prevention or recovery, and help ensure a healthy return and reintegration after conflict. Exploration of these perceived needs within moral injury work has then led—albeit only in initial and undeveloped ways—to attempts to identify practices that can meet the needs, with some writers pointing explicitly to the Old Testament's lament psalms.

The first of the needs that has been emphasized in recent moral injury work is to provide opportunities and encouragement for returning soldiers to speak honestly about their experiences. Those dealing with participation in war need the opportunity to make honest assessments and give candid expression of things they've done, witnessed, or by which they've been affected. Soldiers need help engaging in uninhibited truth telling about particular acts and events, as well as broader circumstances and realities, so that the healing process can begin and they can resist the kinds of negative assessments of self and the world that lead to moral injury. Levine puts it succinctly: "Moral injury cannot be healed without the truthful telling of what has been done by and what has happened to the war veteran."[11]

As Bica asserts, this kind of honesty cuts against a cultural "mythology" associated with the military today, which labels speaking out on the difficulties of war or questioning war's justifications and procedures as unpatriotic or diminishing the sacrifice of others, and thus often prevents soldiers from "confronting and working through the psychological, emotional, and moral (PEM) injuries of war."[12] Against this cultural backdrop, the need for truth telling by returning soldiers sometimes takes the form of the expressions of protest, which give voice to the extreme and dehumanizing evil of war. These acts of protest—sometimes in the form of public grief or mourning—name war's injustices, evils, and sufferings as the first step to moving past denial toward hope for a repaired future.[13] More frequently, however, current moral injury work stresses that the needed truth telling for soldiers is the honest personal processing and expression of emotional suffering, pain, grief, and disillusionment. Ramsay,

*[handwritten margin note: * "We" had trouble doing this w/ COVID]*

for instance, recently defined moral injury in its essence as "an experience of profound loss and grief with individual and systemic consequences."[14] And a recurring theme in much clinical research highlights the need for soldiers to acknowledge candidly and process honestly their experiences of grief and pain because the very ability to feel anguish, hurt, or shame is a sign of hope that their moral conscience remains intact. On all of these counts, moral injury work seeks to enable soldiers to find their voice and to provide them with words that can facilitate the necessary truth telling or honest grieving to allow for a new sense of resilience and hope.[15]

The second and most extensively discussed need of returning soldiers is the need for forgiveness (of self and others). When soldiers experience moral injury, it's often tied to a sense of having violated their own moral conscience and experiencing guilt or shame over their actions, those of others, or the larger circumstances. As a result, moral injury works commonly talk about a felt need for forgiveness (understood in various ways) among returning morally injured soldiers. Lynd and Lynd express the conviction succinctly: "There appears to be general agreement that self-forgiveness and forgiveness of others is central to healing from moral injuries."[16] Even more tellingly, Nash et al.'s analysis of events that potentially cause moral injury concludes that forgiveness is the most important element for helping soldiers struggling with a sense of transgression.[17]

The goal of facilitating experiences of forgiveness isn't simply that soldiers will accept and acknowledge the parts of themselves that were involved in bad acts, but also that they will reclaim a sense of their own humanity and goodness for a different future.[18] The term *forgiveness* in these military moral injury contexts carries the broad meaning of a renewed, positive self-acceptance and empathetic self-understanding, instead of unrelenting self-judgment. Along these lines, many moral injury works identify the act of confession as a primary means to meet the felt need for forgiveness.[19] In these contexts, confession is understood as the honest acknowledgment of acts and circumstances for which a soldier feels responsibility, guilt, or shame. Confession is truth telling with the goal of honest acknowledgment, empathetic self-understanding, and a renewed sense of hope.

Those working on moral injury don't always conceive of the need for forgiveness or the act of confession in religious terms (i.e., the need to repent for sinful actions and receive pardon from a divine power), although this perspective is often present in works within chaplaincy, ministry, and Christian counseling.[20] Approaches that use specifically Christian theological terms may describe objectionable acts done within war as "sins" in need of divine forgiveness or identify the entire enterprise of war as inherently sinful, both of which lead to the conviction that moral injury results, at least to some degree, from sin and thus requires repentance before God. Larson nuances the religious perspective on the need for confession and forgiveness in this way:

> It may not be that the sin resulting in MI [moral injury] requires repentance in the traditional understanding of the term. However, it does surely require the language of confession in the sense that confession explicitly recognizes the causal agency of that event that the MI victim heretofore preferred to leave to her/his internal darkness.[21]

Other articulations of the need for confession and forgiveness draw from moral psychology rather than religion or theology to suggest that the development of positive moral emotions can be a significant part of recovery from moral injury, and this development occurs as a person learns to take responsibility for their own actions and culpability while simultaneously learning to show compassion toward self and others.[22] Similarly, Sherman uses the field of moral philosophy to assert that the needed change in self-evaluation for the morally wounded soldier can be accomplished by honest conversations in which the soldier retells their story to an empathetic listener who can "bear compassionate witness to the pain and... reconstrue what happened in ways that may involve fairer self-judgment."[23] She stresses a legal framework for war—namely, that if a soldier's actions were legal and didn't involve any "intentional wrongdoing," then they weren't a moral offense. Thus, she resists the term

Legally
Moral
or
immoral

- 107 -

forgiveness, but still concludes that morally wounded soldiers have a need to develop "self-empathy" through honest articulation of their experiences in understanding environments.[24]

Similar to Sherman's approach, the Adaptive Disclosure model, one of the most fully developed clinical treatment models for moral injury, emphasizes helping sufferers find forgiveness and empathy (for self and others) through honest dialogue with a compassionate listener.[25] Specifically, this model suggests that morally injured persons engage in "evocative imaginal 'confession' and dialogue with a compassionate and forgiving moral authority in order to begin to challenge and address the shame and self-handicapping that accompany such experiences."[26] This practice moves toward forgiveness through honest expression, but clinicians understand that such confession only begins the moral repair process. The overall goal of dialogue with a compassionate moral authority is to help the person to acknowledge bad actions but also begin to reclaim a sense of moral goodness.

The third need that has been emphasized in recent moral injury work is to help returning soldiers communalize their moral and emotional experiences. The general introduction to moral injury in chapter 2 defined communalization, and Sherman's recent book using moral philosophy suggested communalization as the key to moral repair.[27] This perceived need for veterans involves helping them unpack and discuss their experiences with others. Perhaps even more significantly, however, communalization represents the soldiers' need to have their feelings of pain, grief, and even guilt validated and co-owned by their larger network of family, friends, local communities, societal institutions, and even governmental authorities. There is a need for soldiers to sense that the moral burdens, responsibility, and even guilt for war are shared by those who remained untouched directly by the experience. When others recognize and share in the moral anguish and ethical uncertainties caused by combat by listening to the truth telling of soldiers and veterans, those listeners become witnesses that grant agency and voice to the morally injured and validate their struggles. Moreover, the listeners who attend to the stories of the morally injured may themselves come to sense and experience some of the struggles previously confined to the soldiers alone. As Ramsay states, "Those who recognize suffering through another's 'testimony' step into that inter-human space as witnesses who experience the moral agency such suffering bespeaks and evokes in those who will listen."[28]

The final element of the background of war-related laments in the Old Testament is the attempt that has arisen within moral injury study to identify practices or other means that can, at least partially, meet the needs of returning soldiers for honesty, forgiveness, and community. The current moral injury literature offers fewer insights on this topic than on the needs themselves, admitting that "little is known" about the best practices for promoting things such as forgiveness.[29] Even so, some moral injury works point explicitly to lament—understood as a passionate, sometimes public, expression of grief—as a possible means for meeting these recognized needs. And recently, laments written by soldiers reflecting on their experiences have appeared in print individually and in collections.[30] Fisher, for example, offers a full-scale analysis of poetry written by combat veterans across seven different historical conflicts as a means to study moral injury and repair.[31]

From the perspective of pastoral care and counseling, Graham offers an extended discussion of the use of lamentation ceremonies in the context of public memorials. He argues, "Corporate ritual practices are extremely important for individuals, such as soldiers, who otherwise must bear alone in the intricacies of their brains and psyches the costs of what the body politic as a whole has asked them to shoulder."[32] Doehring highlights the lament-related spiritual care practices of sharing anguish (i.e., compassionately accepting the emotions that accompany moral injury) and interrogating suffering (i.e., exploring values, beliefs, and coping methods).[33] Others look especially to poems, liturgies, and similar written formulations that can serve as expressions of lament for those seeking honesty, forgiveness, and community. These literary expressions articulate ideas, feelings, moods, and experiences known to those affected by moral injury and help their readers process and bear those things. For example, Fawson has recently explored the literary genre of "witness poetry" as a way to recognize and lament the wounds of war.[34] Poems in this genre are written in response to extreme struggle and suffering, and may help soldiers recognize and process the violence, trauma, and loss of war (see further discussion in the "Moral Injury Connections" section below).

The final and most direct background for this exploration of the Bible's war-related laments has appeared in the works on moral injury that have pointed specifically to the laments in the Old Testament book of Psalms as possible examples and resources. Within Christian pastoral care in particular, several works suggest that the forms of lament found in various psalms may provide words to help morally injured persons speak honestly of their suffering as the first step to healing.[35] Brock and Lettini recount the story of a military chaplain who had struggling soldiers read Psalm 51 as a forgiveness liturgy and the so-called imprecatory psalms (or cursing of enemies psalms; see Ps 137) as ways to express the mood, tone, and feelings of having been betrayed.[36] Ramsay provides an article-length study on the use of ritual resources within spiritual care for facilitating grieving and building resilience that emphasizes the usefulness of laments found in the Old Testament psalms, alongside other examples from both Jewish and Christian traditions. She explains that laments function as "witness and testimony" for the suffering and provide the "language of pain that opens a way for healing by helping hope to reemerge, though the path is not simple."[37]

Old Testament Lament

The fifth and final category of Old Testament postwar rituals and symbolic practices, which goes along with purification (of warriors, captives, and objects), appropriation of booty, construction of memorials and monuments, and celebration and procession, consists of several references to the act of lament, offered in response to military defeat or other kinds of war-related personal and communal suffering. These laments are a natural counterpart to the victory songs and celebrations in the preceding category.

Some of the most explicitly war-related laments described in biblical texts appear in the Old Testament Historical Books and the messages attributed to the Old Testament prophets. The major example in the Historical Books occurs in David's lamentation over the deaths of Saul and Jonathan in battle in 2 Samuel 1:19-27. The passage as a whole is an individual lament by David. Note the presence of the opening exclamation, "How" ("How the mighty have fallen!" v. 19; see also vv. 25, 27) *How* known from other biblical lament passages (e.g., Jer 2:21; 9:18; Mic 2:4). David not only grieves the death of Saul and Jonathan, but expresses deep angst over the possibility that Israel's enemies might rejoice over the defeat (v. 20). His lament expresses his own distress and sense of loss at Saul's and Jonathan's deaths in battle (v. 26). Additionally, verses 21-23 go beyond David's personal expressions and seem to envision a communal lament to be given by women (see v. 24). His call for women to weep for Saul represents the inverse of the descriptions mentioned above that portrayed groups of women who led postbattle celebratory songs elsewhere (e.g., Exod 15:20-21; 1 Sam 18:6-9). As noted above, the weeping women reference likely connects to a larger tradition of women fulfilling the role of both postbattle celebrants and designated mourners in ancient Israel and elsewhere in the ancient Near East.[38] Other postbattle laments by David in the Historical Books reflect similar language and themes of personal grief and loss, as well as communal mourning. See, for example, David's laments over the general Abner (2 Sam 3:33-44) and his rebellious son Absalom (2 Sam 18:33).

Laments after defeat also occur among the poetic texts found in the Old Testament prophetic books. Some appear in prophetic pronouncements that fit the genre of so-called city laments (see below). In the Old Testament, these laments treat the subject matter of the destruction of cities (usually due to enemy invasion) and feature themes such as God's abandonment of the city, description of the destruction as divine judgment, assignment of blame for the destruction, and somber expressions of grief, sometimes authentic, sometimes sarcastic. In Amos 5:1-3, for instance, the prophet utters a "lamentation" (v. 1) directed at the "maiden Israel" (v. 2), likely a reference to the capital city of Samaria.[39] The meter of the Hebrew text constitutes a funeral dirge, and Amos speaks of maiden Israel as if she were already dead. He even seems to predict future military defeats for the city.

Biblical readers may also observe prophetic oracles that employ ironic or sarcastic laments to condemn enemy kingdoms such as Babylon, Moab, and Egypt. In Isaiah 14:3-20, for example, the prophet proclaims a taunting song against the fallen king of Babylon. Using the characteristic lament word, "How" (vv. 4, 12), mentioned above in conjunction with David's lament in 2 Samuel 1:19-27, Isaiah mimics a lament, with its expressions of grief and loss (v. 12), but portrays both humans and nature rejoicing over the evil king's fate. Similarly, in Isaiah 15–16, the prophet proclaims a judgment oracle against Moab that takes the form of a postbattle lament over defeat. Isaiah's language reflects typical expressions of grief over the destruction of cities and the fate of refugees (15:5-6; 16:4), as well as personal anguish over the suffering and loss (16:9). The passage is notoriously difficult to interpret, however, with many uncertainties in language, syntax, and tone. Some biblical scholars conclude that when placed in the larger context of the oracles against the nations in the Old Testament prophetic books generally, and the judgment oracles against foreign kingdoms in Isaiah's messages particularly, the passage should be understood as carrying an ironic intention designed to urge Judah's nonalignment with foreign powers during Isaiah's day.[40] From a different perspective, Joel 1:2–2:17 features a prophetic call to Israel's elders for an extended communal lamentation intertwined with references (literal or metaphorical) to an invasion that has devastated the land (see 1:6-8).

As with the other Old Testament postwar rituals and symbolic actions, war-related laments (especially following military failure) also appear in different forms within various ancient Near Eastern writings. Two categories are primary here. First, some epic poetry and ritual texts envision defeat in battle being followed by laments offered by family members of the defeated warrior, often by weeping women. Note, for instance, the presence in ancient Canaanite texts of laments by the deities El and Anat for Baal, or Anat's lament for Aqhat.[41] Second, as referenced above with regard to the Old Testament prophets, the most explicit examples of post-battle laments outside the Bible appear in the so-called Mesopotamian city laments.[42] These texts contain laments over destroyed cities and their sanctuaries (usually due to enemy invasion), and some likely functioned as part of ceremonies accompanying later refounding and restoration. They share common features related to subject, mood, divine abandonment of the city, assignment of responsibility, description of destruction, and a weeping goddess.[43] Five compositions constitute the best representations of the genre: "Lamentation over the Destruction of Ur," "Lamentation over the Destruction of Sumer and Ur," "Nippur Lament," "Eridu Lament," and "Uruk Lament."[44] The similarities shown by certain prophetic oracles (e.g., Amos 5) and other Old Testament texts to these Mesopotamian city laments suggest that Israel developed a city lament tradition of its own between the eighth and sixth centuries BCE.[45]

Alongside the examples found in the Old Testament Historical Books and prophetic texts, the short book of Lamentations represents the most concentrated collection of explicitly war-related laments in the Bible. The book consists of five, multivoiced grief poems about the destruction of Jerusalem by the Babylonians in 586 BCE that give pictures of the horrors of the event and explore its causes and aftermath. The book is the fullest example of the city lament genre in the Old Testament, with many similarities to the Mesopotamian city laments mentioned above, especially in the portrayal of a deity who is said to have withdrawn from the patron city and given it over to enemies. The poems in Lamentations offer ceremonial and, in some cases, communal (especially ch. 5) laments in response to the catastrophe of destruction and exile. They reflect on the military defeat, express the suffering and violence involved, and plead for relief.

In her commentary on Lamentations, O'Connor identifies the grief poems in the book of Lamentations as "truth-filled and faithful prayers" that testify specifically to the ways that experiences of war-related destruction and suffering wreck a person's or community's faith in their own morality and agency and their hope for a positive world in which to live.[46] Specifically, O'Connor notes that the first poem (Lam 1) describes a female figure called "daughter Zion" (v. 6)—a personification of the destroyed city of Jerusalem—whose expressions of grief and hurt over being bereft of children, family, priests, and any other companions represent her sorrow over not having anyone who can witness and validate her pain.[47] Daughter Zion says,

> Is it nothing to you, all you who pass by?
>> Look and see
> if there is any sorrow like my sorrow . . .
> for a comforter is far from me,
>> one to revive my courage;
> my children are desolate,
>> for the enemy has prevailed. (Lam 1:12, 16)

O'Connor then notes that the following poem (Lam 2) relates the voice of a poet who bears witness to and validates Daughter Zion's pain by empathizing with her suffering and acknowledging its enormity.[48] In this acknowledgment, the witness poet even echoes the voice of Daughter Zion from chapter 1 in affirming that Zion's God has acted in wrath and without mercy in this circumstance of suffering (2:1-2; compare 1:12, 15). The poet bears validating witness by saying,

> What can I say for you, to what compare you,
>> O daughter Jerusalem?
> To what can I liken you, that I may comfort you,

- 114 -

O virgin daughter Zion?

For vast as the sea is your ruin;

who can heal you? (Lam 2:13)

Key passage

As Ramsay suggests, this is the crucial practice of witness that is needed for the care of morally injured persons.[49] And this practice is even more vital in Lamentations because there is a complete absence of God's voice in the book—a feature that reflects the inability of many morally injured persons to feel God's presence or even to conceive of the existence or agency of a morally good deity. The witness's voice in chapter 2 not only expresses empathy with Daughter Zion's suffering but also registers a protest against the perceived injustice of the situation and overkill of God's judgment (see 2:3-8).

As a final example from the book of Lamentations, O'Connor notes that the approximate middle of the book (the poem in ch. 3) introduces the voice of another witness (a male speaker) who moves beyond protest to express a tentative hope for the experience of mercy and love from God in the midst of the suffering, pain, and loss (Lam 3:21-33).[50] Two things are notable about this turn in mood. First, the poet here makes a new moral claim about God ("The LORD is good to those who wait for him" v. 25; contrast 2:1-3), which moves toward repair of the sense of God's morality wrecked by the war experiences of pain, loss, and destruction. This claim is an act of reimaging God's presence in the suffering. To this point, the laments have portrayed God as absent, malicious in intent, or excessive in violence. Now the poet in chapter 3 asserts that, in fact, God isn't absent, powerless, or malicious, but responds with goodness to those who wait (persevere) and doesn't willingly hurt or permanently reject anyone (vv. 31-33). The second notable thing about this imaginative turn in mood, however, is that it's based not on any present circumstances or experiences that would suggest hope in a compassionate God, moral world, or restored future. It is based only on memory: "But this I call to mind, and therefore I have hope" (v. 21). Jerusalem's present situation remains unchanged. Even so, the poet calls back to his mind lessons learned from experiences past and testimonies heard from witnesses of old—and thus builds a new hope in a moral and compassionate God.

The most recognizable grouping of Old Testament laments—other than the book of Lamentations—appears in the book of Psalms. The so-called lament psalm is one of the long-established genre classifications of the different psalms that appear in the book (in addition to the hymn of praise, thanksgiving psalm, royal psalm, and more). In general, a lament psalm is a complaint and petition to God over various situations of distress in the life of a person or community. Notably, unlike some of the other Old Testament laments that are personal expressions or addressed to certain groups of people (e.g., 2 Sam 1:19-27), the laments in the book of Psalms are prayers directed to God. They are appeals for divine help in which the worshipper presents her or his condition or circumstances before God and asks for intervention. In this way, the lament psalms represent a different kind of expression of grief, petition, or protest—namely, one that speaks directly to a perceived moral authority who has the presumed ability to hear, help, or forgive.

God hears and we cry out

The lament psalms take different forms and reflect a wide variety of circumstances of distress. The laments that feature an individual who expresses difficulties and appeals to God for assistance make up the largest category of psalms in the book (more than fifty of the 150 psalms). But several laments are communal in nature—prayers in which the community as a whole articulates grief, protest, and petition to God, especially following some disastrous communal or national event. The laments in the Psalter tend to use stereotyped liturgical and theological language and formulas, as prayers in various religious traditions always have. They weren't likely written to be used on only one special occasion; many were probably written by priests and then offered to worshippers as the circumstances warranted.[51] Hence, the lament psalms reflect a wide variety of situations of distress that include oppression by enemies, illness, petition for forgiveness of sin, false accusations, and more. No matter the topic, however, both individual and communal laments typically follow a common pattern that features elements that appear in the structure of the psalm, although not every element is present (or in the same order) in every lament. The common structure of a lament psalm contains the following elements:[52]

1. Address to God

2. Description of Distress

3. Plea for Redemption

4. Statement of Confidence

5. Confession of Sin or Affirmation of Innocence

6. Pledge or Vow

7. Conclusion

As the individual or community moves through these elements of prayer to God, the practice of lament provides a way to express a life disrupted. The common problem that appears in many of these laments is a sense of God's absence—a feeling that God has abandoned the worshipper or community in the midst of distress. The prayers are forthright and direct, but they're not always sensitive or proper. Some of them blame God or express anger at God over the circumstances (e.g., Ps 88), and many of them use hyperbole and vivid, violent metaphors and language (e.g., Ps 137). At the most basic level, the laments express the disconnect often felt by religious persons between what they believe about God's character, power, and actions, and what they actually experience in their lives and world. Ramsay explicitly relates this disconnect to the dynamics of military moral injury in which veterans lose their previous confidence in their "earlier imagination about who God is, how God exercises agency in the world, and the character of God's agency."[53] The laments insist that these experiences of dissonance and disorder should be brought forthrightly before God in prayer. They permit no cover-up or self-deception that pretends all is well; rather, they "insist that the world must be experienced as it really is . . . [and] that all such experiences of disorder are a proper subject for discourse with God."[54] For the lament psalms, such discourse includes the honest expression of grief, pain, protest, anger, betrayal, hopelessness, cynicism, and despair—all addressed directly to God.[55]

In this book, the psalms that are most directly relevant to military moral injury are the several communal laments that relate specifically to ancient Israel's experience of military failure. These psalms constitute inverse counterparts to other psalms (especially so-called royal psalms about the Israelite king and his activities) that express thanksgiving for victory in battle or offer prayers for success in upcoming conflicts.[56] There are some limitations here, however, for intersections with moral injury. For instance, the Bible preserves no laments that follow victory in battle but only those that reflect upon defeat or some other kind of loss. Moral injury, by contrast, is possible whether the soldiers experience victory or defeat. The presence of laments over the dire consequences of war participation even in victory would be a significant resource for reflection on moral injury, but, alas, they're not present in the biblical texts. Additionally, the moral and emotional difficulties expressed in these psalms result from the overall demoralizing effects of defeat, rather than from soldiers' specific conduct in battle or from participation in war as such, which would be more in line with the concentration of moral injury work. Finally, as Brueggemann observes, it might be difficult for readers steeped in Western, individualistic, and "privatistic" ways of thinking to identify meaningfully with the communal (rather than personal) laments or with the sense of shared, public disasters and loss.[57] Insights about the dynamics of moral injury, however, can provide a needed bridge that allows modern readers to resonate with these ancient prayers, think of analogous experiences, and imagine points of contact.

Among the various communal laments within the Psalter (see Pss 12; 44; 58; 60; 74; 79; 80; 83; 90; 137), a plurality reflect "the national calamities and disasters which resulted from warfare and battle."[58] Psalm 44, for example, is a national lament and communal plea for help that refers to the failure of Israel's army and the taking of spoil by the enemy (see

vv. 9-10). No single historical event can be identified as the referent here, but the people's description of their distress (vv. 9-16) is notable because it consists of a direct confrontation and sharp accusations against God as the one who has allowed the defeat to happen.

> Yet you have rejected us....
> You made us turn back....
> You have made us like sheep for slaughter....
> You have sold your people for a trifle. (vv. 9-12)

By contrast, the people maintain their innocence in receiving this undeserved fate (vv. 17-22). The national prayer concludes with a plea for God to awaken from sleep and rescue the people from their distress ("Rouse yourself! Why do you sleep, O Lord?" v. 23).

Psalm 60 offers a communal lament after defeat that expresses the disastrous consequences that have come from God's refusal to grant victory to the army. The prayer identifies God's rejection of the people as the reason for the defeat of Israel's army. Following a complaint against God by the people (vv. 1-4) and a plea for rescue and victory (v. 5), however, this lament includes in vv. 6-8 a divine oracle offered by God in response (perhaps spoken by the priest as part of a communal lament ritual or ceremony).[59] In this divine proclamation, God declares sovereignty over Judah and the surrounding lands, condemning the people's enemies. The prayer then ends with the people's final plea for divine aid (vv. 9-11) and an expression of confidence for future victory with God's help (v. 12).[60]

Psalm 80 contains similar themes but uses the analogy of Israel as God's vineyard to express a communal lament following a national calamity (likely at the hands of enemies, see vv. 6, 16). Among repeated pleas for God to "restore" the people (vv. 3, 7, 19), the prayer describes Israel as a vineyard that has had it walls broken down, its fruit plucked, and its vines cut down and burned (vv. 8-17). This metaphor gives way to a concluding prayer for divine deliverance and an accompanying vow of fidelity by the people to be fulfilled on the other side of their redemption (vv. 17-19).

Psalms 74 and 79 are communal laments concerned with the specific catastrophe of the desecration and destruction of the Jerusalem temple by foreign armies, likely a reference to the Babylonian invasion of Jerusalem in 586 BCE. Psalm 74 focuses on the national humiliation of this experience, underscoring that the temple for ancient Israel was not simply a structure but a "sacral key" that held all parts of life together and without which the world falls apart—not unlike a sense of moral identity or a belief in a moral world.[61] The psalm begins by focusing on God as the one who has allowed the tragedy and the one who can rectify it, even calling on God to go and see firsthand what the enemy has done to the sanctuary (vv. 1-3). The people then painfully describe to God the enemies' destruction and burning of the temple and its aftermath (vv. 4-11) before moving to a hymn that expresses confidence in God as the creator of the world (vv. 12-17). The people conclude with a plea to God to reverse the divine abandonment, "remember" that the enemies' actions are a personal affront to God (not just Israel), and "have regard for your covenant" (vv. 18-23).

Psalm 79 is a more visceral and violent prayer in response to the same situation of the destruction of Jerusalem's temple, which includes pain-filled expressions of desired retaliation and revenge. This prayer focuses less on the temple's destruction and more on the people's suffering. It contains pleas for God to save the people (vv. 9, 11) and includes a communal confession of sin and request for divine forgiveness (vv. 8-9). Yet the emphasis throughout is on depicting the foreign enemies not just as outsiders but as ritually impure, contaminated, and defiled invaders whose presence and acts have rendered the sanctuary unclean and unholy (vv. 1-4). This emphasis gives way to a prayer for God to avenge what has been done, even to the point of a "sevenfold" retaliation (v. 12). This kind of degrading description of foreigners and militant plea for divine vengeance may well give contemporary readers pause. The words and sentiments are, however, honesty in the fullest. As Brueggemann notes, the prayer here expresses a longing that God would "show God's self to friend and foe for who God really is, not to be blasphemed or trifled with, but to be taken with utter seriousness."[62] Perhaps just as importantly, the speakers of this prayer don't hide their longing for such divine demonstration and vengeance. Rather, they are honest and forthright with it. Still, they don't act on that longing; they submit it to God as a prayer and leave it in the divine purview.

Although the communal laments surveyed above are the most obviously relevant for considering military moral injury, we can broaden the dialogue between moral injury and the biblical laments to include some consideration of the personal lament psalms, which aren't so specifically related to warfare experiences and their aftermath. As mentioned above, the personal prayers of distress are the most common type of psalm in the book of Psalms, and although they don't relate overtly to combat experiences, they resonate with some of the things mentioned within moral injury work concerning how individual veterans experience the effects of war, seek to speak truthfully about their grief, and search for compassion in their pain.

The preceding discussion noted that the personal laments in the book of Psalms reflect a variety of circumstances of distress. Among the laments related to situations such as illness and false accusations, two types of laments seem most potentially fruitful for dialogue with moral injury: (1) prayers concerning oppression by enemies; and (2) prayers seeking divine forgiveness.[63]

Many personal laments among the psalms refer to the supplicant being harassed, accused, or oppressed by enemies or adversaries (e.g., Pss 3; 9; 10; 13; 35; 52; 55; 56; 57; 62; 69; 70; 86; 109; 120; 139; 140; 141; 143). These psalms generally share the common structure and elements of the other kinds of lament psalms, and scholars debate how to understand the precise identities of the oppressed and the oppressors in these prayers. The emphasis in these prayers, however, typically falls on the situation of adversity for the worshipper and the enemies' actions that have produced it. The primary pleas include prayers for deliverance, but often feature petitions for the punishment and even destruction of the person's oppressors.

Some psalms describe the oppressors as those outside the community or, at least, outside of the worshipper's immediate circle of neighbors.

Psalm 13 is the textbook example of a brief, personal lament concerning enemies. In six verses, the psalm moves from an opening address to God to complaint to petition to expression of trust to a concluding vow to praise. The psalmist honestly expresses the feeling of God's absence ("How long will you hide your face from me?" v. 1), but emphasizes that an unidentified "enemy" has "prevailed" and the worshipper is "shaken" (v. 4). Psalm 9 is more elaborate and specific in repeatedly identifying the enemies as the "nations" that are oppressing the worshipper (vv. 15, 17, 20). The first half of the prayer (vv. 1-12) expresses thanksgiving to God for past deliverance, seeking in some ways to reaffirm a moral world in which God is an agent of justice in the face of evil. The remainder of the psalm (vv. 13-20) turns this report into a plea for God to recognize the psalmist's suffering at the hands of the enemies and to execute righteous judgment on the wicked entities.

Other lament psalms concerning oppression by enemies have a focus that resembles the dynamics of betrayal noted in some moral injury experiences. These psalms depict the sufferer's enemies not as foreign nations but as neighbors, acquaintances, and friends. Psalm 35, for instance, gives voice to a desperate-sounding situation created by the psalmist's own associates in the community. In this prayer, trouble is close at hand, distaste for the enemies is palpable, and the trust in God is less certain.[64] The psalm uses military language and battle imagery to focus especially on the personally hurtful and destructive actions of the oppressors, pleading with God to fight against the enemies (vv. 1-3). Most notably, the psalm identifies the enemies as those who have betrayed the sufferer by capitalizing upon her or his distress to become "malicious witnesses" (perhaps in court cases; v. 11) and to repay previous acts of kindness toward them when they suffered with treachery and mocking now that the situation is reversed (vv. 12-16, 19-21). Psalm 55 takes the sense of betrayal even farther by depicting the psalmist's oppressor as a former close friend. The worshipper is experiencing "trouble," "fear," and even "horror" (vv. 3, 5). The greatest source of pain, however, is expressed directly to the oppressor in these painful words:

> It is not enemies who taunt me—
>> I could bear that....
> But it is you, my equal,...
>> my familiar friend,
> with whom I kept pleasant company. (vv. 12-14)

The psalmist and the former friend even shared religious devotion together "in the house of God" (v. 14), but now their covenant has been violated (v. 20) and only God can set this right (v. 23).

Within the laments concerned with enemies and adversaries, there is a subcategory of imprecatory (or curse) psalms that often give pause to those who read the texts as part of the Jewish and Christian scriptures. They are laments that go beyond what we've seen in the preceding psalms that ask God to bring defeat on the foes. They are still prayers, but the language in them seems to push the envelope of appropriateness and acceptability because it expresses a level of vitriol and even hatred that comes forth in pleas for God to pay back the enemies for their actions in the most violent and destructive ways. A sense of deep hurt and betrayal is palpable, but a tone of vengefulness permeates some of these psalms, even, at times, including prayers that God would make the offender's family suffer. Even so, these psalms are potentially significant resources for considering the role of honesty, emotion, and protest in the practice of lament.

The communal lament in Psalm 79 discussed above, which reacts to the destruction of Jerusalem's temple, has some of these more visceral and violent elements, including pain-filled expressions of the desire for retaliation and revenge. Psalm 109 is perhaps the harshest plea for the enemy's destruction among the personal lament psalms. As Brueggemann explains, this psalm is "exceedingly problematic for our usual religious understandings" because it is "concerned for *vindictiveness* toward other human beings who have seriously violated the speaker.... It articulates yearning for retaliation and vengeance of the sort that we do not expect to find in the 'edifying' parts of the Bible."[65] The psalmist expresses the theme known from elsewhere that the enemies have repaid good with evil, returning accusations and hatred when the psalmist offered love and support to them (vv. 4-5; see also Ps 35:12-16). Before asking God to deliver from the trouble (vv. 21-31), however, the supplicant pleads for God to curse the adversary's life, family, possessions, and future:

> May his children be orphans,
>> and his wife a widow.
> May his children wander about and beg....
> May the creditor seize all that he has....
> May his posterity be cut off;
>> may his name be blotted out in the second generation. (vv. 9-11, 13)[66]

Throughout these requests is the underlying desire that the enemies would receive the same kind of treatment that they've given to the sufferer.

Psalm 137 is perhaps the most notorious curse psalm. Once again, this pain-filled prayer expresses the people's struggle to come to terms with the destruction of Jerusalem by the Babylonians. This psalm, however, seems to come from the exiled community of Judahites now living in Babylonia. It gives specific voice to the despair, torment, and anger associated with the experience of being exiled to a foreign land and being mocked both by captors and memories of home (vv. 1-6). Out of the crucible of these experiences and feelings, vv. 7-9, the only verses in the psalm that are addressed to God, blurt out a passionate and venom-filled prayer for God to "remember" the treachery of the Edomites and the violence of the Babylonians against Jerusalem, praying that God would bless those who pay them back (vv. 7-8). The cry for retribution against the Edomites (v. 7) may reflect specific feelings of betrayal, since the Old Testament presents the Edomites as a kin group of Israel through Esau, Jacob's brother and the other son of Isaac (see Gen 25).

The curse against the Babylonians in Ps 137, however, seems to spill over into unbridled rage, declaring a blessing on the ones who exact vengeance by bludgeoning to death the innocent children among the Babylonians: "Happy shall they be who take your little ones and dash them against the rock!" (v. 9). No harsher outburst of pain and anger in the face of suffering is imaginable. Brueggemann's words ring true: "I am not sure how such a psalm fits with Christian faith," but "it is not for us to 'justify' such a prayer in the Bible."[67] Even so, in the context of considering moral healing, it's noteworthy that the speaker in the psalm doesn't act to carry out these desires in any way. The psalmist doesn't, in fact, crush Babylonian babies' heads against rocks. The plea, though troubling, remains a prayer that gives honest expression to grief, despair, and rage, yet ultimately is left in God's hands. The psalmist doesn't need to act but must speak honestly in order to survive.

Biblical scholars have acknowledged the difficulties these curse psalms present for those reading the Old Testament as sacred scripture, but have also emphasized the historical contexts that identify these ancient prayers as honest reactions to trauma such as the fall of Jerusalem and the Babylonian exile. These psalms, while violent, often reflect a desire that the enemies would experience as punishment the same kinds of atrocities that they had inflicted on the Israelites. Additionally, the study of ancient Israel's social and political world has revealed that the particular curses and actions described in these psalms often reflect stereotypical patterns and common terminology used in treaties between nations to describe imaginatively the consequences that were to befall those who violated the formal agreements.[68] The language in these prayers may represent common cultural ways of expressing the presumed results of betrayal. At a broader level, however, biblical scholars have also appreciated that the prayers allow the worshippers to express the most realistic and raw feelings that accompany experiences of suffering and betrayal. Even so, recognizing that these psalms are, by genre, only prayers, reminds contemporary readers that the rage expressed in the words is not only brought before God but "submitted" and then "relinquished" to God.[69] Accordingly, the honest expression of such seemingly unorthodox feelings and wishes may keep society from descending into further bloodshed, even as it possibly preserves the one praying from returning violence for violence.

The second major type of lament that seems fruitful for dialogue with moral injury consists of prayers seeking God's forgiveness. These laments—sometimes called penitential psalms—differ from the laments surveyed above because the source of the worshipper's adversity is not external (e.g., mistreatment by enemies). Rather, these prayers identify the trouble as an "internal-spiritual-introspective issue of intimacy."[70] They associate the individual's difficulties with personal sin, readily admit guilt, and feature language that asks God to pardon, wash, purge, and restore for the sake of a new kind of relationship with the divine (e.g., Pss 6; 32; 38; 51; 102; 130; 143). On the surface, these psalms might not seem relevant to moral injury because they don't typically refer to actions taken in combat or feature the community's response to calamities resulting from war. Additionally, the dominant perspective that trouble and adversity are the result of personal sin in need of pardon may be too narrow to apply to the various kinds of shame, guilt, and disorientation experienced as part of moral injury. Even so, for those interested in moral injury, the penitential psalms give voice to the felt needs for forgiveness and cleansing in a way that is unmatched elsewhere in the Bible. Moreover, the description of the sins offered in these psalms usually remains generic and without detail, even when tradition has associated the psalm with some particular event.[71] The use of stereotypical language for sin, without specification, allows these prayers to provide words for those who feel the need for forgiveness and cleansing due to a variety of circumstances.

Psalm 32 opens with a general declaration that the confession and forgiveness of sin is the key for a happy life (vv. 1-2). The prayer's language soon becomes deeply personal, however, as the worshipper offers a first-person description of the experience that has led to this declaration (v. 3). The psalmist describes the distress that accompanied the time when she or he stayed silent about sin and refused the honesty of confession. Especially notable in an exploration of moral injury is that the psalmist describes the distress from lack of confession and forgiveness in terms of physiological suffering: "While I kept silence, my body wasted away...my strength was dried up" (vv. 3-4). In the same ways that moral injury and trauma impact physical and emotional well-being, the body itself pays for silence and suppression with weakness, discomfort, and restlessness.[72] But the answer for the psalmist is striking in its simplicity: "Then I acknowledged my sin to you...and you forgave the guilt of my sin" (v. 5). Here is an after-the-fact psalm meant to serve as a testimony to others who may have similar experiences. The psalmist testifies to the release that came from confession—a release that yielded a new sense of hope and safety ("You are a hiding place for me; you preserve me from trouble" v. 7).

Psalm 38 is less of a testimony about past experiences and more of an immediate plea for forgiveness and restoration. The psalmist gives a first-person description of her or his current suffering seen as the result of God's anger over sin. Once again, the psalmist's words describe a physical toll on the body exacted by unconfessed sin. But the language and imagery here go beyond Ps 32 and cast the effects as wounds and injuries, with some metaphors of weapons and war: "For your arrows have sunk into me" (v. 2); "My wounds grow foul and fester because of my foolishness" (v. 5); "For my loins are filled with burning, and there is no soundness in my flesh. I am utterly spent and crushed; I groan because of the tumult of my heart" (vv. 7-8). The resemblance to the ways that morally injured persons describe the emotional struggles and the effects in everyday life that attend to their suffering is notable (see ch. 2). As befits the genre, however, the psalmist anticipates that honest confession before the divine moral authority will be the key to restored well-being: "I confess my iniquity; I am sorry for my sin....Make haste to help me, O Lord, my salvation" (vv. 18, 22).

The prime example of a penitent lament is Ps 51, a psalm well-known in Jewish and Christian circles because of its traditional association with

David's sexual transgression and subsequent murderous cover-up.[73] This particular lament has come to be seen as both a larger reflection on the nature of sin and a model for practicing confession. The prayer opens with the worshipper's call for God to grant mercy as the sins are confessed—an opening that uses the same commonly established and general vocabulary for wrongdoing that appeared in Ps 32: "transgression," "iniquity," "sin" (vv. 1-2). When the actual confession occurs in vv. 3-5, the psalmist's description of sin is more extensive than in any of the other penitential psalms, claiming that the sin is "ever before me," and expressing the feeling that "I was born guilty" (vv. 3, 5). Rather than taking this description literally as a statement about the nature of human beings or a doctrine of "original sin," contemporary readers should appreciate the words for what they are: a poetic expression and symbolic description that honestly gives voice to the sense of being overwhelmed, even consumed, by an orientation toward wrongdoing that seems to extend as far back as the psalmist can remember.

In terms of resonances with moral injury, however, the most notable element in this psalm's plea for forgiveness and deliverance from sin is the language and imagery of cleansing. The psalmist implores God with imperatives such as "wash," "cleanse," "purge," and "blot out" (see vv. 2, 7, 9), with the expressed desire that "I shall be clean . . . and I shall be whiter than snow" (v. 7). The pleas likely reflect priestly and cultic language from ancient Israel's rituals of washing that symbolized the removal of impurity associated with sin (see Lev 1–7). Beyond the ritual dimensions, the psalmist's confession and pleas reach a climax in verses 10-12 with words that go far beyond asking for pardon: "Create in me a clean heart, O God, and put a new and right spirit within me." The terms "heart" and "spirit" throughout the Old Testament connote the will, intellect, and animating energy that make human living possible. The psalmist asks God for a complete transformation of character and a total renovation of life. Those attuned to the ways that moral injury so often entails the collapse of moral foundations, the loss of a sense of personhood, and the paralysis of lost faith and meaning will recognize here a gut-level yet hopeful plea for renewed personhood, revived emotional and moral energy, and restored capacity for a new beginning.

Moral Injury Connections

Although this chapter also covered the Old Testament's postwar celebrations and processions, recent moral injury works have placed a special emphasis on the notion and practice of lament in a variety of forms. Hence, these concluding reflections will focus on lament and moral injury to connect the dots between the characteristic elements and functions of the Old Testament's war-related laments, particularly the laments in the book of Psalms, and the felt needs of returning soldiers discussed in current moral injury work. As described earlier in the chapter, moral injury work in psychology, veterans' care, and chaplaincy has articulated three major needs that returning soldiers have in order to facilitate healthy reintegration, recovery, and repair: (1) to speak honestly about what has happened; (2) to forgive self and others; and (3) to communalize the moral and emotional experiences. Recent studies have tried—even if only initially—to identify practices that can, at least partially, meet these needs, with some writers pointing explicitly to various examples of lament, including some in the Old Testament psalms.

As a starting point, the Old Testament's laments are, after all, manifestly poems. Poetry—and not just grief-related poetry—makes a special contribution in this context that has to do with the capacity for candid engagement with human affections, passions, and feelings. Reading or writing poetry provides a means not only to express emotions honestly but also to configure them constructively. Poetry of various stripes is a form of expression that "touches the emotions deeply but also shapes and structures them."[74]

Poetry's power in this regard stems, in part, from its words, so often marked by emotive language and imagery. The poetic use of language

- 129 -

offers different ways of speaking candidly about grief, dissonance, and other depths of experience. Poems create a "safe space to name and address emotions" by featuring literary subjects (the speakers in the poems) who speak on behalf of the sufferer, providing her or him with needed language of expression but also allowing some safe distance for one who might not feel comfortable being a full agent of expression for their own grief, shame, or loss.[75] Reading, hearing, and attending carefully to the words of poems can be a way to describe life experiences and resist the temptation to internalize personal struggles or social oppression.[76] Especially with experiences of anguish, trauma, and suffering, however, elements of poetry beyond just the words provide means not only to express but also to begin to give some shape and organization to the sufferer's sense of incoherence and disorientation. As Fawson explains, the "structure of a poem at the level of syntax and line" can function both to express "gaps" and "fragmentation" and to provide some initial "integration" and coherence.[77] From within biblical scholarship, Brueggemann has suggested that biblical poetry, especially the poetic genre of lament and its typical structure, is a way to manage grief.[78]

Honesty

The first of the identified needs mentioned above is for returning soldiers to be able to speak honestly about their experiences—that is, to make truthful assessments and give candid expression of things they've done, witnessed, or by which they've been affected. Soldiers need help engaging in uninhibited truth telling about particular acts and events, as well as broader circumstances and realities, so that the healing process can begin. Laments like those found in the Old Testament provide means and models to meet this need.

At the basic level, the laments give full and sometimes unbridled expression to both personal grief and protest against unjust systems, circumstances, and betrayals. The fact that the Bible contains both individual and communal laments is important for this dimension of moral injury. The lament psalms, for example, provide concrete ways for "individuals and communities to truthfully express the sorrows of the world that have come upon them and to register protest, complaint, and anger at those responsible for them."[79] As mentioned above, at the heart of war-related communal laments such as Psalms 44 and 60, as well as personal laments such as Psalms 13 and 35, is the sense of a disconnect between who the people believe God to be and how they believe God to operate for them in the world versus the realities they're currently experiencing in life. This sense of the tensions in life and morality matches the awareness of a discrepancy between one's beliefs or expectations and realities or experiences that is often felt by those struggling with moral injury. The biblical laments, however, doggedly acknowledge and embrace this moral dissonance and ambiguity, with the expectation that telling the truth is both appropriate and necessary. The communal laments, for instance, give cathartic voice to the community's sense that their moral understanding of how the world should work has been violated, constituting a plea for reordering.

The use of such honest lament prayers is a significant counter to a common tendency within Christian circles to shy away from any embrace of negativity in the experience of God in the world: "We have thought that acknowledgment of negativity was somehow an act of unfaith, as though the very speech about it conceded too much about God's 'loss of control.'"[80] The lament psalms declare otherwise. We may perhaps extend this truth-telling function of lament beyond the church context to speak to the popular cultural sensibilities in the US today that seem also to view any acknowledgment of doubt or negativity about the experiences of war, soldiers, and veterans as unpatriotic, often preferring to mask difficulties with symbolic displays or commemorative ceremonies associated with military service. The lack of transparency and truth telling in such common cultural practices contrasts sharply with the candor of lament. As Frame asserts, in these cultural ceremonies,

> God is mentioned but under the veil of music. There is talk of transcendence but no reassurance of resurrection. The significance of suffering and sacri-

fice, the redeeming features of war, is given prominence while futility and waste, the constant elements of armed conflict, are virtually ignored. The motivating desire is to ennoble what remains irretrievably ignoble: state-sanctioned murder and orchestrated savagery. The absence of opportunities for confession and absolution in government-sponsored commemorative events may eventually render them vacuous.[81]

Seen in these ways as connected to the need for honest expression, the Old Testament's laments function in two important ways. First, they not only acknowledge grief, guilt, contrition, dissonance, and ambiguity, but they do so in formal and stylized ways. The lament psalms, for example, follow a common structure with typical elements and often-ritualized language (as expected given their form as poetry). The use of such stylized formats and expressions to give voice to loss, disaster, sorrow, guilt, or betrayal allows the sufferer to begin to bring a sense of order to the experiences and perhaps provides a way to reign in those experiences for understanding and processing. Second, this very act of lament that facilitates grieving and names suffering can build resiliency. Ramsay proposes that a "renewed sense of resilience" can emerge from candidly and boldly naming one's own agency in destructive events and moral violations, as well as truthfully acknowledging the forces that lie outside of one's control. As she explains, "Resilience describes the ability to temper expectations of mastering the inescapable tensions of historical life while encouraging a hopeful posture about the ways one can exercise freedom and live with hope, meaning, and love."[82]

Biblical readers may see here connections to the ways that the penitential psalms, for example, help a person take responsibility for her or his own behavior when appropriate, while other lament psalms dealing with enemies, oppression, or divine betrayal allow guilt and shame to be externalized onto other agents when warranted.[83] The resilience built through both kinds of lament may also connect to the commonly noted feature that many biblical lament psalms conclude with a sudden turn to praise and confidence (e.g., Pss 13; 22). The origins and explanations for these unexpected changes from plea to praise remain debated.[84] There may have been a community member, sanctuary elder, or priest who offered an unrecorded word of assurance to the Israelite worshipper. Or, perhaps the act of honest lament itself provided an inward, spiritual, or psychological lift that resulted in a new and more positive outlook. Whatever the case, the unexpected shift from complaint to confidence in the lament psalms reflects the ways that resilience built by honest expression may allow those wounded by war's unseen injuries to "reconstruct a hopeful posture" that envisions a more lifegiving future.[85]

If contemporary readers consider these possible connections between the Old Testament texts and the need for honest expression by returning soldiers, the lament psalms in particular may be seen as a type of biblical "witness poetry." As noted earlier in this chapter, Fawson has devoted an article-length study to the literary genre of witness poetry as a way to recognize and lament the wounds of war.[86] Poems of witness are written in conditions of suffering and struggle and reflect these extreme circumstances in their language, structure, and imagery. Fawson explores poems by the North American poets Walt Whitman, Khadijah Queen, Yusef Komunyakaa, and Brian Turner, and concludes that witness poetry serves to acknowledge candidly the trauma and violence of war. Equally important, however, witness poetry functions as a means of "sustaining lamentation." To sustain lamentation is to find ways of living well in spite of what has been lost, and to do so especially by naming forthrightly and thus enduring courageously the disconnects and gaps caused by war's realities—disconnects between the person a soldier had been and who they are now, and gaps between what people had believed and desired and what they've known and experienced. Witness poetry, Fawson concludes, sustains lamentation in these ways precisely because it doesn't "foreclose unresolved grief." The biblical laments may similarly represent poems written out of intense suffering and struggle, which likewise try to give truthful expression to those experiences for the sake of acknowledging pain, maintaining a sense of humanity and community, and rebuilding a moral personhood for the future. Fawson's conclusion about witness poetry applies to the biblical laments, as well:

> In order to witness the gaps created by moral injury, poetry cannot simply comfort or fascinate, nor can it give way too quickly to a summarizing impulse. We want poems that have wrestled with experience, ideas, history, and the speaker's own psychic drama in a way that transforms the drama and utters the complex, varying emotional responses we have.[87]

Forgiveness

The second of the identified needs within moral injury work is for returning soldiers to experience forgiveness (of self and others). This need relates to a soldier's sense of having violated her or his own moral conscience, as well as having experienced guilt or shame because of personal actions, the deeds of others, or the larger circumstances. Among the Old Testament laments, the so-called penitential psalms described above seem to connect particularly well to this felt need. These psalms center on forgiveness as needed and desired, with the same understanding present as in many moral injury conversations—namely, that a sense of forgiveness is what creates mental and emotional space for new understandings of self, community, and circumstances. Some moral injury writers have shied away from the religious overtones of forgiveness (i.e., pardon needed for an intentional wrongdoing), opting instead to talk about the need for "self-empathy" or "self-understanding," since authorized war participation occurs within a legal framework.[88] Yet the specifically theological language and worldview of the biblical laments (seeking divine forgiveness in prayer) may be of special importance for morally injured soldiers who have a distinctively Jewish or Christian moral framework against which they're evaluating their actions and experiences in war (see discussion in ch. 1).

Whether cast in religious or other terms, recent moral injury discussions of the need for forgiveness have emphasized the key role of confession as a means to that end. Moral injury works often view this confession as taking the form of a soldier or veteran candidly recounting her or his experiences to an "empathetic listener" or "compassionate witness" who can receive the testimony with understanding, validate the speaker's perceptions, and help them arrive at a fairer self-assessment.[89] The clinical example mentioned in the background section was the Adaptive Disclosure model. This approach places the practice of confession at the center. The model asks patients to engage in "evocative imaginal 'confession'" by picturing a person they would consider a "compassionate and forgiving moral authority" and then candidly describing their experiences and feelings as if they were sharing their testimony with that imagined authority figure.[90] The underlying conviction here is that the act of honest retelling to someone imagined to be compassionate and with the authority to extend grace allows the sufferer to acknowledge and accept the part of themselves that was involved in moral violations and bears that guilt but also to begin to "reclaim goodness and humanity" as their confession is met with empathy and understanding.[91]

The language, structure, and perspective of the Old Testament lament psalms constitute a theological version of this practice. The penitential psalms in particular give the vocabulary and grammar of confession in a theological perspective. They are concrete, even liturgical, examples of honest confession and truth-telling to a moral authority believed to be benevolent and forgiving. The pleas for forgiveness provide language for acknowledging personal agency and responsibility in a way that morally injured persons may struggle to do, even as the laments over enemies and injustice allow speakers to acknowledge communal, societal, and political forces and situations that were injurious but beyond their control.[92] And the fact that these confessions and pleas are prayers serves implicitly to depict God as compassionate, understanding, and forgiving.

One other dimension of the Old Testament laments connects to the emphasis on forgiveness within moral injury work and provides a segue to the final felt need that is often discussed. The explicitly communal laments highlighted above draw attention to the ways that whole communities

yes

should acknowledge their own complicity in the morally injurious situations and events faced by soldiers, sharing the responsibility and bearing the burdens of war and its actions. They call whole communities to confession. The communal lament psalms constitute ritual practices that allow and encourage communities, even faith communities, to "name and confess our complicity in the moral injury of those who went to war on our behalf."[93] Additionally, the public and communal language of these psalms underscores the emphasis within moral injury work that returning soldiers need persons and communities who will receive their candid testimony as witnesses. If these testimonies are received by the community (or even expressed in communal language), those who listen, affirm, and retell them become witnesses who share in the moral agency and suffering. These witnesses may be the congregation hearing the psalms in ancient Israel or the groups of family, friends, neighbors, and larger society who receive returning soldiers today. In any case, as Ramsay observes, by affirming, retelling, and sharing, the communal witnesses recognize the ones who testify, ratify their testimony, and restore their voice that suffering had silenced.[94]

Community

The third of the identified needs within moral injury work discussed earlier in this chapter is to help returning soldiers communalize their moral and emotional experiences. The Old Testament laments provide language and resources for helping service members and veterans share their experiences in both personal and public ways. More specifically, however, the communal laments in particular speak to the often-expressed need for morally injured persons to have a community that not only hears their confession, offers forgiveness where appropriate, and helps the injured forgive others, but also refuses to distance itself from the moral responsibility of war.[95] The biblical war-related laments may provide the communal vocabulary that is needed to draw larger communities and societies into shared responsibility and agency. This kind of communalization meets the returning soldiers' need to have their feelings of pain, grief, and even guilt validated and co-owned by their larger network of family, friends, local communities, societal institutions, and governmental authorities. The language of communal lament creates a community that is able "to own and to acknowledge its own violence, as embodied in the lives and actions of its soldiers."[96] In so doing, the biblical texts speak at a basic level to the increasing emphasis within moral injury work on broadening the focus beyond merely individual experiences and considering moral injury as something that a group can experience and for which they can collectively seek healing.[97]

Seen in this way, the Old Testament's war-related laments connect to moral healing in particular. At one level, the laments speak to the conviction that a larger community is vital not only for shared responsibility but for moral repair: "It actually takes 'three' to confess and forgive; the sufferer, the caregiver, and a larger spiritual community that embraces and connects all to each other. The injured and the healer both need a keen sense of belonging to something larger and deeper than themselves."[98] Additionally, recent work on moral healing has emphasized that morally injured persons need more than the presence of a larger community; they also need the community's shared traditions upon which they can draw for speech, perspective, and reorientation—traditions with a history that have been rearticulated by generation after generation.[99] Not all communities have such traditions (at least, not healthy traditions). Yet the language of the lament psalms in particular is the language of tradition—it's structured, formal, ritualized, and liturgical. The compositions that now appear in the psalms, for example, were crafted for formal, often public, performance and have been passed down, repeated, and actualized again and again by communities both ancient and modern. They offer the very kinds of time-tested and broadly shared traditions upon which modern people may draw as they seek to acknowledge the moral dissonances, complexities, and disorientations of life and envision a hopeful future into which they can live.

Chapter 6

Injured by the Bible: Do the Biblical Warfare Texts Morally Injure Their Readers?

The Bible, of all books, is the most dangerous one, the one that has been endowed with the power to kill.

—*Mieke Bal*[1]

Throughout history, readers of the Bible have struggled to make sense of the passages of scripture that describe divine and human acts of war and violence. Obviously, exploring the intersections between the Bible and moral injury brings these parts of the Bible to the fore. As we've seen, there are places in the Bible where war is shown to be wrong, but there are other places where sanctioned violence is undertaken by Israel as God's chosen covenant people at God's command and with God's blessing. Other passages go even further and depict God personally and directly killing and destroying. Within the history of Christian interpretation, the Bible's passages that depict these divine and human acts of war and violence have constituted an ongoing dilemma. Interpreters from a wide range of times, places, and traditions have wrestled with their theological and ethical implications. The struggle continues today, even to the point of biblical war and violence constituting a potentially debilitating problem for the church's use of scripture and its witness to a world in need of peace and reconciliation. Creach expresses this dilemma for the Christian church as most pressing:

> One of the greatest challenges the church faces today is to interpret and explain passages in the Bible that seem to promote or encourage violence. It is perhaps not an exaggeration to say that the Bible in this regard is a major problem for Christians, both for the church's own theology (what it says it believes) and for the church's presentation of itself to the world (who the church says it is).[2]

The previous chapters have explored some specific intersections of the Bible and moral injury, but here we pull back to consider the difficulties raised by the presence of violence in the sacred scripture of Judaism and Christianity. Looking at these texts from the perspective of moral injury gives contemporary readers of scripture, especially those who read the Bible as authoritative and inspired revelation, a different way to talk about these biblical depictions and the theological, moral, and ethical problems they present for interpretation. The history of the Bible's reception clearly demonstrates that interpreters both past and present have been troubled by these passages, have tried to explain why and how the passages are troubling, and have offered ideas concerning what readers can do to deal with them as part of their theological, moral, and ethical understanding of God and God's people. The question here is whether perspectives from moral injury can provide a different way to explain why contemporary readers feel troubled by these biblical texts and what, if anything, might be done to help with their interpretation. In other words, could the problem be that the Bible's depictions of war and violence (particularly divinely sanctioned or enacted violence) morally injure their readers? And, if so, how can we use moral injury insights to articulate why these biblical texts are morally injurious, and to consider whether any of the proposed ways to repair moral injury in soldiers might help with interpretation?

To this point, this book has focused on the intersections between biblical texts and the two main trajectories within moral injury study:

(1) creative rereadings of literary texts and characters in light of the experiences of moral injury; and (2) the exploration of rituals and symbolic practices from ancient and traditional cultures (and their writings) for how they might be used today to address the felt needs of morally injured persons. The questions in this chapter move beyond these two trajectories but continue the effort to see how moral injury can be an interpretive lens that brings new meanings out of biblical texts, even as the critical study of the Bible can make substantive contributions to moral injury work.

As in the preceding case study chapters, what follows here isn't a comprehensive analysis but an initial, exploratory, and, I hope, suggestive venture that illustrates how readers of the Bible might look for another set of insights from moral injury work to aid in the understanding of a difficult issue (why readers find the biblical war and violence texts problematic) and the possible ways of dealing with it (how the texts might be interpreted). There is little reason to suspect that insights from moral injury—or from any one perspective—will produce a solution to the issue of God's and people's violence in the biblical texts that will be satisfying to all interested parties. The debate over how to understand why these texts are troubling and what to do about them can and should continue. But in the hopes of advancing the conversation, this chapter will first present the long-discussed problem of the biblical violence texts, survey attempts that have been made to respond to that problem from within biblical interpretation, and then consider how moral injury might offer new perspectives for understanding and response.

A Perennial Problem: Divine and Human Violence in the Bible

Throughout the history of biblical interpretation within Judaism and Christianity, interpreters have wrestled with the Bible's depictions of divine and human violence and their theological, moral, and ethical implications.[3] In the last thirty years, these depictions and their implications have become a central problem, specifically giving rise to the question of how readers, especially Christians, should understand and explain the biblical texts in which human beings enact violence at God's command or with God's endorsement, or in which God directly and personally commits violence. For many today, the problem has risen to the status of being one of the most apparent and unavoidable issues that confronts any reader of the Bible. As Brueggemann asserts, "On the face of it, one must recognize that a violent characterization of Yhwh is present in the Bible, front and center. Anyone who comes 'innocently' to the Old Testament is sure to be surprised or scandalized by such divine behavior."[4]

The issue of violence in biblical texts is certainly poignant for those who read the Bible in faith-based communities as sacred scripture (inspired and authoritative revelation of God's character that is in some way normative for how believers live in the world). The issue of the Bible's problematic elements has also gained a public profile in the aftermath of the events of September 11, 2001, and the nearly two decades of wars in Afghanistan and Iraq, often in public conversations about Islam, Christianity, sacred texts, and religious violence. In a 2010 National Public Radio interview, for instance, historian Philip Jenkins remarked that the Bible contains more violent passages and poses more ethical problems for its readers than the Qur'an.[5] Additionally, the particular issue of the Bible's portrayals of God acting violently has become a commonly cited data point among critics of the Bible operating outside the church. For example, Richard Dawkins, a notable representative of the so-called New Atheism, offered a scathing condemnation of the God portrayed in the Bible:

> The God of the Old Testament is arguably the most unpleasant character in all fiction: jealous and proud of it; a petty, unjust, unforgiving control-freak; a vindictive, bloodthirsty ethnic cleanser; a misogynist, homophobic, racist, infanticidal, genocidal, filicidal, pestilential, megalomaniacal, sadomasochistic, capriciously malevolent bully.[6]

As the above comments indicate, the problem faced by readers of the Bible on this matter is twofold (with plenty of overlap in various passages):

(1) biblical texts that portray human war and violence (notably by God's covenant people) that is commanded, sanctioned, or at least not explicitly condemned by God; and (2) biblical texts that describe God personally and directly carrying out acts of violence against human beings, nature, and even the cosmos. Detailed lists and discussions of the Bible's relevant war and violence texts are readily available and need not be reproduced here.[7] It will suffice to note some representative examples. Contemporary readers of the Old Testament, for instance, might be able to excuse some of the violence depicted early on as being the result of sin or the fallenness of humanity. So, Cain kills Abel (Gen 4), Abram has to go to war to rescue his nephew, Lot (Gen 14), and God destroys pharaoh's army to deliver the Hebrews from slavery in Egypt (Exod 13–14). Even so, readers quickly encounter the flood story (Gen 6–9) in which God destroys not only sinful humanity, but the entire creation of animals, plants, and more. Likewise, God's deliverance of the Hebrew slaves includes the plague of the death of the firstborn enacted on all children and animals in Egypt. And soon enough readers of the Old Testament encounter the stories of the Israelite conquest of Canaan in the book of Joshua, with its depictions of the wholesale slaughter of men, women, children, and animals at God's command and for the sake of religious (and perhaps ethnic) purity (e.g., Josh 6). The acts of war and violence found throughout the books of Joshua, Judges, 1–2 Samuel, 1–2 Kings, 1–2 Chronicles, Ezra, and Nehemiah continue to appear when one moves into the psalms and prophets. As chapter 5 explored, the prayers found in the psalms include stringent pleas for vengeance and the destruction of enemies (e.g., Ps 137), and the prophets proclaim messages of God's judgment upon Israel, the nations, and the natural world that include images of violent destruction (e.g., Ezek 16; 23).

To choose perhaps the most famous (and obviously troubling) example, the Israelites' conquest of Canaan, prescribed and described in the books of Deuteronomy and Joshua, includes the divinely commanded extermination of men, women, children, and animals, the forcible removal of a people from its native land, and the violent subjugation of a population (see Deut 7; 20; Josh 1–12). The stories include descriptions of God personally bringing destruction on the people of the land in order to help the Israelites prevail (e.g., Josh 10:1-15). God's involvement in both commanding the Israelites to conquer the Canaanites and directly participating in the wars against them highlights the issue of divine violence, seemingly portraying a ruthless and genocidal God that is bewildering to some readers who have concentrated on more positive divine depictions elsewhere in scripture. As Creach notes, these very texts that involve God also "describe and advocate what modern people would call war crimes."[8] The portrayals in this part of scripture are even more troubling when combined with other acts of violence directly attributed to God elsewhere: drowning most of humanity (Gen 7:23), burning the cities of Sodom and Gomorrah (Gen 19:24-29), authorizing war against non-Israelites (Num 31:1-2), sanctioning genocide (1 Sam 15:1-3), and slaughtering large numbers of people (2 Sam 24:15; 2 Kgs 19:35).[9] Taken together, an "enormous amount of violence" is ascribed to God throughout nearly every part of the Old Testament and the result is an "inescapable problem that *the God portrayed in the text* appears to be violent."[10]

The problem of violence ascribed to God and God's people in the Bible is also present in the New Testament, though it is usually less recognized by Christian readers. One need only think here of the explicit portrayals of judgment and destruction, often at the cosmic level, in the book of Revelation, or stories such as the divine striking down of Ananias and Sapphira (Acts 5), or the various judgment sayings present in Jesus's own teachings (e.g., Matt 5:25-26; 10:34-36; 16:2-3; 23:1-36; Mark 10:38; Luke 12:49-53; 13:3, 5; 14:25-33). Collins has gone further and argued that what often appear to be anti-violence sentiments in the New Testament—namely, the appeals for Christians not to act in the present age but to leave vengeance to God for the coming age—rely on a belief in eschatological violence that is no less a recourse to violence than immediate and direct action would be. Moreover, he asserts that even Jesus's teachings in the Gospels about loving one's enemies in the here and now are anchored in this belief in a future, final judgment in which violence will be enacted (see Matt 13:24-30, 36-43).[11]

In addition to the basic portrayals of divine and human acts, other dimensions of violence are present in the biblical texts and the social, cultural, and ideological frameworks that underlie them. For example, feminist and gender-focused interpretations—approaches that examine the portrayals and role of gender in the biblical texts and their cultural backgrounds—have noted that much of the violence described and promoted in the Bible is gendered violence in which women are threatened with or portrayed as suffering physical harm as some sort of actual or metaphorical divine judgment or as a result of the people's failure or defeat.[12] Many of these depictions appear in the Old Testament prophetic books and their use of the marriage metaphor that depicts the cities of Samaria and Jerusalem as unfaithful wives of Yhwh who suffer divine punishment for their actions (e.g., Hos 2:1-23; Ezek 16; 23). Likewise, the recent emergence of so-called ecological hermeneutics—an interpretive approach that foregrounds concerns of the earth and nature in both text depictions and modern interpretations—has highlighted that much of the violence committed by human armies and resulting from divine judgment in biblical texts takes the particular form of the devastation of elements of the environment and agriculture such as trees, vineyards, and landscapes.[13] A high number of passages in the Old Testament prophets, for example, employ the imagery of the devastation of nature in the proclamations of divine judgment, including divine threats to render the land desolate, lay waste to crops, and devastate trees and vines (e.g., Isa 13:20-22; Jer 6:6-8; Ezek 6:1-14; 35:1-15; Amos 4:7-9; Nah 1:4-5; Zech 11:2-3).[14]

Even beyond the readily apparent references to divine and human violence, there are thoroughgoing conceptions and frameworks of violence that are at work within and underneath the biblical texts, emerging from the social and cultural worlds that gave rise to them. Collins suggests, for example, that the problem in this regard isn't just with individual texts but that the Bible's repeated use of language and imagery connected to divine and human violence seems implicitly to "endorse and bless the recourse to violence," sometimes in the form of "verbal, symbolic, or imaginary violence," and thus leads its readers, especially those who invest it with authority and normativity, to conceive of God, humanity, and the world as violent.[15]

Similarly, Lemos goes beyond the Bible's military imagery and explicit references to violence to argue that violence manifested in war was not exceptional to normal life and culture in ancient Israel. Rather, the very concept of personhood in ancient Israel's world—and manifested the Bible's descriptions of human persons and social relationships—was based on a "totalizing masculine dominance" that produced a "social organization in which extreme violence was seen as justified not only in war but in the brutal sort of any peace that constituted many areas of quotidian life."[16] This observation means that violence (especially through male dominance) played a determinative role in social relationships, and the Old Testament texts reflect the role of violence and domination in the ways they portray the personhood and relationships of husbands and wives, masters and slaves, and fathers and children.

Alongside all of the above examples of the issue of war, violence, and the Bible, perhaps most problematic for many contemporary interpreters is the knowledge that the biblical depictions of God-sanctioned conquests of indigenous groups have been used throughout history to justify similar acts of aggression and colonization as divinely ordained, especially when done by self-identified Christian groups. For example, Oliver Cromwell saw a parallel between his religious revolution in England and the exodus from Egypt, casting the Catholics of Ireland as the Canaanites. Likewise, the larger English Puritan revolution appealed to biblical analogies such as the "Saints of the Most High" who execute judgment in the book of Daniel, and the Puritans in New England used the conquest stories in Joshua to portray the Native Americans as Canaanites and Amalekites.[17] These historical examples of biblical violence contributing in some way to real-life violence provide all the justification needed for contemporary readers to see the Bible's portrayals as a problem to which they must attend.

Approaches to Biblical War and Violence

Within the field of biblical interpretation, the Bible's depictions of divine and human war and violence surveyed above have produced the felt need to develop strategies for interpreting these passages. There is now a plethora of books and articles available that address this issue from multiple perspectives. Within the last thirty years in particular, numerous works have analyzed these depictions and their implications, attempted to name the problems involved, and proposed ideas concerning how especially Christian readers should understand and explain these biblical texts.

By now, this is well-trodden ground in biblical studies, reflecting a robust history of interpretation, particularly in the church in the post–9/11 era. Along with full-scale individual studies, several convenient overviews and surveys of proposed interpretive strategies are available.[18] Interpreters in evangelical Christian circles, which emphasize the Bible's role as the inspired, authoritative revelation and a norm for believers, have produced a large number of treatments of this subject since the 1980s, many of which are forthright about the theological, moral, and ethical problems created by the biblical texts in question.[19] Rather than reviewing all of the proposals that have emerged in biblical interpretation, this section will highlight some of the more prominent ones and mention two recent representative examples in particular.

The questions about these problematic biblical texts and the effort to develop interpretive strategies for dealing with them didn't originate in the last three decades. Already in the second century CE, for instance, a Christian leader in Rome named Marcion (died in 160 CE) provided an early example when he rejected the entire Old Testament, as well as portions of the New Testament, from being authoritative for Christians because he believed the God portrayed therein was different from the God revealed in Jesus Christ. Although this revision of the canon was rejected by the early church, one still finds today functionally equivalent proposals that dismiss the problematic texts as simply inferior cultural expressions that must be set aside because of the superior revelation now found in Jesus Christ. Boyd's recent and extensive two-volume treatment provides an example of such christological interpretation that sees the crucified Christ as God's definitive self-revelation, a "cross-centered hermeneutic" as the key to interpreting passages of divine violence, and the Old Testament portrayals of God's violence as merely divine accommodation to ancient persons for the sake of instruction and not as definitional for God's true nature.[20]

These kinds of quasi-Marcionite solutions aren't, however, the most prominent perspectives in the interpretive conversation today.[21] Some strategies try to defend the Bible's war ethics and images of violence by emphasizing the wickedness of those who are destroyed, appealing to the hyperbolic nature of the language, or citing the focus on faith over ethnicity as the criterion for destruction in stories such as the conquest of Canaan.[22] Other approaches reject the biblical depictions as merely human projections of God based on ancient cultures and ideologies or as primitive ideas in an evolving religion that would eventually result in something more ethical. As Brueggemann notes, however, these strategies based on evolutionary ideas and cultural relativism are inadequate for those who read the Bible as inspired revelation that discloses the character and ways of God lived with God's people in God's creation.[23]

There are, however, other interpretive strategies that seem to stand on firmer ground. First, at a basic level, readers may note that the conquest command like that given concerning the Canaanites in Deuteronomy and Joshua is never repeated in scripture and isn't given as a model to be followed by any later generation. At most, the conquest appears in the text as a limited, time-bound event that isn't meant to be seen as the paradigmatic way that God works in the world (if anything, God's act to liberate the oppressed in the exodus from Egypt serves as the paradigm of God's ways in the Old Testament; see Exod 13–14; cf. Amos 9:7).[24] Second, questions about the historicity of the events described in Joshua have also been brought to bear upon interpretation. Since the 1980s, a growing consensus in biblical scholarship has concluded that stories such as the conquest and the later exploits of David and Solomon can't be taken at face value as historical accounts.[25] For some interpreters, the ability to say that things such as the slaughter of the Canaanites didn't actually occur but were meant to present theological messages about devotion to God or loyalty to Israelite religion for later times mitigates the negative force of these stories as legitimations and celebrations of violence.

Other strategies take a decidedly big picture approach to the problem texts with an eye toward the Bible as a whole. A holistic perspective stresses the diversity of the portrayals of God and God's ways within the whole canon of scripture, emphasizing that more positive, nonviolent portrayals are in tension with and somewhat relativize the problematic depictions (without, of course, completing negating their force as potential endorsements of violence). Likewise, readers may adopt a "canon within the canon" approach, which emphasizes some texts and portions of the Bible as more authoritative than others and as providing a key for reinterpreting the troubling texts in a more positive way (without advocating their removal from the church's scripture). This approach often views the Old Testament's warfare texts as a truthful and revelatory part of the past realities of God's ways and people but not as normative for the life of God's people today as are the teachings of Jesus and the apostles.

Another big picture type of approach is the recent renewal of the symbolic interpretation of many of the Old Testament's warfare texts that was present in early Christian writings.[26] This interpretation reads things such as the conquest stories in Joshua not as literal or historical accounts but as allegories for the call to defeat sin and overcome evil in believers' lives. The violence is only symbolic and not meant to legitimize any physical actions toward others in the world. A somewhat related interpretive move locates the violent actions by God that are described especially in declarations of divine judgment for sin within the larger covenant framework of the Old Testament.[27] Seen in this way, the violence and destruction that appear as part of God's judgment are only a response called forth as a consequence for human sin, rebellion, and violence within the framework of the covenant between God and God's people. The violence attributed to God is a covenantal response and shouldn't be understood as an inherent part of God's nature.

In addition to these big picture strategies, some interpreters have highlighted certain details within the Bible's violence texts in order to nuance or soften their force.[28] For example, the biblical warfare accounts often use hyperbole in their descriptions of the size, scope, and scale of events. Proclamations of violent divine judgments within the Old Testament prophets also frequently emphasize God's patience in having held off judgment, and some texts portray God as painfully lamenting the necessity of bringing judgment. Other interpreters have focused on the nature and function of the language of divine and human violence. Brueggemann, for instance, asserts that this kind of language in the book of Joshua served as the language of the marginalized and powerless who had no recourse to actual physical force or military aggression against their dominant oppressors. Therefore, the biblical language and imagery can't be legitimately appropriated by powerful empires, states, or people in order to assert or maintain dominance.[29]

I will conclude with two recent representative works that explore many of the approaches mentioned above. Seibert's recent comprehensive survey identifies seven main approaches to the issue of God's violence in the Old Testament.[30] He notes that examples of these approaches appear in a variety of writings, but especially within Christian interpretation. Seibert identifies the seven main approaches as follows:

1. Defending God's Violent Behavior—approaches mostly proposed by conservative Christian interpreters that insist on the Bible's full accuracy and authority in everything said about God. Ways of defending God's actions include emphasizing the following:

    a. just cause for the violence

    b. a greater good served by the acts

    c. a progressive revelation that unfolded over time

    d. symbolic or allegorical interpretations of the acts

    e. trust in God's goodness while acknowledging the questions raised by the violence described

2. Balancing God's Violent Behavior with God's Other Behavior

3. Critiquing God's Violent Behavior—critiques take several forms:

    a. assuming human involvement in the production of the texts and therefore the presence of ancient cultural notions

    b. reader-oriented approaches that welcome critiques based on modern concerns

    c. christological interpretation that critiques Old Testament violence in light of Christ's teachings

    d. feminist approaches that emphasize elements of gender involved in the violence

4. Accepting and Rejecting God's Violent Behavior—approaches that grant a significance to the portrayals of God's actions while also raising moral and ethical questions.

5. Reinterpreting God's Violent Behavior Symbolically—approaches that rely on allegorical or other nonliteral readings.

6. Protesting God's Violent Behavior—approaches that attempt no rehabilitation but simply acknowledge the violence depicted.

7. Celebrating God's Violent Behavior—approaches that explore how such language and imagery can serve the powerless and oppressed, especially through the overthrow of colonial-type subjugation and the establishment of justice.

In one of the most recent book-length treatments of the issue of violence in the Bible, Creach combines a survey of other approaches with a proposal of his own.[31] He argues that when one considers the entire testimony of the Bible as a whole, it becomes apparent that the Bible ultimately "conceives of violence as action that is opposed to God and God's desires for the world."[32] Hence, when the Bible portrays God as enacting violence, these actions occur only as a response to the violence of human beings and as an attempt to reestablish a proper order for creation. Creach reaches this conclusion by relying on the order of the books in the Protestant canon and emphasizing that the Bible opens with stories that demonstrate God's intentions for all creation to live in peaceful and mutually enriching relationships. Additionally, he maintains that the biblical texts endorse some use of human war and violence when it's for the sake of "liberation from oppression."[33] At times, Creach also relies on the ancient reading strategy of "spiritual interpretations" promoted by the early church (especially interpreters such as Origen and Augustine), which saw the war and violence texts as only symbolic, allegorical, or otherwise non-literal in meaning, especially portraying the believer's need to fight against sin and seek a purer faith.[34] By using these interpretive strategies at different times and in different ways, Creach finally and somewhat counterintuitively claims that "the whole of Scripture may be understood rightly as a grand testimony *against* violence."[35]

Moral Injury and the Biblical Warfare Texts

As noted at the outset of this chapter, the primary purpose here is to see if perspectives from emerging work on moral injury have anything to add to the perennial problem of the war and violence present in the Bible and the various strategies that have been proposed for understanding and interpretation. Can moral injury help us understand better, or even somewhat differently, the nature of the problem? Can moral injury help explain *why* the Bible's depictions of divine and human war and violence are a problem for contemporary readers? From the perspective of moral injury work, we could state the question this way: Do the biblical warfare texts morally injure their readers (i.e., is that why many Christian readers today find them so troubling)? And if so, how do these texts cause moral injury (i.e., why are they morally injurious to those who encounter them in present-day, especially faith-based, contexts)?

As a starting point, we may review the ways that moral injury has been said to occur in soldiers in order to ask whether similar things are happening to faith-based readers when they encounter the Bible's war and violence texts, particularly the texts that describe God acting violently in direct and personal ways. The discussion in chapter 2 noted two primary causes that have been identified for the struggles associated with moral injury. A soldier's sense of having been betrayed by an authority figure in a high-stakes situation occupied the initial place among causes of moral injury.[36] The authority acted in ways that were not only perceived by the soldier as immoral and unethical but also led the soldier or others to engage in morally questionable actions. The solider watched a trusted individual violate "what's right," especially the right ways that one should treat and be treated socially, relationally, and interpersonally in difficult situations. The second major cause identified for moral injury had a more personal element and focused on acts done (or allowed or witnessed) by the soldier that violated her or his deeply held moral convictions about self and the world. This view appeared in the most widely accepted clinical definition that mentioned transgressing a person's morals.[37] Here, morals represent the fundamental assumptions about how things should work and how one should behave in the world. Psychologists and other caregivers have noted that the experiences of betrayal and personal violation can cause significant moral dissonance, which can lead to the development of the core symptoms associated with moral injury.

These articulations of how moral injury occurs provide some resources for thinking in new ways about why the biblical war and violence texts are particularly problematic for those who read them as part of sacred scripture within religious contexts. At least in part, these texts morally injure their readers in ways that are similar to military moral injury. For some, especially faith-based, readers today, the portrayals of divine and human war and violence within the Bible create a sense of betrayal and violation of perceived moral convictions about God, people, and the world, some of which are expressed in the Bible itself and others of which come from the readers' religious traditions and practices. We should not overstate this claim. After all, the history of interpretation shows that past generations were able, to a certain level of satisfaction, to arrive at explanations of the violence, suggesting that they didn't (or at least didn't entirely) feel betrayal or violation by these biblical depictions. Likewise, many Christian readers today just assume that God has good reasons for doing whatever God does or commands, even if we don't know those reasons. Even so, although a sense of betrayal due to God's actions and commands may not be pervasive in the history of Christianity or present-day popular understandings, moral injury perspectives suggest that, at least for some believers who have increased awareness of the effects of sustained modern warfare, the theological problem created by these texts is that they seem to violate the operative conviction that God is good and works to bring life rather than death in order to establish a rightly ordered and stable world. The passages raise questions about faith-based understandings of the character and actions of God and the human beings said to be made in God's image.

Let me focus on my own tradition of Protestant Christianity. The ways that the Bible has been commonly interpreted within the primary framework of the Christian tradition past and present have formed Christian readers to believe that their scripture gives a particular moral vision of the character and actions of both God and God's people (i.e., who they are in their nature and how they should act in accordance with that nature). This moral vision isn't entirely self-evident in the texts themselves, but results from the ways that the texts have been collected, organized, and interpreted within Christianity, beginning even with the selection and ordering of the biblical books in the Protestant canon (compared to, say, the Jewish, Roman Catholic, or Orthodox canons).[38] One most clearly sees the Bible's dominant moral understanding of the character and actions of God and God's people on the level of the whole of scripture and not necessarily in any one single passage or verse. When viewed through the lens of moral injury, however, the Bible's many graphic depictions of war and violence enacted by God and God's people—spread as they are throughout nearly every portion of the canon—seem to violate this moral vision.

To explain further, the dominant moral vision of the nature and actions of God and God's people that emerges from Christian scripture has several elements. In short, God's nature is love; God's actions intend to restore humanity and all of creation to a flourishing life of right-relationships with God and each other; and the role of human persons, as those created in God's image, is to love God and others in a way that reflects God's own character and allows for mutual flourishing.[39] A few representative texts illustrate this moral vision. Some of its first expressions in the Old Testament appear in the portion of the story where God is attempting to form the moral and ethical character of the chosen people after their rescue from slavery in Egypt and before their entrance into the promised land. For instance, the general prohibitions of the Ten Commandments in Exodus 20:1-17 (cf. Deut 5:6-21) include commands not to murder or do other forms of violence to members of the community (vv. 13-17). A traditional confession of faith that appears later in Exodus and reappears in various places and forms throughout the Old Testament affirms God's nature as

> merciful and gracious,
> slow to anger,
> and abounding in steadfast love and faithfulness,
> keeping steadfast love for the thousandth generation,
> forgiving iniquity and transgression and sin. (Exod 34:6b-7a)[40]

In one of the more extensive discussions of ethics in the early part of the Old Testament, Leviticus 19 begins with the overall command for the Israelites to imitate God's character and "be holy, for I the LORD your God am holy" (v. 2), before moving on to demand that they deal fairly with the poor and other vulnerable people among them (v. 18). The climax, however, is the command for them not to "hate" or "take vengeance" but to "love your neighbor as yourself" (v. 18). Later in the same chapter, the divine command expands to love not only those who share their citizenship but also to "love the alien [i.e., immigrant, sojourner] as yourself, for you were aliens in the land of Egypt: [and] I am the LORD your God" (v. 34; compare several commands elsewhere not to mistreat the immigrant; e.g., Exod 23:9). Deuteronomy 6:5, one of the most well-known Old Testament passages (part of the so-called Shema in Jewish tradition), makes explicit the command for the Israelites to love God: "You shall love the LORD your God with all your heart, and with all your soul, and with all your might."

Some of the texts among the Old Testament prophets emphasize God's love for the people: "When Israel was a child, I loved him, and out of Egypt I called my son" (Hos 11:1). Likewise, presenting God as speaking in first-person, Isaiah 54:10 says,

> For the mountains may depart
> and the hills be removed,
> but my steadfast love shall not depart from you.

Other prophets, perhaps most well known for their demands for the people to practice justice and righteousness, call the people to treat others rightly and in life-giving ways:

> He has told you, O mortal, what is good;
> and what does the LORD require of you
> but to do justice and to love kindness,
> and to walk humbly with your God? (Mic 6:8)

Even some of the prophets' visions for an ideal future present God's ultimate desire as a world free from war and violence:

> They shall beat their swords into plowshares,
> and their spears into pruning hooks;
> nation shall not lift up sword against nation,
> neither shall they learn war any more. (Isa 2:4; see also Mic 4:3; but
> cf. Joel 3:10)

The overall picture of a loving God who intends a peaceful world and calls believers to act in love is also explicit in the New Testament. Perhaps no clearer statement exists than John 3:16 and its attribution of God's saving actions through Jesus of Nazareth to God's love for creation: "For God so loved the world that he gave his only Son, so that everyone who believes in him may not perish but may have eternal life." But the epistle of 1 John emphasizes this moral vision the most: "For this is the message you have heard from the beginning, that we should love one another" (1 John 3:11); "Beloved, let us love one another, because love is from God; everyone who loves is born of God and knows God. Whoever does not love does not know God, for God is love" (1 John 4:7-8); and most succinctly: "We love because he first loved us" (1 John 4:19). This moral vision finds similar expression in places such as 1 Corinthians 13, a chapter devoted to the nature (see vv. 4-7) and practice (see vv. 1-3) of love in believers' lives. The chapter concludes with the assertion, "And now faith, hope, and love abide, these three; and the greatest of these is love" (v. 13). The admonition in Romans 12:19-20 applies this moral vision specifically to cases of desired vengeance and quotes from Proverbs 25:21-22 in order to extend the practice of love even to one's enemies: "Beloved, never avenge yourselves.... No, 'if your enemies are hungry, feed them; if they are thirsty, give them something to drink; for by doing this you will heap burning coals on their heads.'"

For Christian readers, however, the most compelling indications of a comprehensive moral vision centered on loving actions and right relationships appear in the teachings attributed to Jesus in the New Testament Gospels. The prime example is Jesus's response to a Pharisee lawyer in which he was asked to identify the greatest commandment. Jesus identified two by quoting the passages from Deuteronomy 6:5 and Leviticus 19:18 cited above: "'You shall love the Lord your God with all your heart, and with all your soul, and with all your mind.' This is the greatest and first commandment. And a second is like it: 'You shall love your neighbor as yourself'" (Matt 22:37-39). Most significantly for our purposes, Jesus here identifies these commandments as the overall moral imperative that summarizes the biblical revelation on the whole and as a whole: "On these two commandments hang all the law and the prophets" (Matt 22:40). Other places in the New Testament echo this assertion of the fundamental ethic of loving God and neighbor (e.g., Mark 12:28-34; Luke 10:25-28; John 13:34; Rom 13:9-10). Still others promote a guiding principle of nonviolent response (e.g., Rom 12:14).

The main expressions of this moral vision that conflict with the Bible's depictions of divine and human violence appear in the Sermon on the Mount in Matt 5–7.[41] Here, we again find general principles of nonviolence and admonitions to peacemaking (5:9, 11-12), including the famous "turn the other cheek" response to physical assault (5:39) and the "golden rule" of treating others as you would have them treat you (7:12), both of which reinforce the impression that Jesus's interpretation of the entire biblical tradition is that God acts with unconditional love and God's followers should do the same. Most strikingly, the Sermon on Mount explicitly extends the call for the love of neighbor to include not only foreigners (as present already in the Old Testament texts) but also enemies (see 5:43-48): "You have heard that it was said, 'You shall love your neighbor and hate your enemy.' But I say to you, 'Love your enemies and pray for those who persecute you," (vv. 43-44; see also Luke 6:27-36). This extension, combined with scripture's other moral imperatives concerning love and violence, leave readers with the clear message that Jesus's teachings neither promote nor support the use of force, even in the face of oppression and persecution.[42]

Passages like those mentioned above (particularly the ones found in Jesus's teachings) create the impression for most Christian, especially casual, readers that the Bible presents God and God's people as having a certain moral character with accompanying moral actions. That moral vision is grounded in love: God's nature is love; God acts in love toward creation; and God's people are called to act lovingly toward neighbors, foreigners, and enemies, even in circumstances of persecution. Importantly, we've seen that this moral conviction isn't present in the New Testament alone, but appears throughout the biblical story of God and God's people. The overall moral vision is that God is good, God works to bring life rather than death, God's people should imitate God in this work, and violence represents the opposite of God's nature and intentions for the world. After all, Jesus declared that love for God and neighbor is the true and full summary of the content of scripture's revelation (Matt 22:37-40). When examined as a whole, the "governing center" of scripture's moral vision is to depend on God, respond with love, and resist violence.[43]

Perspectives from moral injury show that the biblical war and violence texts are problematic because they seem to violate the overall moral vision of God and God's people that is derived by many Christian readers from the Bible itself. We might, for instance, say the same thing about the Bible's war and violence texts that the recent Adaptive Disclosure methodology says about the ways that war experiences violate moral sensibilities and create the struggles of moral injury. Just as war does for soldiers, so for many Christian readers the depictions of divine and human war and violence confront people with things "outside what our moral code prepares us to anticipate and cope with."[44] Texts describing God's killing of firstborn babies and animals or the Israelites' mass slaughtering of the Canaanites are at odds with common understandings of Christian morality, especially as seen through the moral imperatives in Jesus's teachings. The depictions of behaviors present in these biblical texts unexpectedly violate the sense of morality previously assigned to the character and actions of God and God's people in the minds of many Christian readers, leaving them to struggle with how to cope and thus leading to proposals of the interpretive strategies surveyed above.

The element of betrayal by an authority figure provides another perspective from moral injury on why the Bible's descriptions of God's violence are problematic. In moral injury terms, such betrayal occurs when an established authority acts in ways that are not only perceived by the soldier as immoral and unethical but also lead the soldier or others to engage in morally questionable actions. For some Christian readers, the Bible's violent depictions of God constitute a betrayal of their core beliefs about who God is and how God works in the world. As Brueggemann states succinctly, the violence attributed to God is "plainly offensive" to sensitive readers because "it does not agree with our sense of the Christian gospel that promotes a God of compassion, gentleness, and forgiveness."[45] We need only think here of the often-echoed description of the character of God in the Old Testament that I mentioned above:

merciful and gracious,
slow to anger,
and abounding in steadfast love and faithfulness,
keeping steadfast love for the thousandth generation,
forgiving iniquity and transgression and sin. (Exod 34:6b-7a)

Seibert goes further and explains that many Christian readers possess an understanding of God that attributes to God a character that is "morally perfect," and they've often developed this view from what they believe to be the Bible's comprehensive and authoritative descriptions of God.[46] Upon close reading, however, they discover a tension between their beliefs and the Bible's portrayals, encountering diverse and contradictory descriptions of God, which they can't easily reconcile with their overall theological convictions. The God they looked to as a moral authority to exemplify life-giving and loving ways in the world betrays their trust in story after story.

The betrayal aspect of moral injury also sheds light on one other element regarding why the biblical war and violence texts are problematic for Christian readers. The experience of betrayal within moral injury involves not simply the immoral or unethical actions of the authority, but also the sense that the authority's actions led others, directly or indirectly, to engage in morally questionable acts. As discussed earlier in this chapter, the biblical war and violence texts, especially those that portray God's direct involvement or sanction, have been used throughout history to justify war, killing, and conquest in different settings. For the Christian reader who looks to the Bible as life-giving revelation of the God who brings salvation, the recognition that the very same book has been weaponized and has helped to cause the suffering and slaughter of others may feel like a deep betrayal. One may conclude that the trusted source of life and redemption has, in fact, been a cause of pain and death. The realization that the biblical texts have the potential within them to be agents of actual harm may register as a betrayal of the believer's highest ideals concerning the nature and function of their sacred scripture—a betrayal that can leave one afraid to take up these texts again, sensing an uncertain morality within them and worrying about their trustworthiness as a life-giving source.

Another perspective gained from moral injury may illuminate why present-day readers struggle with the Bible's war and violence texts in a way not usually considered. Contemporary readers may struggle with these biblical portrayals because of what they reveal about the morality of our own lives, society, and world today. Reading the biblical war and violence texts reminds us that domination-based relationships, war practices, and violent actions are not a thing of the past. They are present in many respects in our society now. The Bible's stark descriptions may make us more aware of the violence that regularly reveals itself among us and may confront us with broken morals and ethics to which we are too easily desensitized. Those attuned to moral injury work will recognize here the dimension in which a morally injured person is no longer able to see themselves as a good person or to see the world as a reliably moral, life-giving place. The Bible's portrayals of God and God's people committing violence wound us in the same way, as they point us to our own personal, relational, and societal violence. In her study of violence and personhood in the Old Testament and its context, Lemos surveys many examples of contemporary violence and domination that have manifested themselves in American culture in recent years.[47] One could think here of the Abu Ghraib prison scandal, dehumanizing treatment in the American prison system, or police violence against African Americans. The ways that the

Bible's violence points us to our own examples of violence remind us that we still face the task of "eliminating the ideologies, the socialization practices, the training, the scarcities, and the structural forms of violence" that exist today.[48] We find the war and violence texts morally injurious because these biblical passages show us the brokenness of humanity and the world—a brokenness that remains today.

I conclude this section with a more general observation. The description of moral injury in chapter 2 suggested that the moral wound suffered is not simply about transgressions; rather, it's the phenomenon of being caught between two moral imperatives, each of which is good but which can't be simultaneously followed in particular instances (e.g., to defend one's family or country and to honor and protect all life as sacred). Seen in this way, moral injury is the experience of being in a moral catch, believing in the virtue of two convictions but recognizing the seemingly irreconcilable conflict between them. This conception accurately describes the moral dilemma sensed by many readers of the biblical war and violence passages. A person operating within a Christian theological framework affirms on the one hand that the fallenness and brokenness of the world results in sinful actions and that a holy God should judge sin and overcome evil, even to the point of bringing down oppressors and destroying evil forces. At the same time, however, the Christian reader believes that God's essential nature is love and God's actions toward people and all creation should always reflect that nature by being consistently loving, indiscriminately merciful, ever redemptive, and life-giving.

Even the testimony of God's people preserved in scripture seems to acknowledge this tension. The core biblical confession of faith about God's character in Exod 34:6-7 mentioned above includes in its fullest formulation a recognition of this tension. The first half of the statement asserts God's loving mercy:

a God merciful and gracious,
slow to anger,
and abounding in steadfast love and faithfulness,

keeping steadfast love for the thousandth generation,
forgiving iniquity and transgression and sin. (vv. 6b-7a)

But the second half asserts God's commitment to acting in judgment:

yet by no means clearing the guilty,
but visiting the iniquity of the parents
upon the children
and the children's children,
to the third and fourth generation. (v. 7b)

The people of God live in this tension within God's essential character. The feeling of being in a moral catch between two virtuous but incompatible convictions may contribute to the difficulties readers have with the Bible's war and violence. And yet this insight also shows that the struggle of present-day readers with these biblical texts is, at its core, a moral struggle.

Moral Repair and the Biblical Warfare Texts

If moral injury helps us understand better, or even somewhat differently, why the Bible's depictions of divine and human war and violence are a problem for contemporary Christian readers, it may also be true that the proposed ways to repair moral injury in soldiers may help those readers struggling with the texts. Here is an initial sketch of some potential contributions from moral injury that could be examined in detail by future studies.[49]

First, work on moral repair for soldiers has emphasized the need for practices that create conversations around the morally injurious experiences. The purpose of such conversation is to provide safe places to express struggles and to move toward healthy perspectives on the experiences. In the same way, readers of these difficult biblical passages may benefit from moving beyond individualistic study and engaging in ongoing conversations with diverse perspectives. Just as in moral repair work with soldiers, such conversations allow both for the forthright critical assessment of the problems presented by the texts and the trying out of creative and positive possibilities in response. Additionally, these kinds of conversations encourage those participating, whether they're discussing war's experiences or the Bible's violent texts, to explore the moral aspects involved (and not simply, for example, the legal aspects). Moral repair tries to help soldiers think not just about legal justifications for combat actions but also about moral dimensions that might be much less clear. The killing of a child who threatens a soldier with a gun might be legally permissible, but its moral correctness is more ambiguous. Conversation permits soldiers and biblical readers alike to engage in moral reasoning. So could God's violent acts in the Old Testament be understood through moral reasoning not as a reflection of an inherently violent divine nature but as the stipulated response of judgment called forth by violations of the particular moral code represented by the covenant?

The practice of conversation connects to another emphasis within moral repair work—namely, the need to communalize morally wounding experiences so that a sense of shared responsibility emerges for both the injurious circumstances and the work of healing and restoration. Perhaps biblical readers can communalize the reception of these troublesome texts for support but also for a more nuanced view of how they're read among different kinds of readers in different contexts. For example, a reader in the First World setting of the US might be seriously troubled by the violence of the plagues against pharaoh and imperial Egypt in Exodus or the overthrow of the powerful Canaanite city-states in Joshua. But conversation in a reading community with a person who has lived through oppression, colonialism, marginalization, and powerlessness in another part of the world may reveal a new perspective about the hope generated by such images and affirmations of God's powerful acts of justice for those who have no recourse to tangible power or physical action. This kind of conversation may then generate further discussion of theological questions such as who would be justified in using this kind of biblical language and its assertions and in what circumstances, as well as, conversely, by whom should this language not be appropriated and why.

Alongside practices of conversation, the related emphasis within moral repair work on the need for honesty concerning war's experiences may offer a helpful resource here as well. At an initial level, we might just encourage readers of the Bible to be honest about the moral difficulties involved with these texts. In moral injury work, such honesty includes the candid naming of what is injurious, as well as the uninhibited criticizing of things seen as morally wrong. This practice of honesty may provide the warrant for those interpreters today who decide the best thing Christian readers can do with the biblical violence texts is simply admit the deeply flawed theology found within them and the immoral effects the texts have had in the hands of believers throughout history. As Brueggemann insists, honesty about these biblical texts and the problems they create demands that Christian readers refuse denial and instead be candid about the memories of God and performances of violence. And this honest processing must include candor about the "residue of hurt" and the "wounding caused by the violence of God" that is part of the church's life and legacy.[50]

A final way to help repair moral injury in soldiers, which is deeply connected to the emphasis on honesty, is the practice of lament. The preceding chapter explored this element in detail, especially in relationship to the Old Testament's postwar laments and the lament psalms. For our purposes here, perhaps those who work with the biblical war and violence texts should simply lament (even publicly) in order somehow to blunt the force of the moral wound. Additionally, lament's connection to confession and repentance (see ch. 5) suggests that readers of the Bible's most problematic texts might engage in repentance for the ways these texts and their portrayals of God have inflicted harm, maybe also seeking means of healing that parallel the performance of acts of repair used in the context of military moral injury. The United Church of Christ, for instance, has issued a formal apology to the native peoples of Hawaii for the exploitative acts done by their missionaries in the past.[51] The concrete expressions of lament may also take the more strident form of protest—something that allows soldiers to dissent and oppose the betrayals and events by which they have suffered moral injury. In the same way, biblical readers may direct protests and petitions to God in prayer over the violence and implore God to "exhibit and perform God's better self toward the world and its vulnerable people."[52]

In the end, several concrete insights and practices from the work of moral repair among soldiers seem helpful for the perennial problem of the Bible's war and violence. But biblical interpreters may be able to learn a more fundamental lesson from the moral injury work that has occurred thus far—namely, that there is no simple solution. Work on understanding these problematic biblical texts, like work on moral injury, remains ongoing and will likely be open-ended and unresolved. Even so, the unresolved nature of the work is itself ethical because it keeps the struggle alive and rejects any attempt to close off the concerns raised by either military moral injury or the Bible's violence. Just as psychologists and other caregivers have worked to get moral injury recognized as an actual phenomenon, so biblical readers may be best served by approaching the Bible's divine and human violence first and foremost as a theological reality to be acknowledged rather than an interpretive problem to be solved.

Conclusion

Present-day readers of scripture may be tempted to dodge the Bible's problematic portrayals of war and violence in favor of some of the more positive moral and ethical passages surveyed above. The intersection with moral injury work, however, suggests that while the biblical texts are troubling, disorienting, and potentially morally wounding, they shouldn't be ignored. Their function for contemporary readers in the late twenty-first century US context may be similar to the important contribution made by acknowledging that moral injury is a present reality. The preceding discussion indicated that these disturbing parts of the Bible remind us of our own society's ongoing brokenness and violence. In so doing, the Bible's uncensored depictions of divine and human violence contrast with modern US culture's propensity to distance itself from, or sanitize for more comfortable consumption, the realities of war. This "distancing and sanitizing" makes war "more bearable for those at home and thus, tragically, far more likely to happen and be accepted."[53] But the biblical texts that present disturbingly violent behavior by God and people don't allow readers to sanitize or distance themselves from the grim realities of war, killing, and death. Their very presence in the sacred scripture that is read every Sunday in houses of worship by those seeking moral guidance gives the realities of war and violence an immediacy for those who live day to day in a society that fights its wars on the other side of the planet. This may be the disconcerting, disorienting, and yet vital contribution made by the biblical portrayals of divine and human violence. As Collins explains, "The power of the Bible is largely that it gives an unvarnished picture of human nature and of the dynamics of history, and also of religion and the things that people do in its name."[54]

Along these lines, Brock and Lettini devote an entire chapter to the need for honesty about the realities of war versus the societal propensity to hide war's wounds.[55] They note that societies employ many strategies to try to mask the harsh realities of war, effectively hiding "the costs and consequences of war from public consciousness," shielding civilians from a sense of communal moral responsibility, and making support for further war efforts more likely.[56] But things such as the candid testimony of soldiers and the unsanitized descriptions of the real-life costs of war on men, women, and children don't allow this kind of cultural concealment: "Speaking about moral injury places morality, justice, and human dignity at the center of public attention and exposes the collective amnesia about war, its victims, and its aftermath."[57] The forthright and sometimes graphic portrayals of war and violence in the Bible may accomplish this same end. We may think of the stark realities and grim descriptions in these biblical texts as functioning analogously to the unfiltered public airing of images of dead soldiers and their coffins arriving home—a practice that was banned by the Bush administration during the conflicts in Afghanistan and Iraq. Such depictions—whether textual or visual—display the savage costs of war and permit no acts of denial.

In the specific context of the Christian tradition, full engagement with the biblical war and violence texts may serve as a check on the ways the just war theory has obstructed the candid assessment of the psychological, emotional, and moral wounds of war. Levine surveys the development and use of the just war theory (particularly within the Western Christian tradition) and concludes that the theory not only assisted in legitimizing war but also created (unintentionally?) a façade that killing done in an acceptable way under certain defined conditions shouldn't produce any injurious effects on the morals, ethics, or psychology of the soldiers involved.[58] By contrast, the Bible's own portrayals of the raw realities of divine and human combat, the negative effects of betrayals and martial actions (as in the Saul story), and the various ritualized efforts to deal with the aftermath of war (as in the Old Testament's postwar rituals) pierce this façade and keep the actual experiences of war ever before those who read them, urging a sense of shared moral responsibility and an appreciation of war's inescapable costliness.

In the end, then, perhaps we can make a particular application of Frechette's recent analogy for the Old Testament as a whole and think of the biblical war and violence texts as a kind of "controlled substance."[59] Much like drugs classified as controlled substances by the US government, the Bible's violent passages can be harmful when handled improperly but can also be helpful and therapeutic when administered carefully. Even when functioning more positively, however, such controlled substances retain the capacity to do harm and always have the potential for accompanying side effects, which necessitates ongoing critical sensitivity and scrutiny.

Chapter 7
Retrospect and Prospect

Moral injury is real. There is no turning away now.

—David Wood[1]

The quote that heads this chapter is not only my conviction; it's also the conclusion that I hope will be increasingly accepted by those who consider the realities and wounds of war. My hope for what may come out of this book is similar. I hope that through the explorations and case studies presented here, those who study the Bible academically or devotionally/pastorally and those who work with morally injured persons as psychologists, chaplains, and other caregivers will become convinced that there are elements of common ground in the efforts to interpret the Bible from new perspectives and to find better ways of addressing moral injury. The analysis of the Bible, whether as a collection of ancient writings, an influential cultural element of Western society, or the theological norm that shapes the lives of soldiers, veterans, and others who identify as confessing believers, can both benefit from and contribute to the efforts to engage moral injury as a reality and to save lives that might otherwise be lost.

Contributions of Biblical Studies to Moral Injury

The overall thesis explored throughout this book is that the engagement between the Bible and moral injury generates a two-way conversation in which perspectives from each offer new insights to the other. From one side, the interpretations of the biblical texts given in the preceding chapters show that moral injury provides a profitable heuristic that yields valuable new insights into these ancient writings. For example, perspectives from moral injury encourage future biblical interpretation to pay more attention to several areas of study concerning the biblical texts related to war and violence in particular. These include the following: (1) the reception history of the Bible's war and violence passages in both premodern and modern contexts (e.g., do previous interpreters of these texts express similar concerns to those raised by moral injury?); (2) connections between moral injury and specific genres within biblical literature (e.g., do biblical poetic texts have special characteristics for engaging moral injury perspectives?); (3) further analysis of the contributions of ritual theory to understanding the functions of rituals in warfare contexts and within the Bible more generally; and (4) motifs and images that are most frequently connected with portrayals that reflect moral injury experiences (e.g., the type scenes of the woman at the window [see Judg 5:28-31] and endangered daughters, concubines, and wives [see Gen 19; Judg 19; 1 Sam 25]).

In this conclusion, however, I'm particularly interested in highlighting some potential contributions that the study of the Bible, especially as done within the field of academic biblical scholarship, might make to the ongoing work on moral injury among psychologists, veterans' workers, moral philosophers, chaplains, and others. My study of the biblical texts in dialogue with moral injury has convinced me of the conviction expressed by McDonald: "In turn, these old texts, always as part of a broader, interdisciplinary effort, make credible contributions to the job of understanding, preventing, and healing moral injury."[2]

In my preview in chapter 1, I mentioned that the most readily apparent contributions involve perspectives related to faith and spirituality. As I noted there, although specific statistics remain uncertain, it seems clear that many US service members self-identify as Christians, come from Christian backgrounds, or at least express interest in spirituality. Several recent studies within moral injury work have paid particular attention to spiritual and faith-based dimensions and have indicated that veterans generally welcome the incorporation of religion and spirituality into psychological counseling concerning moral injury.[3] As the explorations of the Old Testament's Saul story, postwar rituals, and laments have shown, biblical texts have the potential to help those interested in moral injury consider things such as the following: How a person of faith experiences moral violation; what the personal, communal, and religious effects of such an experience are; what the morality of war in and of itself is, and how one responds to having participated in it; what the Bible teaches about forgiveness and healing; and what the place of prayer, honesty, grief, and confession is for those affected by war.

Additionally, as discussed in chapter 1, for those who operate from these faith-based contexts, the Bible might be the source of a starting moral sense of the self and the world—the very core moral identity and ethical framework that gets violated in moral injury in such a way that the person no longer sees it as reliable or functional. The biblical writings offer a particular way in which readers define themselves as persons, structure their world, and live in relationship to the world and others. The damaging of this initial moral sense may be the cause for some of the experiences of moral injury and the object that needs to be recovered and restored in the work of healing.

These possible contributions indicate that the study of the Bible can help answer the call that has been expressed within some circles that while moral injury is manifestly a human wound and not a religious one, we should reserve a place for the insights provided by religious and theological perspectives.[4] There are probably a few reasons why this path of the sustained use of the Bible in moral injury research and treatment hasn't yet been taken, and the reasons reflect tendencies in both psychology and biblical studies. Even though many US service members self-identify as Christians, come from a Christian background, or at least express interest in spirituality, today's psychological and therapeutic community remains largely secular in its approaches. At the same time, biblical interpretation in both academic and ecclesial contexts hasn't yet offered many useable resources concerning the biblical texts and how they might be engaged in this work. I hope that the kinds of interpretive moves I make in this book show that the study of the biblical texts can join in the larger cultural conversation about the moral questions of war, the social responsibility for the experiences, and the possibilities of meaningful spiritual life after war—a conversation that may ultimately serve to save the lives of some of those who've been morally wounded.[5] In this way, the biblical texts, particularly the war-related stories, poems, and rituals, can join with insights from other disciplines to contribute to a new and more wholesome religious and spiritual self-understanding for those who've experienced moral injury. Larson describes the goal here as the development of a new "religious anthropology" that includes the "faith that *this* life can be graced with redemption and positive purpose," and I suggest that critical engagement with the Bible in dialogue with moral injury can be a formative piece in this development effort.[6]

A final contribution to moral injury emerges specifically from the academic study of the Bible as one of the sacred texts of the world's religions and the place of this scholarship within the larger collection of academic disciplines. As chapter 2 indicated, moral injury study thus far has been dominated by mental health, psychology, and related therapeutic contexts, resulting in it often being "medicalized."[7] Academic biblical studies, however, can contribute a particularly humanities-oriented dimension to this clinical and scientific reductionism—that is, the dimension of historians, philosophers, literary critics, artists, theologians, sociologists, and textualists. The human lives and experiences reflected in these ancient biblical writings, whether the lives and experiences of those who are portrayed in the texts or of those who authored and preserved the texts in various communities throughout history, point to the historical and cultural breadth of the moral struggles involved in war. And the biblical texts can place moral injury into contexts that clinical psychology and moral philosophy cannot—contexts of rituals, penance, confession, and narratives about complex moral agency and characters.[8]

Seen in this way, the critical study of the biblical texts as ancient writings can provide a resource for pursuing the goal that Boudreau says we should seek when we talk about moral injury: "We seek a deeper understanding of our humanity."[9] In other words, the kind of interdisciplinary engagement represented in my case studies and other explorations pushes those who study war in the Old Testament or ancient Israel, for instance, to pursue new levels of clarity about the goals of this work. While scholars need not set antiquarian, sociological, theological, or other interests against one another, the interdisciplinary potential of the engagement with moral injury leads students of the biblical writings and ancient warfare toward a more fully orbed study that moves beyond how war was done to how war was conceived, constructed, and experienced personally, socially, culturally, and morally. And this, in turn, opens the door to appreciate the potential relevance of such biblical interpretation to the lives of soldiers in present-day communities who now deal with the experiences of modern warfare. This kind of interdisciplinary study has the potential to recontextualize warfare in the Bible as one manifestation of a human phenomenon known in diverse times and settings, and thus help veterans and others who feel alone in their struggles to see the moral wounds of war as part of a very ancient and human experience.

Here, those working on moral injury today may also find resources for a thicker description of the experience, as well as its causes and effects. The inclusion of insights from the Bible and theology places special emphasis on the nature, purposes, and "proper ends" of human life.[10] Putting these ideas into dialogue with moral injury invites us to reflect explicitly on how war affects our understanding of who we are as human beings, why we are here, and toward what ends we live—the very understandings of the self and the world that war's experiences can alter and even deform. The intersections of the Bible and moral injury invite us into a broader inquiry beyond diagnoses and treatments—an inquiry in which we study war in order to understand more fully what it means to be human.

Pathways for Future Work

Work on military moral injury continues to emerge at a rapid pace, and this work increasingly employs interdisciplinary insights from religious studies, moral philosophy, ethics, biblical studies, and theology (see ch. 2). As more and more people from different contexts become interested in the moral effects of war participation on individuals, communities, and congregations today, this work will continue to expand, opening new pathways for future study that reach beyond the originating discipline of psychology. Biblical interpreters will likely find more opportunities for engagements with moral injury along the lines of what I've attempted in this book, especially in dialogue with the two main trajectories seen thus far: (1) creative rereadings of literary narratives and characters as portrayals of morally injured warriors; and (2) the identification, importance, and implementation of postwar rituals and symbolic practices from ancient and traditional societies and their writings to see how they connect with the felt needs of morally injured persons for forgiveness, purification, communalization, and hope.

In the last few years, however, the notion of moral injury has been appropriated in a growing variety of ways and contexts that may open even broader pathways for future study. In a recent article, Wiinikka-Lydon provides a mapping survey of the multiple discourses that have emerged around the concept of moral injury, especially within the fields of psychology, psychiatry, and moral philosophy.[11] He notes that the behavioral sciences and philosophy use the label *moral injury* in different ways, particularly with regard to how they identify the subjects who suffer moral injury, the sources that cause the injury, what constitutes the injurious violence, and the institutional and social contexts of the injury. In general, philosophy uses moral injury to refer to "the damage one inflicts on another," while psychology uses moral injury primarily in connection with US veterans to refer to the "effects on the felt character that participation in a combat zone can create."[12]

Wiinikka-Lydon observes three broad discourses concerning the understanding and use of moral injury. First, in the "clinical discourse" (represented primarily by the behavioral sciences), "moral injury" is used primarily in the military-type ways discussed in this book via the work of Shay, Litz, and others. Here, as we've seen, soldiers are the subjects of moral injury as a result either of betrayal by an authority or their own actions (or simply the combat environment). The second discourse ("juridical-critical"), however, comes out of moral philosophy and defines moral injury as something done to the subject by others, specifically in the forms of "dehumanizing violence" (e.g., rape, torture), the degradation of self-respect, and the violation of rights (e.g., hate crimes).[13] Due to the more general definition of moral injury as diminishing and demeaning someone's personhood and dignity, the "juridical-critical" understanding doesn't confine the experience to military or combat contexts. In this understanding, moral injury can occur in a wide variety of settings, even within everyday social interactions. The third discourse ("structural") differs from the other two by moving beyond their focus on interpersonal violence as the essence of moral injury. The "structural" understanding of moral injury focuses on ways that social and cultural institutions, structures, and practices cause a loss of trust and healthy social relationships by harming a person's moral subjectivity.[14] Psychologists working within this discourse point, for example, to the ways that children are formed into certain norms concerning gender and how this formation from social pressures can result in the suppression of authentic personhood, feelings, and voice in order to fit into socially acceptable images of womanhood and manhood. This loss of subjectivity is a moral injury caused not by interpersonal violence but by the structural and institutional dynamics of society and culture. The person is harmed by a loss of authenticity and suffers limitations on the "development of orientations of care that allow one to relate more authentically to others."[15]

Wiinikka-Lydon suggests that "constructive comparison" of how moral injury is being used within these different discourses provides one pathway for future study by broadening our ways of understanding and articulating the experience, its subjects, sources, and contexts. With this kind of comparison, we can think critically about the moral dimensions of many different types of violence, environments, and social and political dynamics.[16] Taking a cue from the discourses that say moral injury can result from a wide variety of interpersonal, cultural, and institutional contexts (e.g., social acts of dehumanization and institutions that forcibly strip away personhood and subjectivity), contemporary publications have begun to apply the notion of moral injury to nonmilitary settings. A common element in these settings is the experience of some kind of violence that undermines confidence in the moral goodness of persons, relationships, or the world, harmfully dehumanizes or demeans personhood, or forcibly suppresses or malforms moral subjectivity.

For example, Lynd and Lynd devote a book-length study to applying moral injury to the setting of prisons, especially practices such as mass incarceration and solitary confinement. Like soldiers in combat, prisoners try to cope with morally erosive conditions by seeking ways to "affirm their humanity and establish community with others."[17] At a much broader level within the field of political science, Subotic and Steele have used the notion of moral injury (understood especially as the loss of a sense of control and the ethical and relational strains that accompany it) to explain the anxiety felt in the US today over state and cultural identity and the breakdown of US relations with other international actors.[18] Similar extensions of moral injury into nonmilitary contexts include, for example, its application to child protective services professionals, medical students in pre-hospital care, and journalists covering refugee crises.[19]

For those interested in the intersection of the Bible and moral injury, this recent broadening beyond military contexts opens possibilities for future study to include a broader range of biblical passages. Future work with the Bible might consider how moral injury perspectives could bear upon texts that aren't related to war, soldiers, or military violence. Thus far, most engagements of moral injury from within biblical scholarship have concentrated on the kinds of war-related texts that I've explored in this book. But understandings of moral injury like those in the discourses noted above, perhaps especially the view that moral injury results from interpersonal or structural violence that dehumanizes, degrades, or diminishes moral subjectivity and personhood, could allow readers of the Bible to look to a broader range of material. The possibilities here may include passages that portray experiences such as famine and child loss suffered due to economic or political maneuverings (2 Kgs 6:24-33), the loss of personhood or subjectivity experienced by women in certain contexts (Judg 19–21; Ruth 1–2), dehumanization or social diminishment suffered by the actions of hostile forces (2 Sam 10:1-5), and other kinds of moral extremities.

An additional benefit of the broadening of moral injury beyond war-related contexts may be the ability to do more with New Testament texts in this regard. My work in this book has focused on the Old Testament, in part because there are fewer explicitly war-related texts in the New Testament. A few works from within psychology and pastoral care, as well as biblical studies, have examined the New Testament texts that reflect a military setting. As I mentioned earlier, for example, Larson and Zust used the stories of the Roman centurions and their encounters with Jesus, the disciples, and others in Luke and Acts to consider conscientious military behavior in the context of discussing moral injury.[20] From a different perspective, Yandell has reexamined the story of the Gerasene Demoniac in Mark 5 as the portrayal of a morally wounded veteran of the Roman military, who suffers isolation, self-harming, and aggression as consequences of his war participation.[21] If one broadens beyond just military moral injury, however, new possibilities may emerge among New Testament texts in the same ways I mentioned above for Old Testament texts.

For instance, Carter has moved away from the focus on soldiers and used the lens of moral injury, specifically the element of betrayal, to study the depictions of Peter and Judas in the Gospels of Matthew and John.[22] Peter betrayed his moral convictions based on the values of loyalty and courage, and the Gospels of Matthew and John present different portrayals of the repair he experienced. By contrast, the Gospels portray Judas as ultimately unable to overcome the moral injury that his betrayal caused. These kinds of studies point the way for future work to explore how different kinds of texts can contribute to the conversation on moral injury, particularly by including portrayals of moral wounding and repair that lie outside of combat contexts.

Wiinikka-Lydon's mapping survey points to an additional pathway for future work. As noted above, one of the results of his survey was the conclusion that moral injury has been viewed too narrowly as the result of direct interpersonal violence and, instead, researchers should pay more attention to moral injury as the result of harm done by violent or unjust social and political structures and dynamics. Seen in this way, the very notion of moral injury can serve as a larger critique of some of the social dynamics and cultural practices that are associated with war and the military. This function recovers elements of Shay's original emphasis on betrayal by authorities as the essence of moral injury (see ch. 2), as well as elements of the definition of moral injury within Wiinikka-Lydon's so-called structural discourse, which emphasizes the moral harm done by social and cultural pressures and institutions. The study of the Bible may add some specific elements to this possible critique function of moral injury, perhaps giving the dialogue between biblical texts and moral injury a larger, even prophetic, cultural significance that should be pursued by future work. The Old Testament prophets, for example, challenged the morals and ethics of the people of ancient Israel at both personal and communal levels, questioning contemporary notions of the social body and pushing them to reconsider who they were as God's people and how they should've lived out that identity in the world. Similarly, the intersection of the Bible and moral injury can generate important cultural conversations for us about the moral character of society. These conversations may serve to expose a "collective amnesia about war, its victims, and its aftermath" by placing "morality, justice, and human dignity at the center of public attention."[23]

One way in which this prophetic function may occur is to recapture the specifically political critique that is inherently present within the notion of moral injury. Concerning moral injury in general, Wiinikka-Lydon notes that current understandings "may not pay enough attention to the political aspects of war and violent conflict," specifically the "insights that soldiers have in virtue of their experience of combat regarding our society's effects on the world, and largely unspoken challenges to certain policies and cultural narratives that such experiences may reflect."[24] Future work on biblical texts may make a contribution to the effort to recapture this dimension of moral injury. The stark depictions of war and its effects in the Bible, along with the laments given in response and the rituals that relate to the aftermath, may provide resources for honest discussion about the negative impact on individuals and communities that results even from legal or sanctioned violence. Working with the Bible's narratives, characters, rituals, and laments might provide a way to do what Wiinikka-Lydon advocates with regard to war and moral injury in general—namely, to "form a politically engaged, social ethic...engaging society with an ethic rooted in and formed from critical reflection on their felt experience of war."[25] The war-related texts in the Bible at times confront us directly with the ways that war can create morally erosive situations and have broader effects on society and the world. But the bitter knowledge given by the biblical warfare texts of all varieties may serve to encourage frank conversations about the moral fabric and ethical identity of a society. Or, at least, this bitter knowledge may encourage readers to do what some of the biblical texts themselves do—namely, to bear honest witness to the realities of war and to lament.

Another way that moral injury's potential prophetic critique may function has to do specifically with dominant trends within biblical interpretation. Perspectives from moral injury push contemporary biblical interpreters to examine critically how the current cultural and social paradigms of biblical interpretation function with regard to war and its moral dangers in present-day US culture in particular. Denton-Borhaug has recently examined the use of the New Testament in this regard and noted, for example, that current paradigms tend to present Jesus and his teachings as the archetype that sacralizes the "sacrifices" of war and thus use the Bible to valorize war as a sacred sacrifice.[26] More broadly, the need is to analyze the interpretive frames used culturally to produce socially dominant interpretations of biblical texts that legitimate war and suffering and thus provide a social and cultural backing for the very experiences that cause moral injury. This is a way of inquiring into how the Bible is utilized in connection with the war-culture in the US. The use of perspectives from moral injury, which bring out the difficult realities and harmful experiences attested in some of the war-related biblical texts, can foster criticism of these dominant cultural interpretations. Moral injury's insights into the biblical war and violence texts raise questions about how the biblical interpretations that sacralize war and suffering actually obscure the realities of violence and the questions about its effects and results. Biblical interpretation informed by moral injury can offer a new space for the honest assessment of the realities of war that may lead to more sound moral and ethical reflection on the use of violence.

In the end, then, I hope that what I've tried to do with the biblical texts and moral injury in this book becomes an invitation, especially for those whose primary vocation is biblical interpretation. The invitation is, first, to allow perspectives from moral injury to keep us honest about the fact that the Bible contains narratives, rituals, prayers, and poems that depict the moral harm that so often accompanies the experience of war. When seen through the lens of moral injury, the Bible isn't a legitimation of war but an indirect acknowledgment that war is morally injurious (at least potentially, and perhaps necessarily). But I hope my work here is also an invitation to all biblical interpreters—professional, scholarly, ministerial, devotional, and more—to engage in ongoing reflection on the roles our interpretations play in how people think about war and its effects—morally, ethically, personally, and communally. Given the stark realities attested by the notion of moral injury and the Bible's overall emphasis on love for God and others, our interpretations of the biblical war and violence texts should help people have a more fully orbed understanding of war, including the moral burdens and wreckage it involves. The goal of such interpretation isn't to hide from these realities of war, but to face them full-on with the hope of moral repair. As we consider the dialogue between the Bible and moral injury, we study war and its injuries in order to work for peace and its possibilities.

Appendix

Current Definitions of Moral Injury[1]

(A sampling alphabetized by author)

"Consequences of acting in violation of their moral code, i.e., the dictates of their consciences, the moral foundations by which we structure our lives" (Bica, *Beyond PTSD*, 48).

"Moral injury is . . . the damage done to our moral fiber when transgressions occur by our hands, through our orders, or with our connivance. When we accept these transgressions, however pragmatically (for survival, for instance), we sacrifice a piece of our moral integrity" (Boudreau, "The Morally Injured," 749).

"Moral injury is a wound in the soul, an inner conflict based on a moral evaluation of having inflicted or witnessed harm. . . . Moral injury can result not only from active behavior, such as torturing or killing, but also from passive behavior, such as failing to prevent harm or witnessing a close friend be slain . . . it can (also) involve feeling betrayed by persons in authority" (Brock and Lettini, *Soul Repair*, 1).

"A disruption in an individual's confidence and expectations about one's own or others' motivations or capacity to behave in a just and ethical manner. This injury is brought about by bearing witness to perceived immoral acts, failure to stop such actions, or perpetration of immoral acts, in particular actions that are inhumane, cruel, depraved, or violent, bringing about pain, suffering, or death of others" (Drescher, "Exploration," 9).

"The erosive diminishment of our souls because our moral actions and the actions of others against us sometimes have harmful outcomes" (Graham, *Moral Injury*, xi).

"Moral injury refers to the diminishment of vitality that comes about in our souls and communities when we are unable to do what we believe is right or when doing the right thing results in harm to others and distress to ourselves" (Graham, *Moral Injury*, 78).

"Phenomenologically, *moral injury* represents a particular trauma syndrome including psychological, existential, behavioral, and interpersonal issues that emerge following perceived violations of deeply held moral beliefs by oneself or trusted individuals (i.e., morally injurious experiences). These experiences cause significant moral dissonance, which if unresolved, leads to the development of its core symptoms" (Jinkerson, "Defining and Assessing Moral Injury," 126; italics original).

"The experience of having acted (or consented to others acting) incommensurably with one's most deeply held moral conceptions" (Kinghorn, "Combat Trauma," 57).[2]

"[A] complex 'soul' wound... [that] produces a chain of emotions and maladaptive behaviors that corrode character and damage an individual's capacity for living" (Larson and Zust, *Care for the Sorrowing Soul*, 5).

"A persistent existential crisis that erodes the very fabric of their sense of self... a spiritual and existential ambivalence that leads to a deep identity crisis due to the fact that they have perpetrated, witnessed, or failed to prevent battlefield events that run against the grain of identified or unidentified, but viscerally felt and 'known,' personal moral or ethical views and commitments" (Levine, "Legal War," 220–21).

"Perpetrating, failing to prevent, or bearing witness to acts that transgress deeply held moral beliefs and expectations may be deleterious in the longterm, emotionally, psychologically, behaviorally, spiritually, and socially" (Litz et al., "Moral Injury and Moral Repair," 695).

"In the context of war, moral injuries may stem from direct participation in acts of combat, such as killing or harming others, or indirect acts, such as witnessing death or dying, failing to prevent immoral acts of others, or giving or receiving orders that are perceived as gross moral violation. The act may have been carried out by an individual or a group" (Maguen and Litz, "Moral Injury in the Context of War," 1).

"An act of serious transgression that leads to serious inner conflict because the experience is at odds with core ethical and moral beliefs" (Shira Maguen and Brett Litz, "Moral Injury in Veterans of War," *PTSD Research Quarterly* 23 [2012]:1).

"The violation, by oneself or another, of a personally embedded moral code or value resulting in deep injury to the psyche or soul" (Meagher, *Killing from the Inside Out*, xvi–xvii).[3]

"A betrayal of 'what's right' by someone who holds legitimate authority in a 'high-stakes situation'" (Shay, *Achilles in Vietnam*, 208).

"Roughly speaking, it refers to experiences of serious inner conflict arising from what one takes to be grievous moral transgressions that can overwhelm one's sense of goodness and humanity... [sometimes having] less to do with specific (real or apparent) transgressive acts than with a generalized sense of falling short of moral and normative standards befitting good persons and good soldiers" (Sherman, *Afterwar*, 8).

Notes

Preface and Acknowledgments

1. Albert Einstein, *Why War? The Correspondence between Albert Einstein and Sigmund Freud* (Chicago: Chicago Psychoanalytic Institute, 1978), 1.

1. Introduction

1. Quoted in Rita Nakashima Brock and Gabriella Lettini, *Soul Repair: Recovering from Moral Injury after War* (Boston: Beacon, 2012), 99.

2. See especially Brett T. Litz et al., "Moral Injury and Moral Repair in War Veterans: A Preliminary Model and Intervention Strategy," *Clinical Psychology Review* 29 (2009): 696.

3. For discussion and examples of these societal tendencies, see Brock and Lettini, *Soul Repair*, 93 and the accounts presented throughout that book.

4. Robert Emmet Meagher and Douglas A. Pryer, "Introduction," in *War and Moral Injury: A Reader*, ed. Robert Emmet Meagher and Douglas A. Pryer (Eugene, OR: Cascade, 2018), 1.

5. Larry Kent Graham, *Moral Injury: Restoring Wounded Souls* (Nashville: Abingdon, 2017).

6. See Brad E. Kelle, *Ancient Israel at War 853–586 BC*, Essential Histories 67 (Oxford: Osprey, 2007); Brad E. Kelle, "Dealing with the Trauma of Defeat: The Rhetoric of the Devastation and Rejuvenation of Nature in

Ezekiel," *JBL* 128 (2009): 469–90; Brad E. Kelle, *Ezekiel: A Commentary in the Wesleyan Tradition*, New Beacon Bible Commentary (Kansas City, MO: Beacon Hill, 2013).

7. For recent treatments of moral injury aimed at chaplains and Christian ministers, see Graham, *Moral Injury*; Wollom A. Jensen and James M. Childs, *Moral Warriors, Moral Wounds: The Ministry of the Christian Ethic* (Eugene, OR: Cascade, 2016); Duane Larson and Jeff Zust, *Care for the Sorrowing Soul: Healing Moral Injuries from Military Service and Implications for the Rest of Us* (Eugene, OR: Cascade, 2017); Lindsay B. Carey et al., "Moral Injury, Spiritual Care and the Role of Chaplains: An Exploratory Scoping Review of Literature and Resources," *Journal of Religious Health* 55 (2016): 1218–45; J. M. Childs, "Moral Injury and the Priesthood of All Believers," *Dialog* 57 (2018): 111–19; Lewis Jeff Lee, *Moral Injury Reconciliation: A Practitioner's Guide for Treating Moral Injury, PTSD, Grief, and Military Sexual Trauma through Spiritual Formation Strategies* (London: Jessica Kingsley, 2018); Timothy J. Hodgson and Lindsay B. Carey, "Moral Injury and Definitional Clarity: Betrayal, Spirituality and the Role of Chaplains," *Journal of Religious Health* 56 (2017): 1212–18; Zachary Moon, "'Turn Now, My Vindication Is at Stake': Military Moral Injury and Communities of Faith," *Pastoral Psychology*, November, 21 2017. https://doi.org/10.1007/s11089-017-0795-8.

8. Meagher and Pryer, "Introduction," 3.

9. The next chapter will describe how moral injury has intersected with biblical studies so far. For a convenient example, see Edward Tick, *Warrior's Return: Restoring the Soul after War* (Boulder, CO: Sounds True, 2014). He makes extensive references to Old Testament texts, including the stories of Saul and David (pp. 91–93; 111–15), Job (pp. 199–202), and postwar purification rituals such as Num 31 (pp. 194–98).

10. See information from the Office of Public and Intergovernmental Affairs: "VA Releases National Suicide Data Report," (June 18, 2018). https://www.va.gov/opa/pressrel/pressrelease.cfm?id=4074.

11. M. L. Kelley et al., "Moral Injury and Suicidality among Combat-Wounded Veterans: The Moderating Effects of Social Connectedness and Self-Compassion," *Psychological Trauma*. March 21, 2019. doi: 10.1037/tra0000447.

12. Douglas A. Pryer, "What We Don't Talk about When We Talk about War," in Meagher and Pryer, *War and Moral Injury: A Reader,* 68–69. In 2012, Brock and Lettini (*Soul Repair,* xii) noted veterans' suicides averaged one every eighty minutes. Another study focused on January 2009 through July 2012 reported that the army recorded 933 confirmed or suspected suicides among active duty, national guard, or reserve soldiers during that period (see Warren Kinghorn, "Combat Trauma and Moral Fragmentation: A Theological Account of Moral Injury," *Journal of the Society of Christian Ethics* 32 [2012]: 58).

13. Pryer, "What We Don't Talk About," 69.

14. Jennifer H. Wortmann et al., "Spiritual Features of War-Related Moral Injury: A Primer for Clinicians," *Spirituality in Clinical Practice* 4 (2017): 250.

15. Blair E. Wisco et al., "Moral Injury in U.S. Combat Veterans: Results from the National Health and Resilience in Veterans Study," *Depress Anxiety* 34 (2017): 340. https://doi.org/10.1002/da.22614.

16. William P. Nash and Christa Davis Acampora, "Foreword," in Meagher and Pryer, *War and Moral Injury: A Reader*, xxvi.

17. See discussion of these surveys in Carey et al. "Moral Injury, Spiritual Care," 1218–45.

18. See Brad E. Kelle, *Telling the Old Testament Story: God's Mission and God's People* (Nashville: Abingdon, 2017), 6–7.

19. For the only major recent collection of essays that explores these kinds of connections between moral injury and sacred texts (including but not limited to the Bible), see Joseph McDonald, ed., *Exploring Moral Injury in Sacred Texts*, Studies in Religion and Theology (London: Jessica Kingsley, 2017).

20. Robert Emmet Meagher, *Killing from the Inside Out: Moral Injury and Just War* (Eugene, OR: Cascade, 2014).

21. Meagher, *Killing from the Inside Out: Moral Injury and Just War*, xiv. Meagher concludes that the moral injury frame of reference for scripture and

tradition shows that modern-day military suicide is "not some undecipher-able, modern or even postmodern, aberration, without deep roots in our shared human past. Rather, it is the lamentable legacy of a long tradition of justified war and inevitable moral injury" (p. xvi).

22. As a witness to the prominence of this issue, note the recent reference-type volume published particularly for Christian audiences: Jerome F. D. Creach, *Violence in Scripture*, Interpretation: Resources for the Use of Scripture in the Church (Louisville, KY: Westminster John Knox), 2013.

23. Tom Frame, "Introduction," in *Moral Injury: Unseen Wounds in an Age of Barbarism*, ed. Tom Frame (Sydney, Australia: UNSW Press, 2015), 3.

24. See Frame, "Introduction," 8.

25. E.g., an article examining religious affiliation reporting options in the military identified 40 percent of active duty personnel as evangelical Christian. See Kate Shellnutt, "Why the US Military Wants Fewer Generic Christians," *Christianity Today*, May 30, 2017. https://www.christianitytoday.com/news/2017/may/why-us-military-fewer-generic-christians-216-religions.html.

26. Most notably, Joseph M. Currier et al. ("Military Veterans' Preferences for Incorporating Spirituality in Psychotherapy or Counseling," *Professional Psychology: Research and Practice* 49 [2018]: 39–47) surveyed veterans and found that they ranked the incorporation of spirituality in their psychological treatment as "somewhat" important and supported an approach that allowed for religion and spirituality but without the presumption of its importance in every case. See also Wortmann et al., "Spiritual Features," 249–61; Marek S. Kopacz et al., "Towards a Faith-Based Understanding of Moral Injury," *Journal of Pastoral Care and Counseling* 71 (2017): 217–19; Lee, *Moral Injury Reconciliation*.

27. See Kinghorn, "Combat Trauma," 57–74.

28. Tom Frame ("Moral Injury and the Influence of Christian Religious Conviction," in Meagher and Pryer, *War and Moral Injury: A Reader*, 191) provides the important caveat that people's notions of right and wrong are at

least partially shaped by political, social, and cultural factors, and often lack consistency and coherency.

29. See discussion in Shira Maguen and Brett Litz, "Moral Injury in the Context of War." https://www.ptsd.va.gov/professional/treat/cooccurring/moral_injury.asp.

30. See Brett T. Litz et al., *Adaptive Disclosure: A New Treatment for Military Trauma, Loss, and Moral Injury* (New York: The Guilford Press, 2016), 17, 29–42; Lee, *Moral Injury Reconciliation*, 8–9.

31. Zachary Moon, *Warriors Between Worlds: Moral Injury and Identities in Crisis*, Emerging Perspectives in Pastoral Theology and Care (Lanham, MD: Lexington, 2019).

32. On this point, see Joseph Wiinikka-Lydon, "Moral Injury as Inherent Political Critique: The Prophetic Possibilities of a New Term," *Political Theology* 18 (2017): 222.

33. So Frame, "Moral Injury and the Influence of Christian Religious Conviction," 195.

34. See the definition of moral conscience in Brock and Lettini, *Soul Repair*, 102.

35. Kinghorn, "Combat Trauma," 67.

36. Kinghorn, "Combat Trauma," 70. For other studies that use theological categories such as the image of God and the telos of love for God and neighbor to describe what is violated in moral injury, see Kopacz et al., "Towards a Faith-Based Understanding," 217–19, and Wortmann et al., "Spiritual Features," 249–61. For the most extensive theological engagement of moral injury, particularly using Augustinian theology, see Brian S. Powers, *Full Darkness: Original Sin, Moral Injury, and Wartime Violence* (Grand Rapids: Eerdmans, 2019). See a synopsis of this work in Brian S. Powers, "Moral Injury and Original Sin: The Applicability of Augustinian Moral Psychology in Light of Combat Trauma," *Theology Today* 73 (2017): 325–37. See discussion of Powers's work in ch. 2 to follow.

2. Moral Injury and Biblical Interpretation

1. Camillo Mac Bica, *Beyond PTSD: The Moral Casualties of War*, War Legacy Series: Book Two (Commack, NY: Gnosis, 2016), 80.

2. Rita Nakashima Brock and Gabriella Lettini, *Soul Repair: Recovering from Moral Injury after War* (Boston: Beacon, 2012), xv.

3. The most up-to-date (at the time of this book) review of the literature, especially clinical publications, on moral injury is Brandon J. Griffin et al., "Moral Injury: An Integrative Review," *Journal of Traumatic Stress* (2019). doi: 10.1002/jts.22362. This review identifies 116 epidemiological and clinical studies on moral injury from 2009 to 2019, not counting the numerous non-scientific publications.

4. Pryer (Douglas A. Pryer, "What We Don't Talk about When We Talk about War," in *War and Moral Injury: A Reader*, ed. Robert Emmet Meagher and Douglas A. Pryer [Eugene, OR: Cascade, 2018], 63n7) notes that as early as the 1720s, the sermons of Bishop Joseph Butler contained references to war injuries that were moral in nature (see his Sermon VIII, "Upon Resentment and Forgiveness of Injuries," in Joseph Butler, *Fifteen Sermons* [London: Bell and Sons, 1964]). In modern contexts, the first and most sustained discussions of moral injury appear in the works of VA psychologist Jonathan Shay. See Jonathan Shay, *Achilles in Vietnam: Combat Trauma and the Undoing of Character* (New York: Touchstone, 1994) and Jonathan Shay, *Odysseus in America: Combat Trauma and the Trials of Homecoming* (New York: Scribner, 2002).

5. A 2013 study reported that the Department of Defense was spending $1.5 million on research into the possible treatments for moral injury. See Martha Bebinger, "Defining the Deep Pain PTSD Doesn't Capture," WBUR News, June 24, 2013, www.wbur.org/news/2013/06/24/moral-injury-tyler-boudreau.

6. *Ender's Game* features a young protagonist who completes a series of space war games, culminating with his destroying the enemy's home planet. He later learns that the games were real and that he had destroyed real beings and their planet. This knowledge results in guilt, dysfunction, depression,

and the search for atoning actions within religion and elsewhere, which carry through several subsequent books.

7. William P. Nash and Christa Davis Acampora, "Foreword," in Meagher and Pryer, *War and Moral Injury: A Reader*, xxiv.

8. Nash and Acompora, "Foreword," xxiv.

9. Glenn William Orris, "Moral Injury and PTSD: Toward an Integrated Model of Complex, Combat-related Trauma," (PhD diss., Pacifica Graduate Institute, 2017), iii.

10. The American Psychiatric Association (APA) first accepted PTSD as a diagnosis in 1980, especially in light of the experiences of veterans after the Vietnam War. For a convenient summary of today's prominent theories of PTSD, see Brett T. Litz et al., "Moral Injury and Moral Repair in War Veterans: A Preliminary Model and Intervention Strategy," *Clinical Psychology Review* 29 (2009): 698–99.

11. See Litz et al., "Moral Injury and Moral Repair," 696, 698; Cathy Caruth, *Unclaimed Experience: Trauma, Narrative, and History* (Baltimore: Johns Hopkins University Press, 1996), 11; Judith Herman, *Trauma and Recovery: The Aftermath of Violence—from Domestic Abuse to Political Terror*, 2nd ed. (New York: Basic, 1997).

12. See Daniel L. Smith-Christopher, *A Biblical Theology of Exile*, OBT (Minneapolis: Fortress, 2002); Kathleen M. O'Connor, *Jeremiah: Pain and Promise* (Minneapolis: Fortress, 2011); Brad E. Kelle, *Ezekiel: A Commentary in the Wesleyan Tradition*, New Beacon Bible Commentary (Kansas City, MO: Beacon Hill, 2013).

13. Shay, *Achilles in Vietnam*; Shay, *Odysseus in America*. The definition of PTSD in the *DSM-5* gives criteria that require exposure to actual or threatened fear-inducing events such as death or serious physical injury (see Orris, "Moral Injury and PTSD," 31). By contrast, moral injury is a "value-based injury from severe moral dissonance" (Duane Larson and Jeff Zust, *Care for the Sorrowing Soul: Healing Moral Injuries from Military Service and Implications for the Rest of Us* [Eugene, OR: Cascade, 2017], 59).

14. Litz et. al., "Moral Injury and Moral Repair," 699 (italics original). Recent literature indicates this focus with some new terminology: "collective harmdoing" and "Perpetration-Induced Traumatic Stress." See *Peace and Conflict: A Journal of Peace Psychology* 21 (2015) and Rachel M. MacNair, *Perpetration-Induced Traumatic Stress: The Psychological Consequences of Killing* (Westport, CT: Praeger, 2002).

15. See the recent behavioral science study of the links between moral injury experiences and PTSD factors in Joseph M. Currier et al., "Temporal Associations between Moral Injury and Posttraumatic Stress Disorder Symptom Clusters in Military Veterans," *Journal of Traumatic Stress* (2019). doi: 10.1002/jts.22367. See also the recent discussion of "differentiating" PTSD from moral injury in Larson and Zust, *Care for the Sorrowing Soul*, 59–65.

16. Compare Litz et al., "Moral Injury and Moral Repair"; William P. Nash and Brett T. Litz, "Moral Injury: A Mechanism for War-Related Psychological Trauma in Military Family Members," *Clinical Child Family Psychology Review* 16 (2013): 365–75; Tyler Boudreau, "The Morally Injured," *Massachusetts Review* (Fall–Winter 2011–2012): 746–54.

17. See See discussion in Shira Maguen and Brett Litz, "Moral Injury in the Context of War," 2, https://www.ptsd.va.gov/profesional/treat/cooccurring/moral_injury.asp. Tom Frame, ed., *Moral Injury: Unseen Wounds in an Age of Barbarism* (Sydney, Australia: UNSW Press, 2015), 2; Nash and Acampora, "Foreword," xxv. Perhaps another possibility is to expand the defining criteria of PTSD to include morally injurious events rather than creating a distinct diagnostic category (see Orris, "Moral Injury and PTSD," 29).

18. From Amy Amidon, "Guest Perspective: Moral Injury and Moral Repair," *Center for Deployment Psychology*, January 3, 2016, 1–7. http://deploymentpsych.org/blog/guest-perspective-moral-injury-and-moral-repair.

19. From David Wood, "The Grunts: Damned If They Kill, Damned If They Don't," March 18, 2014, *Huffington Post*, http://projects.huffingtonpost.com/moral-injury/the-grunts.

20. Wood, "The Grunts."

21. Wood, "The Grunts."

22. See, e.g., Bica, *Beyond PTSD*; Brock and Lettini, *Soul Repair*; David Wood, *What Have We Done: The Moral Injury of America's Longest Wars* (New York: Brown and Company, 2016); Karl Marlantes, *What It Is Like to Go to War* (New York: Atlantic Monthly, 2011).

23. Bica (*Beyond PTSD*, 4) explains, "They are as much combat injuries as a shrapnel-broken tibia."

24. See especially Litz et al., "Moral Injury and Moral Repair"; Kent D. Drescher et al., "An Exploration of the Viability and Usefulness of the Construct of Moral Injury on War Veterans," *Traumatology* 17 (2011): 8–13; Nash and Litz, "Moral Injury"; Maguen and Litz, "Moral Injury in the Context of War"; William P. Nash et al., "Psychometric Evaluation of the Moral Injury Events Scale," *Military Medicine* 178 (2013): 646–52; J. M. Currier, J. M. Holland, and J. Malott, "Moral Injury, Meaning Making, and Mental Health in Returning Veterans," *Journal of Clinical Psychology* 71 (2015): 229–40. For an accessible, nontechnical history of the development of the notion of moral injury and its initial clinical treatments within the military, see Wood, *What Have We Done*, 116–32.

25. Shay, *Achilles in Vietnam*; Shay, *Odysseus in America*.

26. Shay, *Achilles in Vietnam*, 208.

27. For these insights and discussion of Shay's formulation compared to more recent formulations, see Orris, "Moral Injury and PTSD," 9–13.

28. Joseph Wiinikka-Lydon, "Moral Injury as Inherent Political Critique: The Prophetic Possibilities of a New Term," *Political Theology* 18 (2017): 219.

29. See Alice Lynd and Staughton Lynd, *Moral Injury and Nonviolent Resistence: Breaking the Cycle of Violence in the Military and Behind Bars* (Oakland, CA: PM Press, 2017), 19.

30. Litz et al., "Moral Injury and Moral Repair," 695.

31. See Orris, "Moral Injury and PTSD," 9.

32. In a more pointed statement, Timothy J. Hodgson and Lindsay B. Carey ("Moral Injury and Definitional Clarity: Betrayal, Spirituality and the

Role of Chaplains," *Journal of Religious Health* 56 [2017]: 1217) assert, "It can be argued that in recent years some researchers have deliberately used Litz et al.'s (2009) clinical description of moral injury to exclude Shay's political and somewhat controversial consideration of 'betrayal' as being caused by legitimate authorities."

33. See Brett Litz, "Moral Injury: Assessment, Conceptualization and Treatment Strategies" (paper presented at the Australian Conference on Traumatic Stress, "Public Issues-Private Trauma," Queensland, Australia, September 8–10, 2016).

34. Amidon, "Guest Perspective," 2.

35. Amidon, "Guest Perspective," 3–4.

36. Maguen and Litz, "Moral Injury in the Context of War," 1.

37. Boudreau, "The Morally Injured," 53–54 (italics original).

38. Sean Levine, "Legal War, Sin, and 'Moral Injury' in the Age of Modern Warfare," in Meagher and Pryer, *War and Moral Injury: A Reader*, 220–21.

39. Larson and Zust, *Care for the Sorrowing Soul*, 5.

40. Larry Kent Graham, *Moral Injury: Restoring Wounded Souls* (Nashville: Abingdon, 2017), xi. For an extended use of "soul" as part of defining moral injury as a "soul wound," see Edward Tick, *Warrior's Return: Restoring the Soul after War* (Boulder, CO: Sounds True, 2014), 5 and Edward Tick, *War and the Soul: Healing Our Nation's Veterans from Post-traumatic Stress Disorder* (Wheaton, IL: Quest, 2005).

41. Nancy Sherman, *Afterwar: Healing the Moral Wounds of Our Soldiers* (Oxford: Oxford University Press, 2015), 8.

42. J. D. Jinkerson, "Defining and Assessing Moral Injury: A Syndrome Perspective," *Traumatology* 22 (2016): 126 (italics original).

43. See Nash and Litz, "Moral Injury," 368; Lynd and Lynd, *Moral Injury and Nonviolent Resistance*, 20.

44. Compare Brock and Lettini, *Soul Repair*, 93–115 and Sherman, *Afterwar*, 103.

45. Recently, see Lynd and Lynd, *Moral Injury and Nonviolent Resistance.* For the role of moral emotions in the preservation of social relationships, see Jacob K. Farnsworth et al., "The Role of Moral Emotions in Military Trauma: Implications for the Study and Treatment of Moral Injury," *Review of General Psychology* 18 (2014): 249–62.

46. Bica, *Beyond PTSD*, 73.

47. Larson and Zust, *Care for the Sorrowing Soul*, 15.

48. See Nikki Coleman, "Moral Status and Reintegration," in Frame, *Moral Injury*, 205–8.

49. Ronnie Janoff-Bulman, *Shattered Assumptions: Toward a New Psychology of Trauma* (New York: The Free Press, 1992), 4–6.

50. Nash et al., "Psychometric Evaluation," 646–52.

51. Litz et al., "Moral Injury and Moral Repair," 696.

52. See the nuanced explanation of the shifting of dynamic "moral orienting systems" and identity as the root of moral injury in Zachary Moon, *Warriors Between Worlds: Moral Injury and Identities in Crisis*, Emerging Perspectives in Pastoral Theology and Care (Lanham, MD: Lexington, 2019).

53. Litz et al., "Moral Injury and Moral Repair," 700–701.

54. Bica, *Beyond PTSD*, 16. So also Frame, "Moral Injury and the Influence of Christian Religious Conviction," in Meagher and Pryer, *War and Moral Injury: A Reader*, 246–47.

55. Bica, *Beyond PTSD*, 18–19. For a comprehensive analysis of the techniques used by the military to break down recruits' moral aversion to killing, see Dave Grossman, *On Killing: The Psychological Cost of Learning to Kill in War and Society*, rev. ed. (New York: Back Bay Books, 2009).

56. Farnsworth et al., "The Role of Moral Emotions," 254–56.

57. Pete Kilner, "Moral Injury: Personal, Organizational, and Divine Betrayals," *Thoughts of a Soldier-Ethicist* (blog), Nov. 1, 2016. http://soldier -ethicist.blogspot.com/2017/03/a-third-form-of-moral-injury.html.

58. For a clinical study related to how morally injured veterans may have a spiritual struggle of turmoil with God or a higher power, see Joseph M. Currier, J. D. Foster, and S. L. Isaak, "Moral Injury and Spiritual Struggles in Military Veterans: A Latent Profile Analysis," *Journal of Traumatic Stress* (March 12, 2019). doi: 10.1002/jts.22378.

59. A comprehensive international clinical study is underway to measure the way that moral injury occurs as an outcome of various potentially morally injurious events, and findings thus far indicate an established connection between such events and the outcomes that reflect psychological, behavioral, social, and spiritual impacts that have been identified under the label *moral injury*. See Julie D. Yeterian et al., "Defining and Measuring Moral Injury: Rationale, Design, and Preliminary Findings from the Moral Injury Outcome Scale Consortium," *Journal of Traumatic Stress* (2019). doi: 10.1002/ jts.22380.

60. Harold G. Koenig et al., "The Moral Injury Symptom Scale—Military Version," *Journal of Religion and Health* 57 (2018): 249–65. For lists of commonly identified symptoms and signs of moral injury, see Hodgson and Carey, "Moral Injury and Definitional Clarity," 1218; Nash and Litz, "Moral Injury," 369.

61. Joseph M. Currier et al., "Development and Evaluation of the Expressions of Moral Injury Scale—Military Version," *Clinical Psychology and Psychotherapy* 25 (2017): 474–88.

62. See Drescher et al., "Exploration," 8; Nash and Litz, "Moral Injury," 369.

63. J. Irene Harris et al., "Moral Injury and Psycho-Spiritual Development: Considering the Developmental Context," *Spirituality in Clinical Practice* 19 (2015): 6

64. Brian S. Powers, *Full Darkness: Original Sin, Moral Injury, and Wartime Violence* (Grand Rapids: Eerdmans, 2019); Brian S. Powers, "Moral In-

jury and Original Sin: The Applicability of Augustinian Moral Psychology in Light of Combat Trauma," *Theology Today* 73 (2017): 325–37.

65. Powers, "Moral Injury and Original Sin," 326.

66. Powers, "Moral Injury and Original Sin," 327.

67. Powers, "Moral Injury and Original Sin," 327.

68. Powers, "Moral Injury and Original Sin," 333. Similarly, Christopher Hansen ("Glimmers of the Infinite: The Tragedy of Moral Injury," *Dialog* 58 [2019]: 64–69. doi.org/10.1111/dial.12454) draws on Paul Tillich's notion of fulfillment coming from placing faith in something that is truly "ultimate" in order to articulate moral injury. Soldiers can suffer moral injury when what was thought to be ultimate (perhaps, in the soldier's mind, the military or its mission) is revealed to be penultimate or even evil.

69. For an accessible survey of the development of healing approaches for moral injury, see Wood, *What Have We Done*, 234–50.

70. Litz et al., "Moral Injury and Moral Repair," 700–701.

71. See the summary of repair approaches linked to particular symptoms in Hodgson and Carey, "Moral Injury and Definitional Clarity," 1218.

72. See Maguen and Litz, "Moral Injury in the Context of War," 3 and Brett T. Litz et al., *Adaptive Disclosure: A New Treatment for Military Trauma, Loss, and Moral Injury* (New York: The Guilford Press, 2016).

73. Wood, *What Have We Done*, 250.

74. For discussion of various approaches to healing and repair, see Cecilia Yocum, *Help for Moral Injury: Strategies and Interventions* (Fayetteville, NC: Quaker House, 2016); Litz et al., "Moral Injury and Moral Repair," 700–701; Graham, *Moral Injury*, 98; Stefan J. Malecek, "The Moral Inversion of War," in Meagher and Pryer, *War and Moral Injury: A Reader*, 292–300.

75. Litz et al., *Adaptive Disclosure*, 17.

76. For example, Shay (*Odysseus in America*, 245) envisioned a "communal ritual with religious force" that could use resources from religion, the arts,

mental health professionals, and elsewhere. See also Litz et al., "Moral Injury and Moral Repair," 704.

77. Shay, *Odysseus in America*, 5–6.

78. Sherman, *Afterwar*, 161. See also Tick, *Warrior's Return*.

79. Boudreau, "The Morally Injured," 55.

80. See Tick, *Warrior's Return*, 212–13.

81. Charles W. Grimsley and Gaylene Grimsley, *PTSD and Moral Injury: The Journey to Healing through Forgiveness* (Mesa, CO: Xulon, 2017), 33–35. They also use Deuteronomy's teaching on remembering, and forgiveness in the passion narratives in the Gospels (p. 67).

82. See Shay, *Odysseus in America*, 152. For similar references to Old Testament rituals, see Tick, *War and the Soul*, 3; Tick, *Warrior's Return*, 194–98, 206–7; Larson and Zust, *Care for the Sorrowing Soul*, 164; Wood, *What Have We Done*, 5; Graham, *Moral Injury*, 135–52.

83. See Tick's (*Warrior's Return*, 91–93, 111–15, 199–202) use of Saul, David, and Job; Larson and Zust's (*Care for the Sorrowing Soul*, 164) use of Saul and David, as well as the Roman centurions in the New Testament (pp. 160–92).

84. Lewis Jeff Lee, *Moral Injury Reconciliation: A Practitioner's Guide for Treating Moral Injury, PTSD, Grief, and Military Sexual Trauma through Spiritual Formation Strategies* (London: Jessica Kingsley, 2018), 27, 100–101.

85. J. M. Childs, "Moral Injury and the Priesthood of All Believers," *Dialog* 57 (2018): 115.

86. Brock and Lettini, *Soul Repair*, 26; Graham, *Moral Injury*, 135–57; Lee, *Moral Injury Reconciliation*, 110–11.

87. Kim S. Geringer and Nancy H. Wiener, "Insights into Moral Injury and Soul Repair from Classical Jewish Texts," *Pastoral Psychology* 68 (2019): 59–75. https://doi.org/10.1007/s11089-018-0848-7.

88. Brad E. Kelle, "Post-war Rituals of Return and Reintegration of Warriors," in *Warfare, Ritual, and Symbol in Biblical and Modern Contexts*, ed. Brad E. Kelle, Frank Ritchel Ames, and Jacob L. Wright, Ancient Israel and Its Literature 28 (Atlanta: Society of Biblical Literature, 2014), 205–42; Brad E. Kelle, "Moral Injury and the Division of Spoils after Battle in the Hebrew Bible," in *Exploring Moral Injury in Sacred Texts*, ed. Joseph McDonald, Studies in Religion and Theology (London: Jessica Kingsley, 2017), 83–102.

89. Nancy R. Bowen, "Sodom and Lot's Family: Moral Injury in Genesis 19," in McDonald, *Exploring Moral Injury in Sacred Texts*, 47–68.

90. David R. Blumenthal, "Soul Repair: A Jewish View," in McDonald, *Exploring Moral Injury in Sacred Texts*, 33–46.

91. Michael Yandell, "'Do Not Torment Me': The Morally Injured Gerasene Demoniac," in McDonald, *Exploring Moral Injury in Sacred Texts*, 135–50. On the New Testament, see also Warren Carter, "Peter and Judas: Moral Injury and Moral Repair," in McDonald, *Exploring Moral Injury in Sacred Texts*, 151–68.

3. Moral Injury and the Case of King Saul

1. Friedrich Nietzsche, *Beyond Good and Evil: Prelude to a Philosophy of the Future*, Dover Thrift Editions (Mineola, NY: Dover, 1997), 52.

2. This chapter is adapted from Brad E. Kelle, "Moral Injury and the Interdisciplinary Study of Biblical War Texts: The Case of King Saul," in *Worship, Women, and War: Essays in Honor of Susan Niditch*, ed. John J. Collins, T. M. Lemos, and Saul M. Olyan, Brown Judaic Studies 357 (Providence, RI: Brown Judaic Studies, 2015), 147–72. Used here with permission.

3. E.g., Jonathan Shay, *Achilles in Vietnam: Combat Trauma and the Undoing of Character* (New York: Touchstone, 1994); Jonathan Shay, *Odysseus in America: Combat Trauma and the Trials of Homecoming* (New York: Scribner, 2002); Nancy R. Bowen, "Sodom and Lot's Family: Moral Injury in Genesis 19," in *Exploring Moral Injury in Sacred Texts*, Studies in Religion and Theology, ed. Joseph McDonald (London: Jessica Kingsley, 2017),135–50;

Michael Yandell, "'Do Not Torment Me': The Morally Injured Gerasene Demoniac," in McDonald, *Exploring Moral Injury in Sacred Texts*, 135–50.

4. Shay, *Odysseus in America*, 3.

5. Shay, *Achilles in Vietnam*, xx.

6. Shay, *Achilles in Vietnam*, 4.

7. Shay, *Odysseus in America*, xv.

8. Shay, *Odysseus in America*, xvi, 2.

9. Peter Meineck and David Konstan, eds., *Combat Trauma and the Ancient Greeks*, The New Antiquity (New York: Palgrave Macmillan, 2014), xi–xii. The essays in this volume originated in a traveling program devoted to bringing veterans together with public readings and theatrical performances of ancient Greek epics and tragedies.

10. See David Konstan, "War and Reconciliation in Greek Literature," in *War and Peace in the Ancient World*, ed. Kurt A. Raaflaub (Oxford: Blackwell, 2007) and Robert Emmet Meagher, *Herakles Gone Mad: Rethinking Heroism in an Age of Endless War* (New York: Olive Branch, 2006).

11. See Sherman, *Afterwar*, 81–97; Pryer, "What We Don't Talk About," 64; Jan Helge Solbakk, "You Can't Go Home Again: On the Conceptualization of Disasters in Ancient Greek Tragedy," in *Disasters: Core Concepts and Ethical Theories*, eds. Dónal P. O'Mathúna, Vilius Dranseika, and Bert Gordijin; Advancing Global Bioethics 11 (Cham, Switzerland: Springer Open, 2018), 87–104.

12. See Nancy Sherman, *Afterwar: Healing the Moral Wounds of Our Soldiers* (Oxford: Oxford University Press, 2015), 114–24, and Robert Emmet Meagher, *Killing from the Inside Out: Moral Injury and Just War* (Eugene, OR: Cascade, 2014), 5–8.

13. Sherman, *Afterwar*, 115.

14. Edward Tick, *Warrior's Return: Restoring the Soul after War* (Boulder, CO: Sounds True, 2014), 60.

15. Charles W. Grimsley and Gaylene Grimsley, *PTSD and Moral Injury: The Journey to Healing through Forgiveness* (Mesa, CO: Xulon, 2017), 36–49.

16. E.g., Tick, *Warrior's Return*, 91–93, 111–15, 199–202; Duane Larson and Jeff Zust, *Care for the Sorrowing Soul: Healing Moral Injuries from Military Service and Implications for the Rest of Us* (Eugene, OR: Cascade, 2017), 164. Larson and Zust (pp. 160–92) also provide a New Testament example by interpreting the stories of the Roman centurions and their encounters with Jesus in Luke and Acts to explore different types of military behavior in the context of a discussion of moral injury.

17. Arthur W. Frank, *The Wounded Storyteller: Body, Illness, and Ethics* (Chicago: University of Chicago Press, 2013), 181–82.

18. See Bowen, "Sodom and Lot's Family"; David R. Blumenthal, "Soul Repair: A Jewish View," in McDonald, *Exploring Moral Injury in Sacred Texts*, 33–46; Warren Carter, "Peter and Judas: Moral Injury and Moral Repair," in McDonald, *Exploring Moral Injury in Sacred Texts*, 151–68; and Yandell, "Do Not Torment Me."

19. See Hanna Liss, "The Innocent King: Saul in Rabbinic Exegesis," in *Saul in Story and Tradition*, ed. Carl S. Ehrlich in cooperation with Marsha C. White, FAT 47 (Tübingen: Mohr Siebeck, 2006), 245–60 and Barbara Green, *King Saul's Asking*, Interfaces (Collegeville, MN: Liturgical, 2003).

20. See, e.g., the presentation of Saul in John Bright, *A History of Israel*, 4th ed., Westminster Aids to the Study of Scripture (Louisville, KY: Westminster John Knox, 2000). For an older reading of Saul as suffering a psychological disorder, see H. C. Ackerman, "Saul: A Psychotherapeutic Analysis," *Anglican Theological Review* 3 (1920): 114–24.

21. For discussion, see David M. Gunn, *The Fate of King Saul: An Interpretation of a Biblical Story*, JSOTSup 14 (Sheffield, UK: JSOT Press, 1980), 23–26.

22. For standard discussions of the literary history issue, see Ralph W. Klein, *1 Samuel*, WBC 10 (Waco, TX: Word, 1983), 101 and Bruce C. Birch, "The First and Second Books of Samuel," in *The New Interpreter's Bible*, vol. 2 (Nashville: Abingdon, 1998), 1031–32. In contrast to some

earlier scholarship, recent commentators do not try to distinguish clearly between supposedly promonarchical and anti-monarchical sources within the text. For an analysis of the text's narrative structure and literary devices, see Diana Vikander Edelman, *King Saul in the Historiography of Judah*, JSOTSup 121 (Sheffield, UK: JSOT Press, 1991).

23. Note, for example, that Saul's anointing by Samuel in ch. 9 is accompanied by three divine signs that confirm Saul's appointment as ruler. For the traditions that preserve more negative assessments of kingship, see 8:1-22 and 10:17-27.

24. On compositional and editorial issues for 1 Sam 12, see P. Kyle McCarter Jr., *I Samuel*, AB 8 (Garden City, NY: Doubleday, 1980), 195.

25. Walter Brueggemann, *First and Second Samuel*, Interpretation (Louisville, KY: Westminster John Knox, 1990), 89.

26. See Brueggemann, *First and Second Samuel*, 92; Klein, *1 Samuel*, 113; Birch, "First and Second Books of Samuel," 1062.

27. See Gunn, *The Fate of King Saul*, 65; Sarah Nicholson, *Three Faces of Saul: An Intertextual Approach to Biblical Tragedy*, JSOTSup 339 (Sheffield, UK: Sheffield Academic, 2002), 106.

28. Scholars have explored the possibility that chs. 13 and 15 may be two versions of the same event. See David Toshio Tsumura, *The First Book of Samuel*, NICOT (Grand Rapids: Eerdmans, 2007), 387.

29. The text clearly represents the theological perspective of the deuteronomistic historians that centers on obedience, disobedience, and retribution and is driven by the commitment to establish David as the one chosen by Yhwh to lead Israel. Many interpreters simply follow this perspective and conclude that Saul lacked faith in Yhwh, failed a test of obedience, and acted selfishly in violation of an earlier prophetic instruction or a more general law concerning legitimate priestly sacrifice (see, e.g., Tsumura, *First Book of Samuel*, 346).

30. See especially Brueggemann, *First and Second Samuel*, 98–101; Gunn, *The Fate of King Saul*, 39; Birch, "First and Second Books of Samuel,"

1071; and David Jobling, *1 Samuel*, Berit Olam (Collegeville, MN: Liturgical, 1998), 81.

31. No such commandment of Yhwh had previously been mentioned in the text, and scholars have proposed a number of hypotheses (see discussion in Tsumura, *First Book of Samuel*, 347–48). On the ambiguity of the period of seven days in 10:8, see Tsumura, *First Book of Samuel*, 290 and Jobling, *1 Samuel*, 81. Robert Polzin (*Samuel and the Deuteronomist: A Literary Study of the Deuteronomic History*, part 2, *1 Samuel* [Bloomington: Indiana University Press, 1989], 107) notes that Samuel's failure to arrive in the time specified by 10:8 actually suggests the prescription in Deut 18:22 that identifies a false prophet as one who speaks a word in Yhwh's name that does not come to pass.

32. Jobling, *1 Samuel*, 81. So also Brueggemann, *First and Second Samuel*, 101; Klein, *1 Samuel*, 127; Nicholson, *Three Faces of Saul*, 57.

33. See Brueggemann, *First and Second Samuel*, 101; Birch, "First and Second Books of Samuel," 1072; John A. Sanford, *King Saul, the Tragic Hero: A Study in Individuation* (New York: Paulist, 1985), 48; Polzin, *Samuel and the Deuteronomist*, 129.

34. The portrayal of Saul in 1 Sam 14 might also be read in a more sympathetic light than is usually the case. Although Saul's actions here certainly seem rash and ill-advised (see McCarter, *I Samuel*, 250), they can also be seen as pious, sincere, and well-intentioned (see Brueggemann, *First and Second Samuel*, 103–5). Saul engaged in two proper (if ill-timed) ritual practices (the vow and offering) and ensured that proper sacrifice was performed when he learned what the troops were doing. At the end of the episode (14:36–46), although Jonathan had broken the vow in ignorance, Saul was willing to insist that the vow be honored even though his own son must die (one may hear resonances of Abraham's willingness to sacrifice Isaac in Gen 22).

35. See the different views in Klein, *1 Samuel*, 147; Birch, "First and Second Books of Samuel," 1087; and Brueggemann, *First and Second Samuel*, 110.

36. Brueggemann, *First and Second Samuel*, 108.

37. See, for example, Brueggemann, *First and Second Samuel*, 111; Gunn, *The Fate of King Saul*, 53. Liss ("The Innocent King," 248) notes that rabbinic and midrashic texts concluded that Saul had been obedient to the halakhah and offered several explanations grounded in halakhic arguments that Saul had to spare Agag for legal reasons.

38. Keith Bodner, *1 Samuel: A Narrative Commentary*, Hebrew Bible Monographs 19 (Sheffield, UK: Sheffield Phoenix, 2008), 156. Note that v. 12 places Saul's construction of a "monument for himself" in Carmel, away from the sacrificial site at Gilgal and not involving the spoils in question.

39. See Birch, "First and Second Books of Samuel," 1090–91; Jobling, *1 Samuel*, 83.

40. The earliest major treatments of Saul from the perspective of tragedy were W. Lee Humphreys, "The Tragedy of King Saul: A Study of the Structure of 1 Samuel 9–31," *JSOT* 6 (1978): 18–27; W. Lee Humphreys, "The Rise and Fall of King Saul: A Study of an Ancient Narrative Stratum in 1 Samuel," *JSOT* 8 (1980): 74–90; Gunn, *The Fate of King Saul*; W. Lee Humphreys, "From Tragic Hero to Villain: A Study of the Figure of Saul and the Development of 1 Samuel," *JSOT* 22 (1982): 95–117; W. Lee Humphreys, *The Tragic Vision and the Hebrew Tradition*, OBT (Philadelphia: Fortress, 1985). For a commentary that represents this approach, see Brueggemann, *First and Second Samuel*. These treatments generally operate from a focus on the final form of the Saul narrative without a concern to identify its earlier sources. (Humphreys's earliest works cited above are the exceptions.)

41. Gunn, *The Fate of King Saul*, 27.

42. Gunn, *The Fate of King Saul*, 28.

43. Gunn, *The Fate of King Saul*, 28. Humphreys ("Tragic Hero," 99–100), while adding an editorial history element, argues that the tragic vision of the Saul narrative holds flaw and fate in tension. Humphreys argues that there was an "early narrative stratum" in 1 Sam 9–31 that presented Saul's rise and fall as a "tragic vision" in line with the characteristics of Aegean, Hittite, and Greek culture. This stratum was subsequently recast by "northern prophetic circles" and then "southern royalist" circles that transformed Saul from a tragic hero into a villain ("Tragic Hero," 95–96).

44. For other works on Saul from the tragedy perspective, see Sanford, *King Saul*; Polzin, *Samuel and the Deuteronomist*; J. Cheryl Exum, *Tragedy and Biblical Narrative: Arrows of the Almighty* (Cambridge: Cambridge University Press, 1992); Edelman, *King Saul*; L. Daniel Hawk, "Saul as Sacrifice: The Tragedy of Israel's First Monarch," *BRev* 12 (1996): 20–25, 56; Nicholson, *Three Faces of Saul*; Barbara Green, *How Are the Mighty Fallen? A Dialogical Study of King Saul in 1 Samuel*, JSOTSup 365 (Sheffield, UK: Sheffield Academic Press, 2003); Green, *King Saul's Asking*; Dawn Maria Sellars, "An Obedient Servant? The Reign of King Saul (1 Samuel 13–15) Reassessed," *JSOT* 35 (2011): 317–38.

45. Humphreys ("Tragic Hero," 102), for example, points for comparison to works of Sophocles and Euripides. See also Tsumura, *First Book of Samuel*, 266; Jobling, *1 Samuel*, 250; Robert L. Duncan, "Jephtha, Saul, and Agamemnon: Anxious Generals, Deadly Fathers" (paper presented at the Midwestern Regional Evangelical Theological Society Meeting, Chicago, March 22–23, 1991). For an early treatment of the comparison with Greek tragedy, see Cyrus H. Gordon, *Before the Bible: The Common Background of Greek and Hebrew Civilisations* (London: Collins, 1962).

46. Exum, *Tragedy and Biblical Narrative*.

47. Herman M. van Praag, "The Downfall of King Saul: The Neurobiological Consequences of Losing Hope," *Judaism* 35 (1986): 414.

48. Brett T. Litz et al., "Moral Injury and Moral Repair in War Veterans: A Preliminary Model and Intervention Strategy," *Clinical Psychology Review* 29 (2009): 700–701.

49. See Brueggemann, *First and Second Samuel*, 101.

50. Drescher et al., "Exploration of the Viability," 8; William P. Nash and Brett T. Litz, "Moral Injury: A Mechanism for War-Related Psychological Trauma in Military Family Members," *Clinical Child Family Psychology Review* 16 (2013): 369. Van Praag ("Downfall of King Saul," 414–28) provides a related yet distinct reading of Saul from the fields of psychiatric research and cognitive science that examines his story for insight into the consequences that losing hope and experiencing chronic despair have on the brain and its behavior regulation.

51. Shay, *Odysseus in America*.

52. Scholars have traditionally identified the subsequent chapters as an originally distinct composition ("the History of David's Rise") whose plot revolves around the tension between Saul and David and David's steady march to the throne. Since the work of Leonhard Rost in 1926 (*The Succession to the Throne of David*, trans. David M. Gunn [Sheffield, UK: Sheffield Almond, 1982]), scholars have often identified a unified composition beginning in ch. 16 but with different identifications of the exact ending. See discussion in Brueggemann, *First and Second Samuel*, 119; Birch, "First and Second Books of Samuel," 1094. Yet the chapters seem to indicate a complex literary history with different traditions concerning how Saul met David. For a reconsideration of the compositional history, see Jacob L. Wright, *David, King of Israel, and Caleb in Biblical Memory* (Cambridge: Cambridge University Press, 2014).

53. Brueggemann (*First and Second Samuel*, 125) similarly describes Saul's condition as "alienation rooted in a theological disorder."

54. D. William Alexander, "Gregory Is My Friend," in *War and Moral Injury: A Reader*, ed. Robert Emmet Meagher and Douglas A. Pryer (Eugene, OR: Cascade, 2018), 199.

55. Shay, *Achilles in Vietnam*, 95.

56. Tick (*Warrior's Return*, 93) actually describes the evil spirit in Saul's story as "the Biblical interpretation of the traumatic wound."

57. See Klein, *1 Samuel*, 188; Brueggemann, *First and Second Samuel*, 136; Green, *King Saul's Asking*, 69. Contrast Birch ("First and Second Books of Samuel," 1121) who sees an "intensifying parallelism" in v. 7. The words of the women's song appear twice more after ch. 18, both times on the lips of the Philistines (21:11; 29:5).

58. Birch, "First and Second Books of Samuel," 1126.

59. See more explicitly 1 Sam 23:17, where Jonathan declares that David will be king of Israel, imagining that he will be second to David rather than to his own father.

60. Shay, *Odysseus in America*, 206.

61. Shay, *Odysseus in America*, 242.

62. Shay, *Odysseus in America*, xv.

63. Scholars typically identify some of these stories as variant tellings of the same tradition (especially the stories of David's sparing Saul's life in chs. 24 and 26). See Tsumura, *First Book of Samuel*, 594; McCarter, *I Samuel*, 379.

64. Brueggemann, *First and Second Samuel*, 192–93.

65. 2 Samuel 1 presents an alternate account of Saul's death in which an Amalekite tells David that he dispatched the wounded Saul at the king's request and has brought the crown to David.

66. Klein, *1 Samuel*, 287.

67. See Litz et al., "Moral Injury," 700–701.

68. See Larson and Zust, *Care for the Sorrowing Soul*, 19–25.

69. Larson and Zust, *Care for the Sorrowing Soul*, 19.

70. See Brian S. Powers, *Full Darkness: Original Sin, Moral Injury, and Wartime Violence* (Grand Rapids: Eerdmans, 2019); Powers, "Moral Injury and Original Sin: The Applicability of Augustinian Moral Psychology in Light of Combat Trauma," *Theology Today* 73 (2017): 325–37.

71. Powers, "Moral Injury and Original Sin," 327.

4. Moral Injury and the Bible's Postwar Rituals

1. Quoted in Jonathan Shay, *Odysseus in America: Combat Trauma and the Trials of Homecoming* (New York: Scribner, 2002), 1.

2. Rita Nakashima Brock and Gabriella Lettini, *Soul Repair: Recovering from Moral Injury after War* (Boston: Beacon, 2012), 42.

3. This chapter contains material adapted from two previous works, used here with permission: Brad E. Kelle, "Post-war Rituals of Return

and Reintegration of Warriors," in *Warfare, Ritual, and Symbol in Biblical and Modern Contexts*, ed. Brad E. Kelle, Frank Ritchel Ames, and Jacob L. Wright, Ancient Israel and Its Literature 28 (Atlanta: Society of Biblical Literature, 2014), 205–42, and Brad E. Kelle, "Moral Injury and the Division of Spoils after Battle in the Hebrew Bible," in *Exploring Moral Injury in Sacred Texts*, ed. Joseph McDonald, Studies in Religion and Theology (London: Jessica Kingsley, 2017), 83–102.

4. J. M. Currier, J. M. Holland, and J. Malott, "Moral Injury, Meaning Making, and Mental Health in Returning Veterans," *Journal of Clinical Psychology* 71 (2015): 238.

5. Camillo Mac Bica, *Beyond PTSD: The Moral Casualties of War*, War Legacy Series: Book Two (Commack, NY: Gnosis, 2016), 96–97; see also Lewis Jeff Lee, *Moral Injury Reconciliation: A Practitioner's Guide for Treating Moral Injury, PTSD, Grief, and Military Sexual Trauma through Spiritual Formation Strategies* (London: Jessica Kingsley, 2018), 112, and the special emphasis on the role of religious communities in Zachary Moon, *Warriors Between Worlds: Moral Injury and Identities in Crisis*, Emerging Perspectives in Pastoral Theology and Care (Lanham, MD: Lexington, 2019).

6. See Amy Amidon, "Guest Perspective: Moral Injury and Moral Repair," *Center for Deployment Psychology*, January 3, 2016, 5, http://deploymentpsych.org/blog/guest-perspective-moral-injury-and-moral-repair; Cecilia Yocum, *Help for Moral Injury: Strategies and Interventions* (Fayetteville, NC: Quaker House, 2016), 34.

7. See Sean Levine, "Legal War, Sin, and 'Moral Injury' in the Age of Modern Warfare," in *War and Moral Injury: A Reader*, ed. Robert Emmet Meagher and Douglas A. Pryer (Eugene, OR: Cascade, 2018), 230; Edward Tick, *War and the Soul: Healing Our Nation's Veterans from Post-traumatic Stress Disorder* (Wheaton, IL: Quest, 2005), 3.

8. For examples, see Brock and Lettini, *Soul Repair*, xviii; Shay, *Odysseus in America*, 244–45; Karl Marlantes, *What It Is Like to Go to War* (New York: Atlantic Monthly, 2011), 205; Yocum, *Help for Moral Injury*, 34–35; Nikki Coleman, "Moral Status and Reintegration," in *Moral Injury: Unseen Wounds in an Age of Barbarism*, ed. Tom Frame (Sydney, Australia: UNSW Press, 2015), 205–19; Duane Larson and Jeff Zust, *Care for the Sorrowing Soul:*

Healing Moral Injuries from Military Service and Implications for the Rest of Us (Eugene, OR: Cascade, 2017), 164. For a chapter devoted to the use of rituals for moral injury from a Christian counseling and pastoral care perspective, see Larry Kent Graham, *Moral Injury: Restoring Wounded Souls* (Nashville: Abingdon, 2017), 135–52.

9. Shay, *Odysseus in America*, 245 (italics original).

10. Nancy Sherman, *Afterwar: Healing the Moral Wounds of Our Soldiers* (Oxford: Oxford University Press, 2015), 19, 161. See also Edward Tick, *Warrior's Return: Restoring the Soul after War* (Boulder, CO: Sounds True, 2014), 162–64. Note the connection here to the recent emphasis within pastoral care that acts of caregiving for moral injury should be done by communities of faith and not simply by individual caregivers (see Zachary Moon, "'Turn Now, My Vindication Is at Stake': Military Moral Injury and Communities of Faith," *Pastoral Psychology*, November, 21 2017, https://doi.org/10.1007/s11089-017-0795-8).

11. Brock and Lettini, *Soul Repair*, 65.

12. E.g., see Yocum, *Help for Moral Injury*, 45; Sherman, *Afterwar*, 161.

13. Alice Lynd and Staughton Lynd, *Moral Injury and Nonviolent Resistence: Breaking the Cycle of Violence in the Military and Behind Bars* (Oakland, CA: PM Press, 2017), 31.

14. Bica, *Beyond PTSD*, 100; Tick, *War and the Soul*, 207–10.

15. Brock and Lettini, *Soul Repair*, xviii.

16. See the survey provided in Lindsay B. Carey et al., "Moral Injury, Spiritual Care and the Role of Chaplains: An Exploratory Scoping Review of Literature and Resources," *Journal of Religious Health* 55 (2016): 1234.

17. Elizabeth A. Liebert, "Accessible Spiritual Practices to Aid in Recovery from Moral Injury," *Pastoral Psychology* 68 (2019): 41–57. https://doi.org/10.1007/s11089-018-0825-1.

18. E.g., Shay, *Odysseus*, 152; David Wood, *What Have We Done: The Moral Injury of America's Longest Wars* (New York: Brown and Company,

2016), 3; Tick, *Warrior's Return*, 194–98, 206–7; Larson and Zust, *Care for the Sorrowing Soul*, 164; Kim S. Geringer and Nancy H. Wiener, "Insights into Moral Injury and Soul Repair from Classical Jewish Texts," *Pastoral Psychology* 68 (2019): 65–67. https://doi.org/10.1007/s11089-018-0848-7.

19. Shay, *Odysseus in America*, 152.

20. Bernard J. Verkamp, *The Moral Treatment of Returning Warriors in Early Medieval and Modern Times*, 2nd ed. (Scranton: University of Scranton Press, 2006).

21. Verkamp, *The Moral Treatment*, 1–2.

22. See Verkamp, *The Moral Treatment*, 8.

23. As a recent example, Mark T. Moitoza ("Fresh Courage for Moral Injury: Sacramental Healing with Returning Veterans" [PhD diss., La Salle University, 2018]) has provided a comprehensive examination of how sacraments within the Catholic tradition, such as rites of penance and the anointing of the sick, can be resources for healing moral injury (with special emphasis on communal rituals in which congregations participate with veterans). See also Christopher Grundy, "Basic Retraining: The Role of Congregational Ritual in the Care of Returning Veterans," *Liturgy* 27 (2012): 27–36.

24. E.g., Shay, *Odysseus in America*, 245; Marlantes, *What It Is Like to Go to War*, 205.

25. E.g., Martin Van Creveld (*The Culture of War* [New York: Ballantine, 2008], 149) surveys the evidence for end of war practices from various historical periods and identifies four things that "must be done, though not necessarily in this order": (1) care for casualties; (2) distribute the spoils and prisoners; (3) celebrate victory with ceremonies to mark the transition from war to peace; and (4) reach a formal agreement to end hostilities.

26. Van Creveld, *Culture of War*, 149. See Carl von Clausewitz, *On War*, trans. O. J. Matthijs Jolles, The Modern Library of the World's Best Books (New York: The Modern Library, 1943).

27. See Gerhard von Rad, *Holy War in Ancient Israel*, trans. Marva J. Dawn (Eugene, OR: Wipf and Stock, 2000; orig. German 1951), 50–51.

28. See Brad E. Kelle, *Ancient Israel at War 853–586 BC*, Essential Histories 67 (Oxford: Osprey, 2007).

29. E.g., see Saul M. Olyan, *Social Inequality in the World of the Text: The Significance of Ritual and Social Distinctions in the Hebrew Bible*, Journal of Ancient Judaism Supplements 4 (Göttingen: Vandenhoeck & Ruprecht, 2011) and James W. Watts, *Ritual and Rhetoric in Leviticus: From Sacrifice to Scripture* (Cambridge: Cambridge University Press, 2007).

30. T. M. Lemos, *Violence and Personhood in Ancient Israel and Comparative Contexts* (Oxford: Oxford University Press, 2017), 17.

31. Two additional texts that relate to possibly recurring postbattle activities are Judg 9:45, which describes sowing the enemy's lands with salt, and Deut 7:1-11, which outlines the procedures for the practice of the total annihilation of the enemy. However, these texts don't deal directly with elements concerning the warriors themselves but focus on actions taken against the enemy or its territory.

32. The traditional view since the time of Martin Noth has been that the passage is one of the latest parts of the Pentateuch, perhaps even a later supplement to the Pentateuch as a whole (see Martin Noth, *Numbers*, OTL [Philadelphia: Westminster, 1968], 229). For more discussion, see Thomas B. Dozeman, "Numbers," in *The New Interpreter's Bible*, vol. 2 (Nashville: Abingdon, 1998), 1–268; W. H. Bellinger Jr., *Leviticus, Numbers*, NIBCOT (Peabody, MA: Hendrickson, 2001); Timothy R. Ashley, *The Book of Numbers*, NICOT (Grand Rapids: Eerdmans, 1993).

33. See David P. Wright, "Purification from Corpse-Contamination in Numbers XXXI 19–24," *VT* 35 (1985): 213–23; David P. Wright, *The Disposal of Impurity: Elimination Rites in the Bible and in Hittite and Mesopotamian Literature*, SBLDS 101 (Atlanta: Scholars Press, 1987), 169–72. For other references to corpse defilement, see Num 6:6-12; 9:6-14; 31:13-24; Lev 10:4-5; 21:1-4, 10-12; 2 Kgs 23:16; Isa 65:4; Ezek 9:6; 39:11-16; 43:7-9; 44:25-27; Hag 2:10-19. Priestly laws concerning pollution through blood and bloodshed may also underlie the ritual in Num 31, although Old Testament texts typically distinguish accidental killing and combat from the type of moral acts such as murder that constitute bloodshed. See Num 35:33; Ps 106:38-39; Isa 59:1-3; Jer 2:34; Lam 4:14.

34. Susan Niditch (*War in the Hebrew Bible: A Study in the Ethics of Violence* [New York: Oxford University Press, 1993], 87) observes that the corpse-contamination laws in Numbers differ from those found in Leviticus. Leviticus typically treats contact with a corpse or blood from a wound as ritually defiling only for priests (e.g., Lev 21:1-11). In Num 5:1-4, the priestly writer extends the defiling nature of corpse contact to all Israelites, and Num 19 develops the notion into a general principle that extends even to aliens in the community.

35. With regard to the demand for the purification of the captive virgin women, Phillip J. Budd (*Numbers*, WBC 5 [Waco, TX: Word, 1984], 334) proposes that the text is expanding the older law in Deut 21:10-14 concerning the transition of a captive woman from a distant city. Niditch's reading (*War in the Hebrew Bible*, 81–87) of Num 31 also focuses on the sparing of the virgin girls and compares the text with Deut 21:10-14. She claims that element reveals the priestly view of the world centered on biological purity of bloodlines.

36. For example, Niditch (*War in the Hebrew Bible*, 78–89) notes the particular contrast on this point between the priestly conception in Num 31 and the holy war or ban traditions in the Old Testament. See also Roland de Vaux, *Ancient Israel*, McGraw-Hill Paperbacks (New York: McGraw-Hill, 1965), 461–62, which interprets the demand for purification in Num 31 as an indication that the warriors needed to desanctify themselves out of a state of holiness now that the battle was over.

37. Emanuel Feldman, *Biblical and Post-biblical Defilement and Mourning: Law as Theology* (New York: Yeshiva University Press, 1977), xix.

38. See E. N. Fallaize, "Purification, Introductory and Primitive," in *Encyclopedia of Religion and Ethics*, ed. James Hastings, vol. 10 (Edinburgh: T&T Clark, 1956), 455–66. Fallaize points out that the identification of death as the ultimate source of defilement is, at times, connected with the notion that postbattle purification rituals for warriors serve to protect the warrior from the ghosts or souls of those he killed (p. 457).

39. Feldman, *Biblical and Post-biblical Defilement and Mourning*, xix, 14. Feldman identifies defilement of the dead—caused by contact with corpses,

carrion, or certain "creeping things"—as the first of three major categories of defilement within Old Testament and rabbinical law (pp. 31–32).

40. The text reflects the priestly legislation as a whole, in which Israelites—even priests—are permitted to defile themselves via contact with a corpse on certain occasions after which specific restrictions are placed upon them (see Lev 21:1-6; Num 19:11-20). In addition to the stipulations to wash and remain outside the camp for seven days—which appear in rituals for nonwar corpse contact in the priestly texts (Num 5; 19)—the use of water as a purifying agent in the ritual in Num 31 appears widely in biblical and extrabiblical texts related to purification, although the use of fire in this text is unique.

41. The booty described in this passage exceeds 800,000 animals and 16,750 shekels of gold (Dozeman, "Numbers," 245).

42. For priestly legislation concerning the priests' portion of offerings in nonwar contexts, see Num 7:1-89; 18:8-32; 28:1-31. For discussion of the levy given to the priests, see Dozeman, "Numbers," 247–48; Ashley, *The Book of Numbers*, 597; Budd, *Numbers*, 331.

43. Reports of the taking of plunder especially appear in the battle texts in Joshua and Judges. Perhaps because of the premonarchic literary setting of the stories, there are no significant rituals of warriors returning to their town, but the postbattle activities often involve booty.

44. In a recent study of textual representations of plunder in Second Temple Period and early Jewish texts, Kvasnica notes these Old Testament examples of plunder with a "pious element" of redistribution to the temple or other people became fully developed in the Jewish exegetical tradition as plundering increasingly came to be seen as an unlawful activity according to the Torah. See Brian Kvasnica, "Shifts in Israelite War Ethics and Early Jewish Historiography of Plundering," in *Writing and Reading War: Rhetoric, Gender, and Ethics in Biblical and Modern Contexts*, eds. Brad E. Kelle and Frank Ritchel Ames (Atlanta: Society of Biblical Literature, 2008), 175–96 (quotation on p. 176). Among these later texts, for instance, 2 Macc 8:21-29 reports that Judas redistributed the booty he claimed at the battle of Ammaus (165 BCE), especially to those who had suffered or were widows and orphans among them (2 Macc 8:28).

45. Some commentators point to other Old Testament passages in which the act of taking a census is sinful and demands atonement (e.g., Exod 30:11-16; 2 Sam 24:1-17). For this view, see Noth, *Numbers*, 232; Ashley, *The Book of Numbers*, 599. Alternatively, other explanations include the soldiers' disregard of the strict ban provision and the sense of having received unmerited divine favor during the battle (see Budd, *Numbers*, 332; Gray, *Numbers*, 425). Norman H. Snaith (*Leviticus and Numbers*, The Century Bible [London: Thomas Nelson and Sons, 1967], 329) proposes that the warriors' motivation is gratitude that their lives have been spared. Yet the context of ch. 31 suggests the need for atonement reflects the sense that participation in the battle was ritually defiling and the offering is part of the purification process (see Dozeman, "Numbers," 248).

46. One might also consider in this category Gen 14:17-24, which depicts Abram giving part of his booty to the priest Melchizedek.

47. These depictions of the captured ark and temple vessels fit within the broader category of the taking of divine images as trophies in the ancient world (see below), but the Old Testament preserves explicit depictions of this ritual only as it was done *to* Israel or Judah in defeat. Perhaps the one-sided portrayal is due to the "ideological prohibition of images" in various biblical traditions that resulted in commands to destroy rather than capture foreign gods and their images (e.g., Exod 34:13; Num 33:52; Deut 7:25). See Kathryn Frakes Kravitz, "Divine Trophies of War in Assyria and Ancient Israel," (PhD diss., Brandeis University, 1999), 118.

48. For a full treatment of this issue, including extended discussion of prebattle, battle, and postbattle practices within the framework of divine war in texts from Mesopotamia, Arabia, Syria-Palestine, and Egypt, see Sa-Moon Kang, *Divine War in the Old Testament and the Ancient Near East*, BZAW 177 (Berlin: de Gruyter, 1989).

49. *COS* 2:243; *ANET*, 556.

50. Tablet VI. *ANET*, 83–84.

51. *COS* 2:243; *ANET*, 267–68, 276, 277, respectively. See Abraham Malamat, "Campaigns to the Mediterranean by Iahdunlim and Other Early Mesopotamian Rulers," in *Studies in Honor of Benno Landsberger on His Seventy-*

Fifth Birthday, ed. H. Gütterbock and T. Jacobsen, The Oriental Institute of Chicago Assyriological Studies 16 (Chicago: University of Chicago Press, 1965), 367. Perhaps the origin of the ritual washing of the weapons lies in the fact that some Assyrian texts depict the weapons used in battle as having been provided by the gods and thus in need of ritual purification after the battle. See Zainab Bahrani, *Rituals of War: The Body and Violence in Mesopotamia* (New York: Zone Books, 2008), 197; Bustenay Oded, *War, Peace, and Empire: Justifications for War in Assyrian Royal Inscriptions* (Wiesbaden: Ludwig Reichert, 1992), 15.

52. E.g., W. Kendrick Pritchett, *The Greek State at War*, part 3, *Religion* (Berkeley: University of California Press, 1979), 202.

53. The text in question is from Aeschylus. The Delphic Oracle, for instance, did not view killing in warfare as causing guilt or defilement.

54. Pritchett, *The Greek State at War*, part 3, *Religion*, 197–98.

55. See Bahrani, *Rituals of War*, 197.

56. Van Creveld, *Culture of War*, 164.

57. Additionally, the typical Roman practice did not reintegrate warriors into the life of the community. Rather, after thirty years of service in the legions, soldiers received a plot of land in a newly conquered territory.

58. Van Creveld, *Culture of War*, 163–64.

59. Jeffrey A. Fadiman, *Meru of Mount Kenya: An Oral History of Tribal Warfare* (Athens: Ohio University Press, 1982), 118–19.

60. See Marlantes, *What It Is Like to Go to War*, 191–92.

61. See Verkamp, *The Moral Treatment*.

62. A letter from Mari contains a king's complaint that he has not received his share of the booty or the portion to be given to the gods from his officers (see Kang, *Divine War*, 47), and Hittite texts describe kings bringing spoils to their palace for the purpose of distribution (p. 71).

63. Elgavish, "The Division of the Spoils," 253–54.

64. See Kvasnica, "Shifts in Israelite War Ethics," 176n7; Edward L. Greenstein and David Marcus, "The Akkadian Inscription of *Idrimi*," *JANES* 8 (1976): 59–96; Elgavish, "The Division of the Spoils," 242–73.

65. Quoted in Kang, *Divine War*, 48.

66. Once the army returned home, the booty became property of the state treasury. See W. Kendrick Pritchett, *The Greek State at War*, part 1 (Berkeley: University of California Press, 1971), 85; Van Creveld, *Culture of War*, 159.

67. See texts discussed in Mark S. Smith, *Poetic Heroes: Literary Commemorations of Warriors and Warrior Culture in the Early Biblical World* (Grand Rapids: Eerdmans, 2014), 18.

68. See Kang, *Divine War*, 46–48.

69. *ARAB II*, 308; quoted in Kang, *Divine War*, 47.

70. Quoted in Kang, *Divine War*, 47. He (p. 106) notes that some Egyptian texts also refer to the postbattle dedication of booty to the gods.

71. For Greek texts related to this aspect, see Pritchett, *The Greek State at War*, part 1, 53–100. For the donation of the tenth, see also Walter Burkert, *Greek Religion*, trans. John Raffan (Cambridge: Harvard University Press, 1985), 267.

72. Pritchett, *The Greek State at War*, part 3, *Religion*, 249, 277–80. Kvasnica ("Shifts in Israelite War Ethics," 180) notes that the practice appears in the earliest Greek texts (see Homer, *Iliad* 10.460) and became a mandatory practice in treaties "for the Athenian league after its victory in the Persian war."

73. See Kravitz, "Divine Trophies." See also Bahrani's (*Rituals of War*, 159–81) discussion of the "assault and abduction of monuments in war."

74. For a survey of the major Assyrian "trophy texts," see Kravitz, "Divine Trophies," 29–117.

75. Kravitz, "Divine Trophies," 6–18.

76. See Kang, *Divine War*, 48, 71.

77. See Kang, *Divine War*, 80, *ANET*, 293, and Kang, *Divine War*, 107, respectively. For the construction of victory stelae and monuments by earlier Assyrian kings such as Ashurnasirpal II and Shalmaneser III, see Kravitz, "Divine Trophies," 29.

78. Pritchett (*The Greek State at War*, part 3, *Religion*, 186) argues that the raising of a battlefield trophy is as old as the time of Homer. The most detailed description appears in Virgil's *Aeneid* (11.4-11) (see Van Creveld, *Culture of War*, 160–61).

79. Burkert, *Greek Religion*, 267; Kravitz, "Divine Trophies," 9n17.

80. Bahrani, *Rituals of War*, 16.

81. Brett T. Litz et al., "Moral Injury and Moral Repair in War Veterans: A Preliminary Model and Intervention Strategy," *Clinical Psychology Review* 29 (2009): 700–701.

82. Lynd and Lynd, *Moral Injury and Nonviolent Resistance*, 1.

83. Brock and Lettini, *Soul Repair*, 81.

84. Levine, "Legal War," 227.

85. See Niditch, *War in the Hebrew Bible*, 87–88.

86. E.g., see Robert Emmet Meagher, *Killing from the Inside Out: Moral Injury and Just War* (Eugene, OR: Cascade, 2014), xviii.

87. Brock and Lettini, *Soul Repair*, 103.

88. Powers, "Moral Injury and Original Sin," 333.

89. Duane Larson, "A Prescription for Moral Injury," *Dialog: A Journal of Theology* 54 (2015): 119, italics original.

90. E.g., Sherman, *Afterwar*; Currier, Holland, and Malott, "Moral Injury," 229–40.

91. Tick, *Warrior's Return*, 212–13.

92. See Brett T. Litz et al., *Adaptive Disclosure: A New Treatment for Military Trauma, Loss, and Moral Injury* (New York: The Guilford Press, 2016).

93. See Sherman, *Afterwar*, 19, 45.

94. See Tick, *Warrior's Return*, 213.

95. See J. Irene Harris et al., "Moral Injury and Psycho-Spiritual Development: Considering the Developmental Context," *Spirituality in Clinical Practice* 19 (2015): 6.

96. Brock and Lettini, *Soul Repair*, 107.

97. Brock and Lettini, *Soul Repair*, 105.

98. See Bessel A. van der Kolk, *The Body Keeps the Score: Brain, Mind, and Body in the Healing of Trauma* (New York: Penguin, 2015) and Shelly Rambo, *Spirit and Trauma: A Theology of Remaining* (Louisville, KY: Westminster John Knox, 2010).

99. van der Kolk, *The Body Keeps the Score*, 3. He suggests physical practices such as yoga, play techniques, and, especially, theatre as a type of communal ritual (see pp. 332–48).

100. van der Kolk, *The Body Keeps the Score*, 337.

5. Moral Injury, Lament, and Forgiveness

1. Ernest Hemingway, introduction to *Treasury for the Free World*, ed. Ben Raeburn (New York: Arco, 1946), xv.

2. This chapter contains material adapted from my previous work, used here with permission: Brad E. Kelle, "Post-war Rituals of Return and Reintegration of Warriors," in *Warfare, Ritual, and Symbol in Biblical and Modern Contexts*, ed. Brad E. Kelle, Frank Ritchel Ames, and Jacob L. Wright, Ancient Israel and Its Literature 28 (Atlanta: Society of Biblical Literature, 2014), 205–42.

3. For an overview listing, see Leland Ryken, James C. Wilhoit, and Tremper Longman III, eds., *Dictionary of Biblical Imagery* (Downer's Grove,

IL: InterVarsity, 1998), 78–79. For an earlier version of the discussion in this section, see Kelle, "Postwar Rituals," 205–41 (adapted here with permission).

4. The overall textual evidence in the Old Testament (especially the tradition of early heroic poetry) suggests that postbattle songs were the particular domain of women in ancient Israel. See Mark S. Smith, "Warfare Song as Warrior Ritual," in Kelle, Ames, and Wright, *Warfare, Ritual, and Symbol in Biblical and Modern Contexts*, 165–86. See also Athalya Brenner and Fokkelien van Dijk-Hemmes, *On Gendering Texts: Female and Male Voices in the Hebrew Bible*, BInS 1 (Leiden: Brill, 1993), 1–42 and Sherry Lou Macgregor, *Beyond Hearth and Home: Women in the Public Sphere in Neo-Assyrian Society*, SAAS 21, Publications of the Foundation for Finnish Assyriological Research 5 (Helsinki: The Neo-Assyrian Text Corpus Project and the Foundation for Finnish Assyriological Research, 2012), 29–54. On the topic of women celebrating victory, see Eunice B. Poethig, "The Victory Song Tradition of the Women of Israel," (PhD diss., Union Theological Seminary, 1985) and Carol Meyers, "Mother to Muse: An Archaeomusicological Study of Women's Performance in Israel," in *Recycling Biblical Figures: Papers Read at a NOSTER Colloquium in Amsterdam, 12–13 May 1997*, ed. Athalya Brenner and Jan Willem van Henten, Studies in Religion and Theology 1 (Leiden: Deo, 1999), 50–77.

5. See Carly L. Crouch, *War and Ethics in the Ancient Near East: Military Violence in Light of Cosmology and History*, BZAW 407 (Berlin: Walter de Gruyter, 2009), 76.

6. The Hebrew term used here is "shatter," but most translators follow the Greek, Syriac, and Targum that suggest a term meaning "bathe" (see NRSV).

7. See T. M. Lemos, "Shame and Mutilation of Enemies in the Hebrew Bible," *JBL* 125 (2006): 225–41.

8. See Sa-Moon Kang, *Divine War in the Old Testament and the Ancient Near East*, BZAW 177 (Berlin: de Gruyter, 1989), 105–6. For example, one text records the gods extolling Ramses II upon his return in victory: "Welcome, our beloved son, King *Usermare-sotpenre*, the Son of Re, Ramses, Beloved of Amun, given life!" (quoted on p. 106).

9. See Walter Burkert, *Greek Religion*, trans. John Raffan (Cambridge: Harvard University Press, 1985), 267. For a list of Greek texts referring to a

postbattle sacrifice, see W. Kendrick Pritchett, *The Greek State at War*, part 3, *Religion* (Berkeley: University of California Press, 1979), 187–89.

10. See H. S. Versnel, *Triumphus: An Inquiry into the Origin, Development, and Meaning of the Roman Triumph* (Leiden: Brill, 1970); Kathryn Frakes Kravitz, "Divine Trophies of War in Assyria and Ancient Israel," (PhD diss., Brandeis University, 1999), 9n17; Martin Van Creveld, *The Culture of War* (New York: Ballantine, 2008), 164.

11. Sean Levine, "Legal War, Sin, and 'Moral Injury' in the Age of Modern Warfare," in *War and Moral Injury: A Reader*, ed. Robert Emmet Meagher and Douglas A. Pryer (Eugene, OR: Cascade, 2018), 228. See also Rita Nakashima Brock and Gabriella Lettini, *Soul Repair: Recovering from Moral Injury after War* (Boston: Beacon, 2012), 81.

12. Camillo Mac Bica, *Beyond PTSD: The Moral Casualties of War*, War Legacy Series: Book Two (Commack, NY: Gnosis, 2016), 106.

13. See J. M. Childs, "Moral Injury and the Priesthood of All Believers," *Dialog* 57 (2018): 115; Nancy J. Ramsay, "Moral Injury as Loss and Grief with Attention to Ritual Resources for Care," *Pastoral Psychology* (Dec 2018). doi: https://doi.org/10.1007/s11089-018-0854-9.

14. Ramsay, "Moral Injury as Loss and Grief."

15. See Ramsay, "Moral Injury as Loss and Grief," and Larry Kent Graham, *Moral Injury: Restoring Wounded Souls* (Nashville: Abingdon, 2017), 78.

16. Alice Lynd and Staughton Lynd, *Moral Injury and Nonviolent Resistence: Breaking the Cycle of Violence in the Military and Behind Bars* (Oakland, CA: PM Press, 2017), 31. See also Duane Larson and Jeff Zust, *Care for the Sorrowing Soul: Healing Moral Injuries from Military Service and Implications for the Rest of Us* (Eugene, OR: Cascade, 2017), 195.

17. William P. Nash et al., "Psychometric Evaluation of the Moral Injury Events Scale," *Military Medicine* 178 (2013): 646–52.

18. Brett T. Litz et al., *Adaptive Disclosure: A New Treatment for Military Trauma, Loss, and Moral Injury* (New York: The Guilford Press, 2016), 5.

19. See, for example, Litz et al., *Adaptive Disclosure*, 5 and Warren Kinghorn, "Combat Trauma and Moral Fragmentation: A Theological Account of Moral Injury," *Journal of the Society of Christian Ethics* 32 (2012): 69.

20. See, for example, Levine, "Legal War," 228 and Larson and Zust, *Care for the Sorrowing Soul*, 195–96.

21. Duane Larson, "A Prescription for Moral Injury," *Dialog: A Journal of Theology* 54 (2015): 118.

22. Jacob K. Farnsworth et al., "The Role of Moral Emotions in Military Trauma: Implications for the Study and Treatment of Moral Injury," *Review of General Psychology* 18 (2014): 257–58.

23. Nancy Sherman, *Afterwar: Healing the Moral Wounds of Our Soldiers* (Oxford: Oxford University Press, 2015), 93.

24. Sherman, *Afterwar*, 101.

25. Litz et al., *Adaptive Disclosure*, 5. See also the clinical treatment model in Cecilia Yocum, *Help for Moral Injury: Strategies and Interventions* (Fayetteville, NC: Quaker House, 2016), 15, 24–26.

26. Litz et al., *Adaptive Disclosure*, 5.

27. Sherman, *Afterwar*.

28. Ramsay, "Moral Injury as Loss and Grief," n.p.

29. So Lynd and Lynd, *Moral Injury and Nonviolent Resistance*, 31.

30. For a collection of such poetry related to moral injury, see the poems collected in Meagher and Pryer, *War and Moral Injury: A Reader*, 11–34.

31. David Lawrence Fisher, *"Dulce et Decorum est*: Moral Injury in the Poetry of Combat Veterans" (PhD diss., Pacifica Graduate Institute, 2019). He gives detailed analyses of twenty-one poems (three from each major conflict included) and argues that this combat poetry expresses the ontology of moral injury, with special emphasis on the importance of memory and honest expression for repair.

32. Graham, *Moral Injury*, 137 (for full discussion of lamentation rituals, see pp. 135–57). See a similar emphasis on lament practices for moral repair in Lewis Jeff Lee, *Moral Injury Reconciliation: A Practitioner's Guide for Treating Moral Injury, PTSD, Grief, and Military Sexual Trauma through Spiritual Formation Strategies* (London: Jessica Kingsley, 2018), 110–11.

33. Carrie Doehring, "Military Moral Injury: An Evidenced-Based and Intercultural Approach to Spiritual Care," *Pastoral Psychology* 68 (2019): 15–30. https://doi.org/10.1007/s11089-018-08135.

34. Shawn Fawson, "Sustaining Lamentation for Military Moral Injury: Witness Poetry that Bears the Traces of Extremity," *Pastoral Psychology* (Nov 2018). doi: https://doi.org/10.1007/s11089-018-0855-8.

35. See Childs, "Moral Injury and the Priesthood of All Believers," 115; Wollom A. Jensen and James M. Childs, *Moral Warriors, Moral Wounds: The Ministry of the Christian Ethic* (Eugene, OR: Cascade, 2016), 102–6; Elizabeth A. Liebert, "Accessible Spiritual Practices to Aid in Recovery from Moral Injury," *Pastoral Psychology* 68 (2019): 51–53; Kim S. Geringer and Nancy H. Wiener, "Insights into Moral Injury and Soul Repair from Classical Jewish Texts," *Pastoral Psychology* 68 (2019): 63.

36. Brock and Lettini, *Soul Repair*, 26.

37. Ramsay, "Moral Injury as Loss and Grief."

38. On women as the primary celebrants of postbattle victory songs, see the discussion of celebrations and processions above, as well as Smith, "Warfare Song as Warrior Ritual," 165–86. For depictions of women as mourners, see 2 Sam 1:24; 2 Chr 35:25; Jer 9:17-21; Ezek 32:16. For the ancient Near Eastern tradition of women as designated mourners, see F. W. Dobbs-Allsopp, *Weep, O Daughter Zion: A Study of the City-Lament Genre in the Hebrew Bible*, BibOr 44 (Rome: Biblical Pontifical Institute, 1993).

39. For other possible examples, see Nah 3; Ezek 16 and 23.

40. See Brian C. Jones, *Howling over Moab: Irony and Rhetoric in Isaiah 15–16*, SBLDS 157 (Atlanta: Scholars Press, 1996). For other possibly ironic or sarcastic laments over enemy kingdoms in the prophets, see Jer 48 and Ezek 32:1-16.

41. KTU 1.5 VI 11-25; 1.5 VI 31—1.6 I 6-8; 1.18 IV 39.

42. See Dobbs-Allsopp, *Weep, O Daughter of Zion*. The genre consists of distinct but related types, and the label "city lament" most often refers to literary laments related to the destruction of the city of Sumer at the end of the Ur III period (ca. 2000 BCE) (p. 13).

43. Dobbs-Allsopp, *Weep, O Daughter of Zion*, 30–31.

44. For translations, see *ANET*, 455–63.

45. So Dobbs-Allsopp, *Weep, O Daughter of Zion*, 156.

46. Kathleen O'Connor, *Lamentations: The Tears of the World* (Maryknoll, NY: Orbis, 2002), 124 (see also pp. 7–8, 98).

47. O'Connor, *Lamentations*, 98. See also Ramsay, "Moral Injury as Loss and Grief."

48. O'Connor, *Lamentations*, 100.

49. Ramsay, "Moral injury as Loss and Grief."

50. O'Connor, *Lamentations*, 122.

51. See discussion in John H. Hayes, *Understanding the Psalms* (Valley Forge, PA: Judson, 1976), 57–58.

52. Hayes, *Understanding the Psalms*, 58–59.

53. Ramsay, "Moral Injury as Loss and Grief."

54. Walter Brueggemann, *The Message of the Psalms: A Theological Commentary* (Minneapolis: Augsburg, 1984), 52.

55. Many of the biblical psalms now include a superscription (an unnumbered opening verse or verses in English Bibles) that associates the psalm with some specific figure, group, or circumstance within ancient Israel (116 of the 150 psalms). Specifically, seventy-three psalms have a superscription that associates them with David, and sixteen of those superscriptions associate the psalm with some event from David's life told in the books of 1 and 2 Samuel. Biblical scholarship generally regards these superscriptions as instructive for

the history of the interpretation of the psalms but doesn't view them as original to the text or as accurate indicators of historical backgrounds. Rather, they represent the efforts of the collectors and editors of the biblical psalms to link together different parts of their sacred texts and traditions in the hopes of finding enhanced and deeper meanings. The superscriptions are best thought of not as historical data but as clues to how the texts have been read within the tradition.

56. E.g., Ps 18 is a thanksgiving for victory in battle; Ps 20 is a petition for the king prior to going to war; and Ps 144 is likely a royal prayer for safety and victory in battle.

57. Brueggemann, *The Message of the Psalms*, 67.

58. Hayes, *Understanding the Psalms*, 118.

59. Hayes, *Understanding the Psalms*, 121.

60. Psalm 89 is personal, rather than communal, in form, but similarly focuses on the defeat and humiliation of the Israelite king and a plea for the reversal of royal fortune.

61. Brueggemann, *The Message of the Psalms*, 68.

62. Brueggemann, *The Message of the Psalms*, 72.

63. Recall the note above that identified the superscriptions that appear on many of these psalms as the result of the efforts of the later collectors and editors of the biblical psalms to link together different parts of their sacred texts and traditions in the hopes of finding enhanced and deeper meanings.

64. Brueggemann, *The Message of the Psalms*, 63.

65. Brueggemann, *The Message of the Psalms*, 81–82 (italics original).

66. The entire curse section in vv. 6-19 may be read either as the sufferer's own plea to God or as a quotation of the curses that the adversaries have made against the sufferer. In any case, v. 20 indicates that the psalmist wants God to bring these very things on the foes.

67. Brueggemann, *The Message of the Psalms*, 77, 76, respectively.

68. See Hayes, *Understanding the Psalms*, 81.

69. Brueggemann, *The Message of the Psalms*, 85.

70. Brueggemann, *The Message of the Psalms*, 95.

71. For example, the superscription on Ps 51 associates the prayer with David's sexual transgressions against Bathsheba, but the language in the psalm makes only generic references to "transgressions," "iniquity," and "sin" (see vv. 1-2).

72. See Brueggemann, *The Message of the Psalms*, 96.

73. See the superscription at the beginning of Ps 51 (an unnumbered verse in English translations). See the stories about David in 2 Sam 11–12.

74. Brock and Lettini, *Soul Repair*, 90.

75. Fawson, "Sustaining Lamentation," n11. Fawson notes that practical theologians have also used poetry as a source for doing contextual practical theology (n11) and that pastoral theologians have applied the same kind of close attention to language in the study of narrative as a means to express experiences of suffering and oppression (n7).

76. Fawson, "Sustaining Lamentation," n7.

77. Fawson, "Sustaining Lamentation."

78. Walter Brueggemann, "The Formfulness of Grief," in *The Psalms and the Life of Faith*, ed. Patrick D. Miller (Minneapolis: Fortress, 1995), 84–97.

79. Graham, *Moral Injury*, 138.

80. Brueggemann, *The Message of the Psalms*, 52.

81. Frame, "Moral Injury and the Influence of Christian Religious Conviction," in Meagher and Pryer, *War and Moral Injury: A Reader*, 195.

82. Ramsay, "Moral Injury as Loss and Grief."

83. Ramsay, "Moral Injury as Loss and Grief."

84. See Brueggemann, *The Message of the Psalms*, 57.

85. Ramsay, "Moral Injury as Loss and Grief."

86. Fawson, "Sustaining Lamentation."

87. Fawson, "Sustaining Lamentation."

88. See Sherman, *Afterwar*, 93–101.

89. Sherman, *Afterwar*, 93.

90. Litz et al., *Adaptive Disclosure*, 5.

91. Litz et al., *Adaptive Disclosure*, 5.

92. For these perspectives on the theological function of laments, see Larson and Zust, *Care for the Sorrowing Soul*, 196.

93. Ramsay, "Moral Injury as Loss and Grief."

94. Ramsay, "Moral Injury as Loss and Grief."

95. Brock and Lettini, *Soul Repair*, 110.

96. Kinghorn, "Combat Trauma," 69.

97. See Lynd and Lynd, *Moral Injury and Nonviolent Resistance*, 1n5.

98. Larson and Zust, *Care for the Sorrowing Soul*, 200.

99. Larson and Zust, *Care for the Sorrowing Soul*, 202.

6. Injured by the Bible

1. Mieke Bal, *Anti-covenant: Counter-Reading Women's Lives in the Hebrew Bible* (Sheffield, UK: Almond, 1989), 14.

2. Jerome F. D. Creach, *Violence in Scripture*, Interpretation (Louisville, KY: Westminster John Knox, 2013), 1.

3. For overall representative reviews and surveys, see, e.g., Creach, *Violence in Scripture*; John J. Collins, *Does the Bible Justify Violence?*, Facets (Minneapolis: Fortress, 2004); Heath A. Thomas, Jeremy Evans, and Paul Copan,

eds., *Holy War in the Bible: Christian Morality and an Old Testament Problem* (Downer's Grove, IL: IVP Academic, 2013); and Eric A. Seibert, "Recent Research on Divine Violence in the Old Testament (with Special Attention to Christian Theological Perspectives)," *CBR* 15 (2016): 8–40.

4. Walter Brueggemann, "Making Sense of God's Violent Actions in the Old Testament," *The Thoughtful Christian* (2013):2. http://www.thethoughtfulchristian.com/products/TC0532/making-sense-of-gods-violent-actions-in-the-old-testamnt.aspx.

5. Cited in Creach, *Violence in Scripture*, 1.

6. Richard Dawkins, *The God Delusion* (New York: Houghton Mifflin, 2006), 31. See also Regina M. Schwartz, *The Curse of Cain: The Violent Legacy of Monotheism* (Chicago: The University of Chicago Press, 1997).

7. See, for example, Creach, *Violence in Scripture* and Seibert, "Recent Research on Divine Violence."

8. Creach, *Violence in Scripture*, 97. For Creach's full discussion of the specific issue of God's violent portrayals, see pp. 17–96; for his discussion of the conquest of Canaan stories, see pp. 97–124.

9. Seibert, "Recent Research on Divine Violence," 9.

10. First quote: Seibert, "Recent Research on Divine Violence," 9; second quote: M. Daniel Carroll R. and J. Blair Wilgus, "Introduction: What Do We Do with the God of the Old Testament?," in *Wrestling with the Violence of God: Soundings in the Old Testament*, eds. M. Daniel Carroll R. and J. Blair Wilgus, Bulletin for Biblical Research Supplement 10 (Winona Lake, IN: Eisenbrauns, 2015), 4.

11. Collins, *Does the Bible Justify Violence*, 23–24.

12. See Gale A. Yee, ed., *The Hebrew Bible: Feminist and Intersectional Perspectives* (Minneapolis: Fortress, 2018); Susanne Scholz, ed., *Feminist Interpretation of the Hebrew Bible in Retrospect*, vol. 1, *Biblical Books*, Recent Research in Biblical Studies 5 (Sheffield, UK: Sheffield Phoenix, 2017); Julia M. O'Brien, *Challenging Prophetic Metaphor: Theology and Ideology in the Prophets* (Louisville, KY: Westminster John Knox, 2008).

13. See David G. Horrell, *The Bible and the Environment: Towards a Critical Ecological Biblical Theology*, Biblical Challenges in the Contemporary World (New York: Routledge, 2014); David G. Horrell, Cherryl Hunt, Christopher Southgate, and Francesca Stavrakopoulou, eds., *Ecological Hermeneutics: Biblical, Historical, and Theological Perspectives* (London: T&T Clark, 2010); and Norman C. Habel, ed., *The Earth Story in the Psalms and Prophets*, The Earth Bible 4 (Sheffield, UK: Sheffield Academic, 2001).

14. For a detailed study of this imagery in Ezekiel in comparison to the other prophetic books, see Brad E. Kelle, "Dealing with the Trauma of Defeat: The Rhetoric of the Devastation and Rejuvenation of Nature in Ezekiel," *JBL* 128 (2009): 469–90.

15. Collins, *Does the Bible Justify Violence*, 2–3.

16. T. M. Lemos, *Violence and Personhood in Ancient Israel and Comparative Contexts* (Oxford: Oxford University Press, 2017), 18.

17. See Collins, *Does the Bible Justify Violence*, 19–20 and Brueggemann, "Making Sense," 1.

18. See most especially Seibert, "Recent Research on Divine Violence" and E. W. Davies, "An Examination of Some Proposed Solutions," *CBR* 3 (2005): 197–228. See also Thomas, Evans, and Copan, *Holy War in the Bible*; Carroll and Wilgus, "Introduction," 1–14; Richard S. Hess and Elmer A. Martens, eds., *War in the Bible and Terrorism in the Twenty-First Century*, Bulletin for Biblical Research Supplement 2 (Winona Lake, IN: Eisenbrauns, 2008). For a survey of approaches to the study of warfare in particular in the Old Testament, see Charles Trimm, "Recent Research on Warfare in the Old Testament," *CBR* 10 (2012): 171–216.

19. See, e.g., Eric A. Seibert, *Disturbing Divine Behavior: Troubling Old Testament Images of God* (Minneapolis: Fortress, 2009); Kenton L. Sparks, *Sacred Word, Broken Word: Authority and the Dark Side of Scripture* (Grand Rapids: Eerdmans, 2012); Christopher J. H. Wright, *The God I Don't Understand: Reflections on Tough Questions of Faith* (Grand Rapids: Zondervan, 2008); Douglas S. Earl, *Reading Joshua as Christian Scripture*, JTISup 2 (Winona Lake, IN: Eisenbrauns, 2010); and David T. Lamb, *God Behaving Badly: Is the God of the Old Testament Angry, Sexist and Racist?* (Downer's Grove,

IL: InterVarsity, 2011). For older treatments in this same vein, see Peter C. Craigie, *The Problem of War in the Old Testament* (Grand Rapids: Eerdmans, 1978); T. R. Hobbs, *A Time for War: A Study of Warfare in the Old Testament* (Wilmington, DE: M. Glazier, 1989); M. C. Lind, *Yahweh Is a Warrior: The Theology of Warfare in Ancient Israel* (Scottsdale, PA: Herald, 1980); Tremper Longman III and Daniel G. Reid, *God Is a Warrior*, Studies in Old Testament Biblical Theology (Grand Rapids: Zondervan, 1995); and C. Sherlock, *The God Who Fights: The War Tradition in Holy Scripture*, Rutherford Studies in Contemporary Theology 6 (Lewiston, NY: E. Mellen, 1993).

20. Gregory A. Boyd, *Crucifixion of the Warrior God: Interpreting the Old Testament's Violent Portraits of God in Light of the Cross*, 2 vols. (Minneapolis: Fortress, 2017). Similarly, see the perspectives debated in C. S. Cowles, et al., *Show Them No Mercy: Four Views on God and Canaanite Genocide* (Grand Rapids: Zondervan, 2003).

21. Most of these approaches deal with the violence texts in the Old Testament. For a discussion of perspectives on divine violence in the New Testament, see T. R. Y. Neufeld, *Killing Enmity: Violence and the New Testament* (Grand Rapids: Baker, 2011).

22. Trimm, "Recent Research on Warfare in the Old Testament," 184–85.

23. Brueggemann, "Making Sense," 2–4.

24. For a discussion of interpretive strategies for the Canaanite conquest stories in particular, see Brad E. Kelle, *Telling the Old Testament Story: God's Mission and God's People* (Nashville: Abingdon, 2017), 119–23.

25. For detailed discussion, see Megan Bishop Moore and Brad E. Kelle, *Biblical History and Israel's Past: The Changing Study of the Bible and History* (Grand Rapids: Eerdmans, 2011).

26. For examples, see Creach, *Violence in Scripture*, and Seibert, "Recent Research on Divine Violence," 8–40.

27. See, e.g., Brad E. Kelle, *Ezekiel: A Commentary in the Wesleyan Tradition*, New Beacon Bible Commentary (Kansas City, MO: Beacon Hill, 2013), 147–48.

28. M. Daniel Carroll R. (Rhodas), "'I Will Send Fire': Reflections on the Violence of God in Amos," in Carroll and Wilgus, *Wrestling with the Violence of God*, 113–32.

29. Walter Brueggemann, *Divine Presence amid Violence: Contextualizing the Book of Joshua* (Eugene, OR: Cascade, 2009).

30. Seibert, "Recent Research on Divine Violence."

31. Creach, *Violence in Scripture*.

32. Creach, *Violence in Scripture*, 4.

33. Creach, *Violence in Scripture*, 10.

34. Creach, *Violence in Scripture*, 8.

35. Creach, *Violence in Scripture*, 4; italics original.

36. See Jonathan Shay, *Achilles in Vietnam: Combat Trauma and the Undoing of Character* (New York: Touchstone, 1994), 208.

37. Brett T. Litz et al., "Moral Injury and Moral Repair in War Veterans: A Preliminary Model and Intervention Strategy," *Clinical Psychology Review* 29 (2009): 695.

38. For example, Christian canonical collections (both Roman Catholic and Protestant) present the main storyline of the Bible as describing an ideal creation that becomes distorted by a human "fall" into sin, which is followed by prophetic pronouncements of a new saving act by God that then give way to the New Testament's announcements that Jesus is the fulfillment of that promised saving act. For more on this issue of how the organization and interpretation of the different canons of scripture affect theological understandings and moral perspectives, see Kelle, *Telling the Old Testament Story*, 9–10.

39. For a detailed description of how this interpretation emerges from the study of the Old Testament in particular, see Kelle, *Telling the Old Testament Story*.

40. For discussion of the remainder of this affirmation in v. 7, see below.

41. See Creach, *Violence in Scripture*, 218–26.

42. Creach, *Violence in Scripture*, 221.

43. Creach, *Violence in Scripture*, 234.

44. Brett T. Litz et al., *Adaptive Disclosure: A New Treatment for Military Trauma, Loss, and Moral Injury* (New York: The Guilford Press, 2016), 124.

45. Brueggemann, "Making Sense," 1.

46. Seibert, "Recent Research on Divine Violence," 10.

47. Lemos, *Violence and Personhood*, 178–96.

48. Lemos, *Violence and Personhood*, 195.

49. See ch. 2 for the full discussion of practices of moral repair within current moral injury work.

50. Brueggemann, "Making Sense," 4.

51. Brueggemann, "Making Sense," 4.

52. Brueggemann, "Making Sense," 4.

53. Robert Emmet Meagher and Douglas A. Pryer, "Introduction," in *War and Moral Injury: A Reader*, ed. Robert Emmet Meagher and Douglas A. Pryer (Eugene, OR: Cascade, 2018), 6.

54. Collins, *Does the Bible Justify Violence*, 31.

55. Rita Nakashima Brock and Gabriella Lettini, *Soul Repair: Recovering from Moral Injury after War* (Boston: Beacon, 2012), 93–115.

56. Brock and Lettini, *Soul Repair*, 95.

57. Brock and Lettini, *Soul Repair*, 112.

58. See Robert Emmet Meagher, *Killing from the Inside Out: Moral Injury and Just War* (Eugene, OR: Cascade, 2014).

59. Christopher Frechette, "The Old Testament as Controlled Substance: How Insights from Trauma Studies Reveal Healing Capacities in Potentially Harmful Texts," *Interpretation* 69 (2015): 20–34.

7. Retrospect and Prospect

1. David Wood, *What Have We Done: The Moral Injury of America's Longest Wars* (New York: Brown and Company, 2016), 261.

2. Joseph McDonald, "Introduction," in *Exploring Moral Injury in Sacred Texts*, ed. Joseph McDonald, Studies in Religion and Theology (London: Jessica Kingsley, 2017), 32.

3. Most notably, Joseph M. Currier et al., "Military Veterans' Preferences for Incorporating Spirituality in Psychotherapy or Counseling," *Professional Psychology: Research and Practice* 49 (2018): 39–47; Jennifer H. Wortmann et al., "Spiritual Features of War-Related Moral Injury: A Primer for Clinicians," *Spirituality in Clinical Practice* 4 (2017): 249–61; Marek S. Kopacz et al., "Towards a Faith-Based Understanding of Moral Injury," *Journal of Pastoral Care and Counseling* 71 (2017): 217–19; Lewis Jeff Lee, *Moral Injury Reconciliation: A Practitioner's Guide for Treating Moral Injury, PTSD, Grief, and Military Sexual Trauma through Spiritual Formation Strategies* (London: Jessica Kingsley, 2018).

4. Tom Frame, "Moral Injury and the Influence of Christian Religious Conviction," in *War and Moral Injury: A Reader*, ed. Robert Emmet Meagher and Douglas A. Pryer (Eugene, OR: Cascade, 2018), 195.

5. Rita Nakashima Brock and Gabriella Lettini, *Soul Repair: Recovering from Moral Injury after War* (Boston: Beacon, 2012), 128.

6. Duane Larson, "A Prescription for Moral Injury," *Dialog: A Journal of Theology* 54 (2015): 117; italics original.

7. Frame, *Moral Injury*, 8.

8. For a specific plea for the use of the humanities and religion in moral injury work, see Douglas A. Pryer, "What We Don't Talk about When We Talk about War," in Meagher and Pryer, *War and Moral Injury: A Reader*, 64.

9. Tyler Boudreau, "The Morally Injured," *Massachusetts Review* (Fall–Winter 2011–2012): 754.

10. Warren Kinghorn, "Combat Trauma and Moral Fragmentation: A Theological Account of Moral Injury," *Journal of the Society of Christian Ethics* 32 (2012): 59.

11. Joseph Wiinikka-Lydon, "Mapping Moral Injury: Comparing Discourses of Moral Harm," *Journal of Medicine and Philosophy* 44 (2019): 175–91.

12. Wiinikka-Lydon, "Mapping Moral Injury," 175–76.

13. Wiinikka-Lydon, "Mapping Moral Injury," 180.

14. Wiinikka-Lydon, "Mapping Moral Injury," 184–85.

15. Wiinikka-Lydon, "Mapping Moral Injury," 185.

16. Wiinikka-Lydon, "Mapping Moral Injury," 187.

17. Alice Lynd and Staughton Lynd, *Moral Injury and Nonviolent Resistence: Breaking the Cycle of Violence in the Military and Behind Bars* (Oakland, CA: PM Press, 2017), 9.

18. Jelena Subotic and Brent J. Steele, "Moral Injury in International Relations," *Journal of Global Security Studies* 3 (2018): 387–401.

19. Wendy Haight, Erin P. Sugrue, and Molly Calhoun, "Moral Injury among Child Protection Professionals: Implications for the Ethical Treatment and Retention of Workers," *Children and Youth Services Review* 82 (2017): 27–41. E. Murray, C. Krahé, and D. Goodsman, "Are Medical Students in Pre-hospital Care at Risk of Moral Injury?" *Emergency Medicine Journal* 35 (2018): 590–94. Anthony Feinstein, Bennis Pavisian, and Hannah Storm, "Journalists Covering the Refugee and Migration Crisis Are Affected by Moral Injury Not PTSD," *Journal of the Royal Society of Medicine* 9 (2018). doi:10.1177/2054270418759010.

20. Duane Larson and Jeff Zust, *Care for the Sorrowing Soul: Healing Moral Injuries from Military Service and Implications for the Rest of Us* (Eugene, OR: Cascade, 2017), 160–92.

21. Michael Yandell, "'Do Not Torment Me': The Morally Injured Gerasene Demoniac," in McDonald, *Exploring Moral Injury in Sacred Texts*, 135–50.

22. Warren Carter, "Peter and Judas: Moral Injury and Moral Repair," in McDonald, *Exploring Moral Injury in Sacred Texts*, 151–68.

23. Brock and Lettini, *Soul Repair*, 112.

24. Wiinikka-Lydon, "Moral Injury as Inherent Political Critique," 219–20.

25. Wiinikka-Lydon, "Moral Injury as Inherent Political Critique," 220.

26. Kelly Denton-Borhaug, "'Like Acid Seeping into Your Soul': Religio-Cultural Violence in Moral Injury," in McDonald, *Exploring Moral Injury in Sacred Texts*, 111–34.

Appendix

1. This sample listing is adapted from Hodgson and Carey, "Moral Injury and Definitional Clarity," 1215–16.

2. Warren Kinghorn, "Combat Trauma and Moral Fragmentation: A Theological Account of Moral Injury," *Journal of the Society of Christian Ethics* 32 (2012): 57–74.

3. Robert Emmet Meagher, *Killing from the Inside Out: Moral Injury and Just War* (Eugene, OR: Cascade, 2014).

Select Bibliography

Bica, Camillo Mac. *Beyond PTSD: The Moral Casualties of War.* War Legacy Series: Book Two. Commack, NY: Gnosis, 2016.

Blumenthal, David R. "Soul Repair: A Jewish View." In *Exploring Moral Injury in Sacred Texts*, edited by Joseph McDonald, 33–46. Studies in Religion and Theology. London: Jessica Kingsley, 2017.

Boudreau, Tyler. "The Morally Injured." *Massachusetts Review* (Fall–Winter 2011–2012): 746–54.

Bowen, Nancy R. "Sodom and Lot's Family: Moral Injury in Genesis 19." In *Exploring Moral Injury in Sacred Texts*, edited by Joseph McDonald, 47–68. Studies in Religion and Theology. London: Jessica Kingsley, 2017.

Brock, Rita Nakashima, and Gabriella Lettini. *Soul Repair: Recovering from Moral Injury after War.* Boston: Beacon, 2012.

Carey, Lindsay B., Timothy J. Hodgson, Lilian Krikheli, Rachel Y. Soh, Annie-Rose Armour, Taranjeet K. Singh, and Cassandra G. Impiombato. "Moral Injury, Spiritual Care and the Role of Chaplains: An Exploratory Scoping Review of Literature and Resources." *Journal of Religious Health* 55 (2016): 1218–45.

Carter, Warren. "Peter and Judas: Moral Injury and Repair." In *Exploring Moral Injury in Sacred Texts*, edited by Joseph McDonald, 151–68. Studies in Religion and Theology. London: Jessica Kingsley, 2017.

Caruth, Cathy. *Unclaimed Experience: Trauma, Narrative, and History.* Baltimore: Johns Hopkins University Press, 1996.

Childs, J. M. "Moral Injury and the Priesthood of All Believers." *Dialog* 57 (2018): 111–19. https://doi.org/10.1111/dial.12391.

Coleman, Nikki. "Moral Status and Reintegration." In *Moral Injury: Unseen Wounds in an Age of Barbarism*, edited by Tom Frame, 205–19. Sydney, Australia: UNSW Press, 2015.

Collins, John J. *Does the Bible Justify Violence?* Facets. Minneapolis: Fortress, 2004.

Creach, Jerome F. D. *Violence in Scripture*. Interpretation: Resources for the Use of Scripture in the Church. Louisville, KY: Westminster John Knox, 2013.

Currier, Joseph M. et al. "Development and Evaluation of the Expressions of Moral Injury Scale—Military Version." *Clinical Psychology and Psychotherapy* 25 (2017): 474–88.

Currier, Joseph M., J. D. Foster, and S. L. Isaak. "Moral Injury and Spiritual Struggles in Military Veterans: A Latent Profile Analysis." *Journal of Traumatic Stress*. March 12, 2019. doi: 10.1002/jts.22378.

Currier, Joseph M., J. M. Holland, and J. Malott. "Moral Injury, Meaning Making, and Mental Health in Returning Veterans." *Journal of Clinical Psychology* 71 (2015): 229–40.

Currier, Joseph M., Timothy D. Carroll, Michelle Pearce, and Harold G. Koenig. "Military Veterans' Preferences for Incorporating Spirituality in Psychotherapy or Counseling." *Professional Psychology: Research and Practice* 49 (2018): 39–47.

Denton-Borhaug, Kelly. "'Like Acid Seeping into Your Soul': Religio-Cultural Violence in Moral Injury." In *Exploring Moral Injury in Sacred Texts*, edited by Joseph McDonald, 111–34. Studies in Religion and Theology. London: Jessica Kingsley, 2017.

Doehring, Carrie. "Military Moral Injury: An Evidenced-Based and Intercultural Approach to Spiritual Care." *Pastoral Psychology* 68 (2019): 15–30. https://doi.org/10.1007/s11089-018-0813-5.

Drescher, Kent D. et al. "An Exploration of the Viability and Usefulness of the Construct of Moral Injury in War Veterans." *Traumatology* 17 (2011): 8–13.

Farnsworth, Jacob K., Kent D. Drescher, Jason A. Nieuwsma, Robyn B. Walser, and Joseph M. Currier. "The Role of Moral Emotions in Military Trauma: Implications for the Study and Treatment of Moral Injury." *Review of General Psychology* 18 (2014): 249–62.

Fawson, Shawn. "Sustaining Lamentation for Military Moral Injury: Witness Poetry That Bears the Traces of Extremity." *Pastoral Psychology*. November 2018. doi: https://doi.org/10.1007/s11089-018-0855-8.

Fisher, David Lawrence. "*Dulce et Decorum est*: Moral Injury in the Poetry of Combat Veterans." PhD diss., Pacifica Graduate Institute, 2019.

Frame, Tom. Introduction to *Moral Injury: Unseen Wounds in an Age of Barbarism*, edited by Tom Frame. Sydney, Australia: UNSW Press, 2015.

———. "Moral Injury and the Influence of Christian Religious Conviction." In *War and Moral Injury: A Reader*, edited by Robert Emmet Meagher and Douglas A. Pryer, 187–96. Eugene, OR: Cascade, 2018.

———, ed. *Moral Injury: Unseen Wounds in an Age of Barbarism*. Sydney, Australia: UNSW Press, 2015.

Frechette, Christopher. "The Old Testament as Controlled Substance: How Insights from Trauma Studies Reveal Healing Capacities in Potentially Harmful Texts." *Interpretation* 69 (2015): 20–34.

Geringer, Kim S., and Nancy H. Wiener. "Insights into Moral Injury and Soul Repair from Classical Jewish Texts." *Pastoral Psychology* 68 (2019): 59–75. https://doi.org/10.1007/s11089-018-0848-7.

Graham, Larry Kent. *Moral Injury: Restoring Wounded Souls*. Nashville: Abingdon, 2017.

Griffin, Brandon J. et al. "Moral Injury: An Integrative Review." *Journal of Traumatic Stress*. 2019. doi: 10.1002/jts.22362.

Grimsley, Charles W., and Gaylene Grimsley. *PTSD and Moral Injury: The Journey to Healing through Forgiveness*. Maitland, FL: Xulon, 2017.

Grossman, Dave. *On Killing: The Psychological Cost of Learning to Kill in War and Society*. Rev. ed. New York: Basic, 2009.

Grundy, Christopher. "Basic Retraining: The Role of Congregational Ritual in the Care of Returning Veterans." *Liturgy* 27 (2012): 27–36.

Hansen, Christopher. "Glimmers of the Infinite: The Tragedy of Moral Injury." *Dialog* 58 (2019): 64–69. doi.org/10.1111/dial.12454.

Harris, J. Irene, Joseph M. Currier, Crystal L. Park, Timothy J. Usset, and Cory D. Voecks. "Moral Injury and Psycho-Spiritual Development: Considering the Developmental Context." *Spirituality in Clinical Practice* 19 (2015): 1–11.

Herman, Judith. *Trauma and Recovery: The Aftermath of Violence—from Domestic Abuse to Political Terror*. 2nd ed. New York: Basic, 1997.

Hodgson, Timothy J., and Lindsay B. Carey. "Moral Injury and Definitional Clarity: Betrayal, Spirituality and the Role of Chaplains." *Journal of Religious Health* 56 (2017): 1212–18.

Janoff-Bulman, Ronnie. *Shattered Assumptions: Toward a New Psychology of Trauma*. New York: The Free Press, 1992.

Jensen, Wollom A., and James M. Childs. *Moral Warriors, Moral Wounds: The Ministry of the Christian Ethic*. Eugene, OR: Cascade, 2016.

Jinkerson, J. D. "Defining and Assessing Moral Injury: A Syndrome Perspective." *Traumatology* 22 (2016): 122–30.

Kelle, Brad E. *Ancient Israel at War 853–586 BC*. Essential Histories 67. Oxford: Osprey, 2007.

————. "Dealing with the Trauma of Defeat: The Rhetoric of the Devastation and Rejuvenation of Nature in Ezekiel." *JBL* 128 (2009): 469–90.

————. *Ezekiel: A Commentary in the Wesleyan Tradition.* New Beacon Bible Commentary. Kansas City, MO: Beacon Hill, 2013.

————. "Moral Injury and the Division of Spoils after Battle in the Hebrew Bible." In *Exploring Moral Injury in Sacred Texts*, edited by Joseph McDonald, 83–102. Studies in Religion and Theology. London: Jessica Kingsley, 2017.

————. "Moral Injury and the Interdisciplinary Study of Biblical War Texts: The Case of King Saul." In *Worship, Women, and War: Essays in Honor of Susan Niditch*, edited by John J. Collins, Saul M. Olyan, and T. M. Lemos, 147–72. Brown Judaic Studies 357. Providence, RI: Brown Judaic Studies, 2015.

————. "Post-war Rituals of Return and Reintegration of Warriors." In *Warfare, Ritual, and Symbol in Biblical and Modern Contexts*, edited by Brad E. Kelle, Frank Ritchel Ames, and Jacob L. Wright, 205–42. SBL Ancient Israel and Its Literature 28. Atlanta: SBL Press, 2014.

————. *Telling the Old Testament Story: God's Mission and God's People.* Nashville: Abingdon, 2017.

Kelley, M. L. et al. "Moral Injury and Suicidality among Combat-Wounded Veterans: The Moderating Effects of Social Connectedness and Self-Compassion." *Psychological Trauma.* March 21, 2019. doi: 10.1037/tra0000447.

Kinghorn, Warren. "Combat Trauma and Moral Fragmentation: A Theological Account of Moral Injury." *Journal of the Society of Christian Ethics* 32 (2012): 57–74.

Koenig, Harold G. et al. "The Moral Injury Symptom Scale—Military Version." *Journal of Religion and Health* 57 (2018): 249–65.

Kolk, Bessel A. van der. *The Body Keeps the Score: Brain, Mind, and Body in the Healing of Trauma.* New York: Penguin, 2015.

Kopacz, Marek S., Courtney Ducharme, David Ani, and Ahmet Atlig. "Towards a Faith-Based Understanding of Moral Injury." *Journal of Pastoral Care and Counseling* 71 (2017): 217–19.

Larson, Duane. "A Prescription for Moral Injury." *Dialog: A Journal of Theology* 54 (2015): 115–20.

Larson, Duane, and Jeff Zust. *Care for the Sorrowing Soul: Healing Moral Injuries from Military Service and Implications for the Rest of Us.* Eugene, OR: Cascade, 2017.

Lee, Lewis Jeff. *Moral Injury Reconciliation: A Practitioner's Guide for Treating Moral Injury, PTSD, Grief, and Military Sexual Trauma through Spiritual Formation Strategies.* London: Jessica Kingsley, 2018.

Lemos, T. M. "Shame and Mutilation of Enemies in the Hebrew Bible." *JBL* 125 (2006): 225–41.

———. *Violence and Personhood in Ancient Israel and Comparative Contexts.* Oxford: Oxford University Press, 2017.

Levine, Sean. "Legal War, Sin, and 'Moral Injury' in the Age of Modern Warfare." In *War and Moral Injury: A Reader*, edited by Robert Emmet Meagher and Douglas A. Pryer, 219–30. Eugene, OR: Cascade, 2018.

Liebert, Elizabeth A. "Accessible Spiritual Practices to Aid in Recovery from Moral Injury." *Pastoral Psychology* 68 (2019): 41–57. https://doi.org/10.1007/s11089-018-0825-1.

Litz, Brett T. "Moral Injury: Assessment, Conceptualization and Treatment Strategies." Paper presented at the Australian Conference on Traumatic Stress, "Public Issues—Private Trauma." Queensland, Australia. September 8–10, 2016.

Litz, Brett T. et al. "Moral Injury and Moral Repair in War Veterans: A Preliminary Model and Intervention Strategy." *Clinical Psychology Review* 29 (2009): 695–706.

Litz, Brett T., Leslie Lebowitz, Matt J. Gray, and William P. Nash. *Adaptive Disclosure: A New Treatment for Military Trauma, Loss, and Moral Injury.* New York: The Guilford Press, 2016.

Lynd, Alice, and Straughton Lynd. *Moral Injury and Nonviolent Resistance: Breaking the Cycle of Violence in the Military and Behind Bars.* Oakland, CA: PM Press, 2017.

MacNair, Rachel M. *Perpetration-Induced Traumatic Stress: The Psychological Consequences of Killing.* Westport, CT: Praeger, 2002.

Maguen, Shira, and Brett T. Litz. "Moral Injury in the Context of War." https://www.ptsd.va.gov/professional/treat/cooccurring/moral_injury.asp.

Maguen, Shira, and Brett T. Litz. "Moral Injury in Veterans of War." *PTSD Research Quarterly* 23 (2012): 1–6.

Malecek, Stefan J. "The Moral Inversion of War." In *War and Moral Injury: A Reader,* edited by Robert Emmet Meagher and Douglas A. Pryer, 292–300. Eugene, OR: Cascade, 2018.

Marlantes, Karl. *What It Is Like to Go to War.* New York: Atlantic Monthly, 2011.

McDonald, Joseph. *Exploring Moral Injury in Sacred Texts.* Studies in Religion and Theology. London: Jessica Kingsley, 2017.

———. Introduction to *Exploring Moral Injury in Sacred Texts,* edited by Joseph McDonald. Studies in Religion and Theology. London: Jessica Kingsley, 2017.

Meagher, Robert Emmet. *Killing from the Inside Out: Moral Injury and Just War.* Eugene, OR: Cascade, 2014.

Meagher, Robert Emmet, and Douglas A. Pryer. Introduction to *War and Moral Injury: A Reader,* edited by Robert Emmet Meagher and Douglas A. Pryer. Eugene, OR: Cascade, 2018.

Meagher, Robert Emmet, and Douglas A. Pryer, eds. *War and Moral Injury: A Reader.* Eugene, OR: Cascade, 2018.

Moitoza, Mark T. "Fresh Courage for Moral Injury: Sacramental Healing with Returning Veterans." PhD diss., La Salle University, 2018.

Moon, Zachary. "'Turn Now, My Vindication Is at Stake': Military Moral Injury and Communities of Faith." *Pastoral Psychology.* Nov. 21, 2017. http://dx.doi.org/10.1007/s11089-017-0795-8.

—. *Warriors Between Worlds: Moral Injury and Identities in Crisis.* Emerging Perspectives in Pastoral Theology and Care. Lanham, MD: Lexington, 2019.

Moore, Megan Bishop, and Brad E. Kelle. *Biblical History and Israel's Past: The Changing Study of the Bible and History.* Grand Rapids: Eerdmans, 2011.

Nash, William P., and Brett T. Litz. "Moral Injury: A Mechanism for War-Related Psychological Trauma in Military Family Members." *Clinical Child Family Psychology Review* 16 (2013): 365–75.

Nash, William P., and Christa Davis Acampora. Foreword to *War and Moral Injury: A Reader*, edited by Robert Emmet Meagher and Douglas A. Pryer. Eugene, OR: Cascade, 2018.

Nash, William P. et al. "Psychometric Evaluation of the Moral Injury Events Scale." *Military Medicine* 178 (2013): 646–52.

Orris, Glenn William. "Moral Injury and PTSD: Toward an Integrated Model of Complex, Combat-Related Trauma." PhD diss., Pacifica Graduate Institute, 2017.

Powers, Brian S. *Full Darkness: Original Sin, Moral Injury, and Wartime Violence.* Grand Rapids: Eerdmans, 2019.

—. "Moral Injury and Original Sin: The Applicability of Augustinian Moral Psychology in Light of Combat Trauma." *Theology Today* 73 (2017): 325–37.

Pryer, Douglas A. "What We Don't Talk about When We Talk about War." In *War and Moral Injury: A Reader*, edited by Robert Emmet Meagher and Douglas A. Pryer, 60–73. Eugene, OR: Cascade, 2018.

Rambo, Shelly. *Spirit and Trauma: A Theology of Remaining.* Louisville, KY: Westminster John Knox, 2010.

Ramsay, Nancy J. "Moral Injury as Loss and Grief with Attention to Ritual Resources for Care." *Pastoral Psychology.* December 2018. doi: https://doi.org/10.1007/s11089-018-0854-9.

Seibert, Eric A. *Disturbing Divine Behavior: Troubling Old Testament Images of God.* Minneapolis: Fortress, 2009.

———. "Recent Research on Divine Violence in the Old Testament (with Special Attention to Christian Theological Perspectives)." *CBR* 15 (2016): 8–40.

Shay, Jonathan. *Achilles in Vietnam: Combat Trauma and the Undoing of Character.* New York: Touchstone, 1994.

———. *Odysseus in America: Combat Trauma and the Trials of Homecoming.* New York: Scribner, 2002.

Shellnutt, Kate. "Why the US Military Wants Fewer Generic Christians." *Christianity Today.* May 29, 2017. https://www.christianitytoday.com/news/2017/may/why-us-military-fewer-generic-christians-216-religions.html.

Sherman, Nancy. *Afterwar: Healing the Moral Wounds of Our Soldiers.* Oxford: Oxford University Press, 2015.

Smith, Mark S. *Poetic Heroes: Literary Commemorations of Warriors and Warrior Culture in the Early Biblical World.* Grand Rapids: Eerdmans, 2014.

Tick, Edward. *War and the Soul: Healing Our Nation's Veterans from Post-traumatic Stress Disorder.* Wheaton, IL: Quest, 2005.

———. *Warrior's Return: Restoring the Soul after War.* Boulder, CO: Sounds True, 2014.

Verkamp, Bernard J. *The Moral Treatment of Returning Warriors in Early Medieval and Modern Times.* 2nd ed. Scranton: University of Scranton Press, 2006.

Wiinikka-Lydon, Joseph. "Mapping Moral Injury: Comparing Discourses of Moral Harm." *Journal of Medicine and Philosophy* 44 (2019): 175–91.

———. "Moral Injury as Inherent Political Critique: The Prophetic Possibilities of a New Term." *Political Theology* 18 (2017): 219–32.

Wisco, Blair E., Brian P. Mark, Casey L. May, Brenda Martini, John H. Krystal, Steven M. Southwick, and Robert H. Pietrzak. "Moral Injury in U.S. Combat Veterans: Results from the National Health and Resilience in Veterans Study." *Depress Anxiety* 34 (2017): 340–47. https://doi.org/10.1002/da.22614.

Wood, David. "The Grunts: Damned If They Kill, Damned If They Don't." March 18, 2014. https://projects.huffingtonpost.com/moral-injury/the-grunts.

———. *What Have We Done: The Moral Injury of Our Longest Wars*. New York: Little, Brown, and Company, 2016.

Wortmann, Jennifer H., Carol Hundert, Mark W. Smith, Ethan Eisen, Alexander H. Jordan, William P. Nash, and Brett T. Litz. "Spritual Features of War-Related Moral Injury: A Primer for Clinicians." *Spirituality in Clinical Practice* 4 (2017): 249–61.

Yandell, Michael. "'Do Not Torment Me': The Morally Injured Gerasene Demoniac." In *Exploring Moral Injury in Sacred Texts*, edited by Joseph McDonald, 135–50. Studies in Religion and Theology. London: Jessica Kingsley, 2017.

Yeterian, Julie D. et al. "Defining and Measuring Moral Injury: Rationale, Design, and Preliminary Findings from the Moral Injury Outcome Scale Consortium." *Journal of Traumatic Stress*. 2019. doi: 10.1002/jts.22380.

Yocum, Cecilia. *Help for Moral Injury: Strategies and Interventions*. Fayetteville, NC: Quaker House, 2016.

CPSIA information can be obtained
at www.ICGtesting.com
Printed in the USA
LVHW042300171219
640716LV00002BA/2/P

9 781501 876288